LANDLORD AND TENANT SERIES

Assured Tenancies

LANDLORD AND TENANT SERIES

Assured Tenancies

by

Stuart Bridge

Fellow of Queens' College, Cambridge
Lecturer in Law, University of Cambridge
Barrister, of the Middle Temple

BLACKSTONE
PRESS LIMITED

First published in Great Britain 1999 by Blackstone Press Limited, Aldine Place, London W12 8AA. Telephone: 0181-740 2277 www.blackstonepress.com

ISBN: 1 85431 978 7

British Library Cataloguing in Publication Data
A CIP catalogue record for this book is available from the British Library.

Typeset by Montage Studios Ltd, Horsmonden, Kent
Printed by Bell & Bain Limited, Glasgow

Contents

Preface

Ten years after Part I of the Housing Act 1988 came into force seems an opportune time to publish a book on Assured Tenancies, and it is a happy coincidence that Blackstone Press is launching its new Landlord and Tenant Series.

While 15 January 1989 has come to be recognised as the beginning of the end of private sector rent control in England and Wales, the overall picture of residential security remains complex and confused, and statutory intervention has not been lacking in the interim. However, as the dust gradually settles, the need for a broadly based book such as my *Residential Leases* (Blackstone, 1994) has become less apparent, and a closer concentration on the assured tenancy more necessary. The current book strives to set out, as clearly as possible, the principles affecting assured and assured shorthold tenancies, giving some practical assistance to practitioners who may not be in day-to-day contact with the operative legislation. Appended to the book are some basic precedents, Part I of the Housing Act 1988 as amended, and relevant statutory instruments and rules of practice. Account has been taken of the Civil Procedure Rules which took effect on 26 April 1999.

I am, as always, grateful to Blackstone Press for their encouragement, support, and patience. Phil Kenny, the General Editor, has been of considerable assistance in reading and commenting upon the manuscript, as well as guiding me on the more practical aspects of precedent drafting.

I have attempted to state the law as at 1 May 1999.

Stuart Bridge
Queens' College
Cambridge

Abbreviations

CPR	Civil Procedure Rules
FLA 1996	Family Law Act 1996
HA	Housing Act (1988 to 1996)
LGHA 1989	Local Government and Housing Act 1989
para.	paragraph
PD	Practice Direction
r.	rule
reg.	regulation
RA 1977	Rent Act 1977
s.	section
Sch.	Schedule

Table of Cases

Table of Statutes

Table of Secondary Legislation

CHAPTER ONE

Introduction

1.1 THE HISTORICAL BACKGROUND

The assured tenancy, the subject matter of this book, is currently the most important form of letting in the private sector of residential property in England and Wales. While the assured tenancy is itself a relative innovation, the history of residential lettings in the twentieth century is complex and colourful, and it is impossible to understand fully the present system, in which evidence of previous legislation is still very apparent, without some awareness of the past.

1.1.1 The introduction of the Rent Acts

At the time of the enactment of the first Rent Act in 1915, the private sector formed by far the largest part (of the order of 90 per cent) of the entire housing stock in England and Wales. There was a shortage of urban housing, and the Act was passed, as a war-time 'emergency' measure, in order to avert rent strikes threatened by munitions workers and others who responded angrily to their landlords' attempts to exploit the situation by increasing rents. Thus the Rent and Mortgage Interest Restrictions Act 1915 froze rents and, in an attempt to prevent consequential mass evictions, conferred protection on occupying tenants. Although the measure was perceived as being a temporary answer to an immediate and pressing social need, the housing shortage did not end with the War, and measures passed shortly afterwards further improved the security of the residential tenant. The 1920 Rent Act, for instance, introduced protection for widows of deceased tenants, and increased the number of dwellings to which the Acts applied. The years between the wars saw a gradual whittling away at tenant protection by Parliament. From 1923, landlords were given an incentive to repossess, as new lets were taken outside rent control. The Acts of 1933 and 1938 were similarly regressive. But at no stage did wholesale repeal, and thereby complete deregulation, take place.

The commencement of hostilities in 1939 required Parliament to step in again to assist the residential tenant, and the majority of houses were brought under control. In 1946, a statutory code for furnished tenancies, previously excluded from protection, was introduced, conferring some rent control and security of tenure. The first concerted post-war attack on the Rent Acts came in 1957, the Conservative administration providing for immediate deregulation of higher value houses, and for phased deregulation of the rest. However, the legislation did not survive the Wilson Labour Government, which largely returned the Acts to the *status quo*, adding further layers of complexity by introducing a distinction between 'controlled' and 'regulated' tenancies, and responding to the much publicised forced evictions (for which phased deregulation was held partly to blame) by creating criminal offences of unlawful eviction and harassment. There followed the Rent Act 1974, bringing furnished tenancies into the Rent Acts proper, and creating at the same time an exclusion in favour of 'resident landlords', a concept which was to spawn much litigation. The Rent Act 1977, and the Protection from Eviction Act 1977, consolidated that which had gone before. By the time of the 1979 election, the law of private sector residential leases was in a reasonably coherent and comprehensible state, but it was not to last for long.

1.1.2 The developing public sector

Since 1945, changes of government policy had actively promoted the public sector. Councils and similar bodies, burdened with wider public duties to house, began to accumulate a substantial body of housing, as the contemporaneous mass house-building programmes resulted in the construction of a vast number of publicly owned dwellings. By 1966, the public rented sector had grown to 27 per cent of the nation's housing stock, and now exceeded the private rented sector (at 24 per cent). Parliament consistently maintained a policy of non-intervention, and allowed councils to regulate their own affairs. But the retention of residential property by the councils came to be identified with the retention of political power, and under the Thatcher administration public sector tenants were given significant legally enforceable rights. Her Government initiated the most radical legislative programme to affect housing in this country.

The two most important housing measures of the Thatcher administration were the Housing Acts of 1980 and 1988. The Act of 1980 (subsequently consolidated in the Housing Act 1985) contained the public sector tenant's charter, most notably the politically popular 'right to buy', whereby tenants were entitled to compel their local authority landlords to sell the freehold reversion in their dwellings to them, at a discount calculated with reference to the length of time they had been public sector tenants. In addition, tenants of local authorities and other public sector bodies were given statutory security (as 'secure tenants') for the first time. The introduction of the right to buy had an inevitable, and intended, impact on the quantity of housing stock held by local authorities, but more was to come, as by further legislation local authorities were first given the power, and then placed under a duty, to sell their interests in housing to private sector purchasers. The effect has been substantial. Between 1981 and 1997, the number of dwellings rented from English local authorities (and new town corporations) fell from 5,118,000 to 3,604,000. As a percentage of the housing stock, the public rented sector declined from over 28 per cent to below 18 per cent.

1.1.3 The attack on the Rent Acts

The Thatcher Government sought at the same time to encourage private sector, and housing association, lettings. The 1980 Act made small but significant amendments to the Rent Act 1977, introducing the protected shorthold tenancy as a means for landlords to let dwellings without conferring security of tenure. Much more radical was the approach of Part I of the Housing Act of 1988, which sought to phase out Rent Act tenancies, with their restrictive rent controls, and introduce as the major form of private sector tenure the assured tenancy. As the 1988 Act did not repeal the Rent Acts, the two systems continue to operate in tandem. However, the number of Rent Act regulated tenancies is slowly but inevitably diminishing. The first question a practitioner will need to ask when faced with a problem concerning a private sector residential lease will be 'When was the lease granted?'. If before 15 January 1989 (the day Part I of the Housing Act 1988 came into force, and a date to remember), the lease is likely to be governed by the Rent Act 1977. If on or after 15 January 1989, the lease will in all likelihood be an assured tenancy.

The 1988 Act also created, as a sub-species of assured tenancy, a new form of tenure for landlords seeking to avoid the conferment of security on the tenant: the assured shorthold tenancy. This device proved very attractive to landlords, as it enabled them to recover possession without difficulty at the end of the term. The most recent legislation in this area, the Housing Act 1996, has made the assured shorthold tenancy the 'default mode' of letting in the residential sector. If a landlord lets a dwelling-house following the coming into force of the relevant provisions (28 February 1997), the assured tenancy will in most cases be an assured shorthold tenancy without further ado.

1.2 THE TYPES OF TENANCY

One of the greatest initial difficulties in this area is the accurate identifica-tion of the type of tenancy. In many cases it will be straightforward. It may be very clear that the tenancy, granted in the last 12 months to a tenant who had not previously been occupying premises owned by this landlord, is an assured shorthold tenancy. But where the landlord–tenant relation-ship (in its widest terms, allowing for possible succession by the current tenant on the death of his or her predecessor) pre-dates the coming into force of ss. 96 to 104 of the Housing Act 1996 (28 February 1997) then resolution of the problem will be more difficult. If, which is by no means impossible, the relationship may be traced back to a time prior to the coming into force of Part I of the Housing Act 1988 (15 January 1989), the tenancy may be regulated under the Rent Act 1977 as a protected or statutory tenancy. It is therefore important to be aware of how the assured tenancy, and its sub-species the assured shorthold tenancy, relates to the earlier legislation.

1.3 THE MACHINERY OF THE RENT ACTS

A brief explanation of the structure of Rent Act regulation may be useful. We shall refer to those tenancies which remain subject to Rent Act control as being 'Rent Act regulated'. The 'regulated tenancy' is in fact a generic term for the two stages of Rent Act status, the 'protected tenancy' and the 'statutory tenancy'. In essence, while the tenant holds under the contract of tenancy, he is, in the event of the Rent Act applying to him, a 'protected tenant'. On termination of his contractual tenancy, he will become a 'statutory tenant' provided that the conditions laid down in the 1977 Act are satisfied, most particularly the condition that he occupies the dwell-ing-house in question as his residence. Regulated tenants, whether protected or statutory, enjoy rent control, together with security of tenure.

1.4 TRANSITIONAL PROVISIONS

The Rent Act 1977 (RA 1977) was not amended substantially by the Housing Act 1988 (HA 1988). However, the intention of the latter Act being to phase out the former, immediate attention must be drawn to s. 34 of the 1988 Act, which prevents almost all tenancies entered into on or after 15 January 1989 from being protected tenancies. It may at first seem surprising that there is no similar prohibition regarding statutory tenancies. The point is that such tenancies are entirely derivative from protected tenancies: they take effect 'by operation of law' on the termination of a protected tenancy. The general policy of the HA 1988 is to keep existing regulated tenancies within the Rent Act. In that sense, the 1988 Act does not 'deregulate'. Thus on termination of a protected tenancy on or after 15 January 1989, which tenancy must (subject to certain exceptions) by definition have been entered into before the 1988 Act came into force, the tenant will hold over as statutory tenant under the 1977 Act. If and so long as the tenant continues to occupy the dwelling-house as his residence, the statutory tenancy will remain in being. Should a regulated tenant die, the 1977 Act will dictate whether any succession to that tenancy will occur. In certain circumstances, a successor will take as assured tenant rather than as statutory tenant, and then the 1988 Act will come into operation.

Section 34(1) of the HA 1988 contains a list of qualifications to the general rule, detailing those tenancies which may be protected tenancies despite being entered into after the 1988 Act came into force on 15 January 1989 (see 1.4.1 to 1.4.4 below).

1.4.1 Tenancies entered into in pursuance of a contract made before 15 January 1989

The HA 1988, s. 34(1)(a) was primarily intended to prevent landlords agreeing to let before the 1988 Act came into force, but delaying the execution of the lease until afterwards. It is of course essential that an enforceable contract be proved. However, the contract need not satisfy s. 2 of the Law of Property (Miscellaneous Provisions) Act 1989 (which does not apply anyway in relation to certain short leases: see s. 2(5)), as that provision has no application to contracts made before 28 September 1989. Reference should be made instead to its statutory predecessor, s. 40 of the Law of Property Act 1925.

1.4.2 Tenancies granted to Rent Act regulated tenants

A tenancy may be a protected tenancy if it is 'granted to a person (alone or jointly with others) who, immediately before the tenancy was granted,

5

was a protected or statutory tenant and is so granted by the person who at that time was the landlord (or one of the joint landlords) under the protected or statutory tenancy' (HA 1988, s. 34(1)(b)). This provision is a similar, essential, anti-avoidance device. A landlord cannot by the simple expedient of offering a new tenancy to his existing Rent Act regulated tenant after the 1988 Act is in force claim that the new tenancy is no longer Rent Act regulated. An example of the operation of this provision is provided by the county court decision of *Kotecha* v *Rimington* (1991) March 1991, Legal Action 15. The tenant was granted a protected tenancy in 1984. The premises were sold, and, after the coming into force of the 1988 Act, the new landlord purported to grant an assured shorthold tenancy. Judge Appleby held, applying s. 34(1)(b) of the 1988 Act, that the new tenancy was a Rent Act protected tenancy. The intention of Parliament in passing the 1988 Act 'was not to release [onto the market] property which was already protected, but to encourage landlords to release property not already let'.

If there is a period of time between the ending of the regulated tenancy and the commencement of the new tenancy, this provision will not apply, as the tenant must have been a protected or statutory tenant 'immediately before' the grant of the new tenancy. But such a situation would be very difficult for the landlord to engineer: it would require the tenant to go out of occupation altogether, as otherwise on termination of the protected tenancy by whatever means the tenant will hold over as statutory tenant. Where the new tenancy is offered by a different landlord, the tenancy cannot be protected. It is not clear what the position would be if the old landlord assumed a new identity, for example where an individual landlord began trading as a company.

Section 34(1)(b) is not restricted to the dwelling-house which has been let on the protected or statutory tenancy. A county court decision, *Goringe* v *Twinsectra Ltd* (1994) June 1994, Legal Action 11, supports the view that where the landlord grants the tenant a new tenancy of different accommodation subsequent to 15 January 1989, it will remain subject to the Rent Acts. Thus landlords would be deprived of the incentive to move tenants around their properties to take them outside the protection of the Rent Acts.

Section 34(1)(b) does not apply where the regulated tenancy was a protected shorthold tenancy. If the landlord grants a protected shorthold tenant (or a statutory tenant holding over following expiry of a protected shorthold fixed term) a new tenancy on or after 15 January 1989, that tenancy will be an assured shorthold tenancy (HA 1988, s. 34(2), (3)).

1.4.3 Tenancies of 'suitable alternative accommodation'

The tenancy may be a protected tenancy if it is granted to a person (alone or jointly with others) in the following circumstances—

(a) prior to the grant of the tenancy, an order for possession of a dwelling-house was made against him (alone or jointly with others) on the court being satisfied as mentioned in section 98(1)(a) of, or Case 1 in Schedule 16 to, the Rent Act 1977 or Case 1 in Schedule 4 to the Rent (Agriculture) Act 1976 (suitable alternative accommodation available); and

(b) the tenancy is of the premises which constitute the suitable alternative accommodation as to which the court was so satisfied; and

(c) in the proceedings for possession the court considered that, in the circumstances, the grant of an assured tenancy would not afford the required security and, accordingly, directed that the tenancy would be a protected tenancy ... (HA 1988, s. 34(1)(c))

This provision contemplates the court, after the coming into force of the 1988 Act, making an order for possession against a protected or statutory tenant on the basis that suitable alternative accommodation is available for the tenant (and that it considers it reasonable to make such an order) (RA 1977, s. 98(1)(a)). The tenancy of the alternative accommodation, being entered into on or after 15 January 1989, would normally be an assured tenancy. If, however, the court takes the view that an assured tenancy does not afford 'security reasonably equivalent to the security afforded' by the 1977 Act to protected tenants (other than protected tenants who have been served with written notices pursuant to Cases 11 to 20 of Sch. 15 to the 1977 Act) then it has jurisdiction to order that the tenancy of the alternative accommodation is to be protected under the 1977 Act. If the court could not do this it would not be able to make an order, as it is strongly arguable that assured tenancies do not as a matter of course confer 'equivalent security' to that enjoyed by such protected tenants. In *Laimond Properties Ltd* v *Al-Shakarchi (No. 2)* (1998) 30 HLR 1099, landlords sought possession of the flat let to the defendant on a protected tenancy, on the grounds that they wished to refurbish the building and that they could provide her with suitable alternative accommodation. The Court of Appeal upheld the decision of the first instance judge that the alternative accommodation could be on an assured tenancy, as it offered the defendant the required security.

1.4.4 New town corporation lettings

By s. 38 of the 1988 Act, on transfer of a tenancy from the public to the private sector on or after 15 January 1989, the tenancy may become an assured tenancy even though it was entered into before that date (see further 3.1.1 below). It cannot in those circumstances be a protected tenancy. There is a saving in relation to transfers of reversions by new town corporations: see further HA 1988, s. 34(1)(d).

1.5 SOCIAL LANDLORDS

There has been a voluntary sector of housing in this country for centuries, but it has never been more important, or substantial, than today. The expansion can be dated from the Housing Act 1974, which introduced a new system of funding for housing associations, and the encouragement for this sector by the subsequent Conservative administration, which perceived it to be more acceptable than local authorities as a large-scale housing provider. The Housing Corporation (and in Wales, Housing for Wales) is a statutory body which maintains a register of housing associations and has an overall supervisory juridiction. It issues management guidance to housing associations, and is responsible for determining whether a particular association (or other person or body) should be approved to enable it to purchase local authority housing stock.

The Housing Acts of 1988 and 1996 made highly significant changes to the funding of housing associations, as a result of which they have come to be viewed by government as belonging to the private rather than the public sector. Similar changes were made in relation to the legal effect of their tenancies. Prior to 1989, housing associations, depending on their precise legal definition, would let either on secure tenancy, conferring on the occupier a security of tenure, as well as in some cases the right to buy, or on 'housing association tenancy', pursuant to provisions contained in Part VI of the RA 1977 which afforded the housing association tenant the benefits of rent control. (Many lettings by housing associations would fall within both definitions.) Part I of the HA 1988 provided that new tenancies granted by housing associations would in general not be 'secure', nor would Part VI of the RA 1977 apply to them, and since then most tenancies granted by housing associations have been on assured tenancy terms.

The Housing Act 1996 (HA 1996) created a new status of 'registered social landlord', comprising not only housing associations but also societies and companies which satisfy numerous statutory conditions (notably that they are non-profit making), and which are duly registered by the Housing Corporation. Regulatory control of registered social landlords is vested in the Corporation, which issues guidance from time to time, and requires such landlords to grant tenancies on certain terms. Since 1989, the Housing Corporation has disapproved of lettings on assured shorthold tenancy, initially requiring all such grants by housing associations to be specifically approved. However, a more liberal approach is now apparent. There is general dispensation to registered social landlords to grant assured shorthold tenancies in the case of supported housing providing temporary accommodation, and where tenants who have a care package under the community care framework are allocated general needs housing. Where a registered social landlord provides housing for homeless persons pursuant to arrangements with a housing authority, the tenancy must be an assured shorthold (HA 1996, s. 209, on which see 3.14 below). Otherwise, with few exceptions, lettings by registered social landlords are expected to be assured periodic tenancies, thereby requiring those granting tenancies on or after 28 February 1997 to make specific provision excluding shorthold status.

1.6 LONG LEASEHOLDERS

The long leaseholder is in many ways closer to a person who owns the freehold rather than a tenant. The leasehold will be relatively freely assignable, the leaseholder will have paid a substantial premium in much the same way that a freehold purchaser pays for his property. Yet the law has recognised the need to accord him greater protection in the form of statutory security and rights to expand or extend his interest. Treatment of the long leaseholder by Parliament has been uneven and inconsistent. The position has now been reached where most long leaseholders have a form of statutory security (generally under Part I of the Landlord and Tenant Act 1954) and some method of compelling the freeholder either to sell the freehold to them, or to grant a new or extended lease. The statutes do not provide a code which is either rational or readily comprehensible. The latest Parliamentary offering, the Leasehold Reform, Housing and Urban Development Act 1993, is the least user-friendly of them all.

1.7 AGRICULTURAL TIED COTTAGES

A separate regime for agricultural workers occupying tied accommodation modelled on the Rent Acts was contained in the Rent (Agriculture) Act 1976. This scheme is now being phased out, and such occupiers are now accorded a security which is provided to 'assured agricultural occupancies' (closely related to that enjoyed by assured tenants) by the HA 1988, ss. 24 to 26.

1.8 THE CURRENT STATE OF THE HOUSING STOCK

The quarterly Government publication *Housing and Construction Statistics* indicates that the housing stock of England is in a state of some flux. In 1981, in the early days of the Thatcher administration, 57.7 per cent of the housing stock was owner-occupied (and therefore outside the scope of this book), 11.4 per cent was rented privately (or with a job or business), 2.3 per cent was rented from housing associations and 28.6 per cent was rented from local authorities or housing associations. The impact of the Housing Acts of 1988 and 1996 is difficult to assess, as many other factors have been influential over the period in question. Legislative promotion of the tenant's right to buy council housing has led to a substantial increase in owner-occupation, and consequential dimunition in local authority-owned residential property. The private sector has remained a relatively constant presence during this time. It can be argued that the Housing Acts have arrested its decline. Furthermore, governmental advocacy of and support for the voluntary sector of housing has led to a large increase in the number of dwellings held by housing associations. By the end of 1988, the private rented sector in England had fallen to some 1,848,000 dwellings, amounting to 9.6 per cent of the overall stock. It had risen by 1997 to 2,095,000, or 10.1 per cent. Housing associations saw an increase, over the same period from 534,000 to 988,000 dwellings, from 2.8 per cent to 4.8 per cent of the housing stock, while the share of local authorities fell from 22.1 per cent to 17.4 per cent.

Thus by 1997, owner-occupation accounted for 67.6 per cent, the private rented sector for 10.1 per cent, housing associations for 4.8 per cent, and the public sector for 17.4 per cent. The most dramatic changes have been the fall in public sector housing, and the increase in owner-occupation and housing association lettings, both clear legacies of government policy. The balance between private sector (if we include housing associations) and public sector is becoming rather fine: as at 1997, 14 per cent as against 18.6 per cent. Owner-occupation remains, and no doubt will continue to be, the most popular method of land-holding in this country. But the rented sector, comprising as it does almost one-third of all houses and flats in this country, is hugely significant, and it is likely to remain so for the foreseeable future.

CHAPTER TWO

The Definition of Assured Tenancy

2.1 INTRODUCTION

The term 'assured tenancy' was devised by the draftsmen of the Housing Act 1980 to describe a special status of residential tenancy. At that time, the majority of private sector residential tenancies were regulated under the Rent Acts, and the rent chargeable subject to control. In this, the Thatcher Government's first piece of housing legislation, landlords were given an incentive to bring property onto the market. Only landlords specifically approved by Parliament could grant assured tenancies, and initially the dwelling had to be newly erected. This enabled approved landlords to charge their tenants a rent outside the constraints of the Rent Act, the tenant in return obtaining security of tenure modelled on the statutory code which applies to business tenants. These '1980 Act assured tenancies' were in turn phased out by the HA 1988 (ss. 1(3), 37), such that no tenancy entered into on or after 15 January 1989 could be a 1980 Act assured tenancy, and that all existing 1980 Act assured tenancies were (with one transitional exception which is no longer of importance) converted into assured tenancies under the 1988 Act (see further HA 1988, ss. 1(4), 1(5), 37(5)). It is therefore hard to conceive of any circumstances in which a practitioner might now encounter a 1980 Act assured tenancy. Despite the use of the same terminology, the statutory codes contained in the 1980 and 1988 Acts were wholly different.

Part I of the HA 1988 (which came into force on 15 January 1989) was enacted in an attempt by the Thatcher Government to revitalise the private sector of residential housing, most notably by permitting landlords to let at a commercial rent. Thus, although the assured tenant has security of tenure, whereby the landlord cannot normally recover possession without obtaining a possession order from the court on proof of certain prescribed grounds, the statute imposes few restraints beyond this. The sub-species of assured tenant known as the assured shorthold tenant was legislatively created in the 1988 Act. Assured shorthold tenants have no effective security of tenure, but there is limited (albeit largely ineffective) rent control.

Provisions contained in the HA 1996 (which came into force on 28 February 1997) made the assured shorthold tenancy the default mode of letting in the private sector so that the majority of private sector residential tenancies now being granted are assured shorthold tenancies. The statutory regime which governs the recovery of possession from assured shorthold tenants, and the reference of excessive rents to rent assessment committees, is now to be found in the HA 1988, ss. 19–23, as amended by the 1996 Act. Indeed, there are now for all practical purposes two kinds of assured shorthold tenancy, which we shall refer to as '1988 Act shortholds' and '1996 Act shortholds'. Shortholds are an attractive proposition to landlords, as they facilitate the recovery of possession at little cost. However, it must be realised that they are themselves assured tenancies. This has particular significance in the following circumstances:

(a) *In determining whether a tenancy is an assured shorthold tenancy.* A tenancy cannot be an assured shorthold unless it is an assured tenancy, and a failure to realise this can prove costly to the landlord. If, therefore, a landlord grants a tenancy which is excluded from assured tenancy status (by HA 1988, Sch. 2), it cannot be an assured shorthold, and the landlord will not be able to utilise the shorthold provisions (or the accelerated possession procedure) to recover possession.

(b) *In recovering possession where the shorthold comprises a fixed term which has not expired.* The only effective route to recovery of possession at this time will be pursuant to the HA 1988, s. 7(6), a highly significant provision which has general application to all fixed-term assured tenancies, shorthold and non-shorthold. Forfeiture as such is not available as a method of terminating assured tenancies.

But many assured tenancies will not be shortholds. Assured tenancies granted between 15 January 1989 and 28 February 1997 will normally be shorthold only where the landlord has served a notice to such effect before the tenancy is entered into. Residential tenancies granted on or after 28

February 1997 are more likely to be, but are not necessarily, shorthold. In particular, the landlord may contract out of the shorthold status, and most landlords in the voluntary sector of housing will do so as a matter of course.

2.2 ASSURED TENANCY: DEFINITION

A tenancy under which a dwelling-house is let as a separate dwelling is an assured tenancy if and so long as three conditions are satisfied:

(a) The tenant, or each of the joint tenants, is an individual;
(b) The tenant, or at least one of the joint tenants, occupies the dwelling-house as his only or principal home; and
(c) The tenancy is not one which cannot be an assured tenancy (HA 1988, s. 1(1)).

2.3 TENANCY

An assured tenancy must be a tenancy (or 'lease'). 'Tenancy' includes a sub-tenancy and an agreement for a tenancy or a sub-tenancy (HA 1988, s. 45(1)). Although it may include a tenancy at will or by sufferance (see the analogous Rent Act cases of *Artizans, Labourers and General Dwellings Co. Ltd v Whitaker* [1919] 2 KB 301 and *Chamberlain v Farr* (1942) 112 LJ KB 206), it certainly does not include a mere licence to occupy. An agreement will comprise a tenancy if it grants exclusive possession for a term, and there will usually be a reservation of rent (*Street v Mountford* [1985] AC 809). Although rent is not a *sine qua non* of tenancy, a rent-free tenancy cannot be an assured tenancy (HA 1988, Sch. 1, para. 3). It is essential to realise that there is now far less incentive for landlords to attempt to avoid the application of the statutory regime than was the case when rent control was at stake. Although the courts are still required to be vigilant to detect sham devices and pretences which are designed to avoid the protective legislation, they encounter them relatively infrequently.

Since *Street* v *Mountford* most agreements for the occupation of residential property will be tenancies, but it remains important to define a tenancy or lease clearly, and to make the distinction between tenancy or lease and licence. The case law which is now described has a much broader utility, and application, than the definition of assured tenancy, as most significant statutory rights are conferred exclusively on tenants.

In *Street* v *Mountford*, a landlord conferred exclusive possession of two furnished rooms on an occupier pursuant to a written agreement whereby the occupier agreed to pay a 'licence fee' of £37 per week. The agreement was expressed to be terminable at 14 days' notice, and the occupier expressly accepted 'that a licence in the above form does not and is not intended to give me a tenancy protected under the Rent Acts'. The House of Lords decided nevertheless that the agreement did create a tenancy. The three vital elements were present, namely:

(a) exclusive possession;
(b) for a term;
(c) at a rent.

The clear evidence from the written agreement that the parties did not intend to create a tenancy was irrelevant, in so far as they did intend exclusive possession to be granted. However, Lord Templeman, giving the only reasoned speech in the House of Lords, conceded that there were certain restricted circumstances in which the presence of the three indicia would not be decisive:

(a) *'Sometimes it may appear from the surrounding circumstances that there was no intention to create legal relationships'*. This must be distinguished from situations (of which *Street* v *Mountford* is of course one) where the parties do not intend to create a lease. Lord Templeman contemplates informal family arrangements where the motive has been affection, kindness or generosity, and where no legal relationship giving rise to enforceable rights and obligations is envisaged. Examples are *Booker* v *Palmer* [1942] 2 All ER 674 (cottage owner agreed to allow a friend to instal an evacuee in the cottage rent free for the duration of the war); *Marcroft Wagons Ltd* v *Smith* [1951] 2 KB 496 (landlord allowed daughter of deceased tenant to occupy a property temporarily, albeit paying for the privilege, while they considered her position); and *Heslop* v *Burns* [1974] 1 WLR 1241 (family occupying cottage rent free). The scope of this exception is limited.

(b) *'Sometimes it may appear from the surrounding circumstances that the right to exclusive possession is referable to a legal relationship other than a tenancy. Legal relationships to which the grant of exclusive possession might be referable and which would or might negative the grant of an estate or interest in the land include ...'*

(i) *'occupancy under a contract for the sale of the land'*. In *Isaac* v *Hotel de Paris Ltd* [1960] 1 WLR 239, an employee agreed 'subject to contract' to purchase shares in his employer's company, and was allowed to run their nightclub (and pay the rent under the employer's lease) in the expectation that the share purchase would be completed. The Privy Council held that he was not a tenant but was occupying pursuant to the informal, and unenforceable, agreement with his employer. In *Bretherton* v *Paton* (1986) 18 HLR 257, although there had been negotiations with a view to a purchase of the freehold by the occupier, the parties never agreed a price. The occupier, who enjoyed exclusive possession and made a periodic payment of £1.20 per week in respect of her occupation, was held by the Court of Appeal to be a tenant.

(ii)   *'occupancy pursuant to a contract of employment or occupancy referable to the holding of an office'*. Where an employee is accommodated by his employer, he will be a licensee (a 'service occupier') if the employer requires him to occupy the premises in order the better to perform his contractual duties (*Smith* v *Seghill Overseers* (1875) LR 10 QB 422). There must be something more than mere convenience to the employee. In *Norris* v *Checksfield* (1991) 63 P & CR 38, an employer allowed his employee, a semi-skilled mechanic, into possession of a bunga-low on condition that he would, in the future, drive coaches for the employer's business. The employee's occupation of the bungalow was not necessary but was desirable: the employer required him to occupy the premises for the better performance of his duties, as he would then be available at short notice to drive coaches. Although, being disqualified from driving, a fact unknown to the employers when engaging him, the employee could not lawfully perform this duty, it was enough that the employer contemplated the employee fulfilling this role. The Court of Appeal held that the employee was a licensee rather than a tenant.

2.3.1 Owner lacks power to grant a tenancy

A grant of exclusive possession will not create a tenancy where the grantor has no capacity to grant a tenancy, or where the grantor has no interest in the land out of which a tenancy could be 'carved'. However, a tenancy by estoppel may arise between the grantor and the grantee where, in such circumstances, there is a representation that a tenancy is being conferred. In *Bruton* v *London and Quadrant Housing Trust* [1997] 4 All ER 970, a housing trust, given permission by a local authority to use short-life properties as temporary accommodation for homeless persons, entered an agreement with the plaintiff for the grant of occupation of one of the properties. Although exclusive possession was conferred on the plaintiff, the agreement recited that the property was on licence from the council pending development. The Court of Appeal held that as the trust did not purport to grant a tenancy, and did not have an estate or interest in the property, neither tenancy nor tenancy by estoppel was created. See also *Redbank Schools Ltd* v *Abdullahzadeh* (1995) 28 HLR 431.

2.3.2 Proof of intention

A major practical problem is working out exactly what the 'landlord' and 'tenant' did 'intend'. The occupier may have gone into occupation having been told by word of mouth what rent he must pay, when he must pay it, and nothing else: there may be no written agreement at all. On the other hand, there may be a lengthy document which purports to inform the occupier in detail what his rights (if any) are, and what his (somewhat more extensive) obligations are. Or the situation may be one where some of the terms of the agreement are oral, and some are in writing. Ultimately, the question is the same: does the agreement as a whole grant exclusive possession of the premises to the occupier, that exclusive possession being for a term at a rent? Matters are complicated by the tendency of many private landlords to attempt to obviate the effect of what they perceive to be legislation which protects the tenant. While they operated under the shadow of rent control, landlords would commonly seek by their written agreements to confer a licence or some other interest falling short of a tenancy on their occupier: indeed, that was the very tactic of the landlord (himself a solicitor) in *Street* v *Mountford*. Written agreements are therefore carefully examined by the courts: 'an express statement of intention is not decisive and ... the court must pay attention to the facts and surrounding circumstances and to what people do as well as to what people say' (*per* Lord Templeman in *AG Securities* v *Vaughan* [1990] 1 AC 417).

There is less incentive now for landlords to beat the system. The absence of rent control means that the assured tenancy is not the item of value which the Rent Act protected tenancy was (and continues to be). The assured shorthold frankly offers little more by way of 'assurance' than a mere licence to occupy does. But the words of Lord Templeman in *Street* v *Mountford* remain of relevance (replacing 'Rent Acts' with 'Housing Act' where appropriate):

Although the Rent Acts must not be allowed to alter or influence the construction of an agreement, the court should, in my opinion, be astute to detect and frustrate sham devices and artificial transactions whose only object is to disguise the grant of a tenancy and to evade the Rent Acts.

2.3.3 Sham transactions

A 'sham' in its strictest sense connotes 'acts done or documents executed by the parties to the "sham" which are intended by them to give to third parties or to the court the appearance of creating between the parties legal rights and obligations different from the actual legal rights and obligations (if any) which the parties intend to create' (*per* Diplock LJ in *Snook* v *London & West Riding Investments Ltd* [1967] 2 QB 786, at 802). As the parties to a purported licence will have a common intention to create a licence rather than a tenancy, this test will rarely be satisfied. However, if a court finds that a written agreement is not a sham, it may still refuse to apply the terms of the agreement which appear in documentary form. The court must apply the same rules of construction as it would apply to any other legal document, bearing in mind that the situation may be as envisaged by Mustill LJ in *Hadjiloucas* v *Crean* [1988] 1 WLR 1006, at 1019, that is:

> ... one in which the document does precisely reflect the true agreement between the parties, but where the language of the document (and in particular its title or description) superficially indicates that it falls into one legal category whereas when properly analysed in the light of the surrounding circumstances it can be seen to fall into another.

The consolidated appeals before the House of Lords in *AG Securities* v *Vaughan; Antoniades* v *Villiers* [1990] 1 AC 417 saw Lord Templeman moderating his choice of words. His Lordship considered that 'fewer misunderstandings would have been caused' if in *Street* v *Mountford* he had used the word 'pretence' to describe a written agreement or clause which was intended to act as a smokescreen obscuring the parties' real intentions. Moreover, in determining whether an agreement or clause is a 'pretence', the court may look at the conduct of the parties subsequent to the agreement in question as evidence of whether they genuinely intended to act upon it. Thus, in the *Antoniades* v *Villiers* appeal, a clause whereby an occupier could be required to share the premises with the landlord or any nominee of his was struck down partly because the landlord, who might be expected to make the maximum profit out of the property, never sought to exercise this right.

2.3.4 Exclusive possession

Exclusive possession was not itself in issue in *Street* v *Mountford*. It has caused difficulties before and since. It is generally recognised that the tenant has exclusive possession if he can lawfully exclude all others, including the landlord, from the property. The landlord (or others) may reserve rights of entry, for example in order to inspect the state of repair, but such rights should be restricted and well defined. Landlords should be aware that attempts to exclude exclusive possession may be subjected to rigorous scrutiny by the courts as they examine whether they are nothing more than 'shams' which the landlord does not intend to invoke.

A bald statement that the agreement does not confer exclusive possession on the occupier will be carefully scrutinised. In *Skipton Building Society* v *Clayton* (1993) 66 P & CR 223, a written agreement purported to confer on a married couple a licence to occupy a dwelling-house for their joint lives and the life of the survivor. A clause vesting 'possession management and control' of the property in the defendants was rejected as a sham, as it did not accord with the parties' true intentions (as evidenced by their subsequent conduct).

In *Crancour Ltd* v *Da Silvaesa* [1986] 1 EGLR 80, a written agreement purported to require the occupier to vacate the property for one and a half hours each day. If this were a genuine term, it would no doubt rebut exclusive possession. It was, however, held to be a sham, as was the case in *Aslan* v *Murphy (No. 1); Duke* v *Wynne* [1990] 1 WLR 766, where the Court of Appeal described the term as 'wholly unrealistic and clearly a pretence'. In *Aslan* v *Murphy*, the Court evaluated the significance of the landlord's retention of a key to the premises. It did not have any magic in itself, and would be significant only if the purpose of keeping the key was to enable the landlord to provide services such as 'frequent cleaning, daily bed-making, the provision of clean linen at regular intervals and the like'.

2.3.5 Tenant or lodger

If extensive services are provided by the landlord, the occupier may not then have exclusive possession. In *Huwyler* v *Ruddy* (1995) 28 HLR 550, a landlord purported to create a licence to use a room. He provided the occupier with clean bed linen weekly, and had the room cleaned. A key was retained to enable the landlord to perform these services, and to give him the unrestricted access which he required to the property. The Court of Appeal held that the occupier had not been granted exclusive possession and that he was a licensee. It could be argued that, in colloquial terms, the occupier was a 'lodger'. A 'lodger' is a licensee rather than a tenant. He is not a tenant because he does not have exclusive possession, the owner retaining control and unrestricted access for the purpose of providing attendance and services (see Lord Templeman in *Street* v *Mountford* at 818).

The extent of services required to render the occupier a licensee is a matter of degree, and no hard and fast rules can be given. Access needs to be 'unrestricted' in so far as the landlord requires 'to go into and out of the lodger's rooms at the convenience of the landlord and without the lodger being there to let the landlord in' (*per* Ralph Gibson LJ in *Crancour Ltd v Da Silvaesa* at 273). But not all licensees are lodgers. In *Brooker Settled Estates Ltd v Ayers* (1987) 19 HLR 246, the county court judge, having held that the occupier was not a lodger, concluded that she must be a tenant. The Court of Appeal allowed the appeal, and ordered a re-hearing. The lodger is but one kind of licensee.

2.3.6 Exclusive possession and multiple occupiers

The landlord who attempts to deny the occupier exclusive possession by insisting that he share with another individual runs the very substantial risk that the two occupiers will together be deemed to be joint tenants. The high-water mark of so-called 'non exclusive occupation agreements' was the Court of Appeal decision in *Somma v Hazelhurst* [1978] 1 WLR 1014. A young unmarried couple shared a double bedsitting room, each signing identical documents whereby they agreed to share the room with the landlord (termed 'the licensor') 'and with such other licensees or invitees whom the licensor shall from time to time permit to use the room'. They were held to be licensees as neither occupier had the individual right to exclusive possession. This decision was over-ruled in *Street v Mountford*, as (in Lord Templeman's words, at 825) 'the agreements signed by H and S [the occupiers] constituted the grant to H and S jointly of exclusive possession at a rent for a term for the purposes for which the room was taken and the agreement therefore created a tenancy'.

Street v Mountford was not itself concerned with multiple occupiers of one dwelling. However, in *Antoniades v Villiers* the House of Lords had to consider whether agreements which were very similar to those in *Somma v Hazelhurst* created a joint tenancy or two licences to occupy in respect of a single room furnished with a double bed. A clause permitting the landlord to occupy the rooms himself at any time and to permit other persons to use them together with the licensee was a pretence, and should be disregarded. The two agreements were interdependent. Reading them together, in the light of the surrounding circumstances (the physical lay-out and size of the flat, and the fact that the occupiers, though not married, were living together as husband and wife), it was clear that the landlord did not genuinely intend them to be a true statement of the nature of the possession to be enjoyed by the occupiers. Evidence of their sham nature was provided by the physical arrangement of the premises (unsuited for the sharing the agreements contemplated), the lack of any discussion between the parties as to how the clause might operate, not to mention that the landlord never attempted to obtain increased income from the flat by introducing further occupiers (as by the agreements he was allegedly entitled to do). The true effect of the agreement between the parties was to confer on the occupiers a joint right to exclusive possession of the flat, and they were accordingly joint tenants.

In *Mikeover Ltd* v *Brady* [1989] 3 All ER 618, the Court of Appeal distinguished *Antoniades* v *Villiers*. A clause imposing an obligation on the occupier to share with those 'who have been granted' a like right did not permit the landlord to introduce further occupiers in the future, and so, as a matter of construction, did not itself derogate from a grant of exclusive possession. However, the agreements, in providing for the occupiers to make separate payments of rent, imposed several rather than joint liability for the rent. The occupiers could not be joint tenants as they lacked the requisite unity of interest, and the Court of Appeal decided that they were accordingly licensees only. Particularly striking on the facts was the landlord's refusal to accept the proferred payment of the whole rent by the occupier who remained following the departure of her fellow occupier.

Mikeover Ltd v *Brady* is an authority which should be treated with care. In a similar case, a court may well find the purported imposition of several rather than joint liability on two or more occupiers a pretence or a sham, as it was not seriously intended to be so enforced. This was so in several other cases (most notably *Antoniades* v *Villiers*, where the agreements *prima facie* indicated several liability for a half share of the rent). Alternatively, a court may infer that a periodic tenancy has been created by the acceptance of rent proferred by the remaining occupier to the landlord.

The effect of these decisions can be summarised as follows. If the agreement, or agreements read together in the light of the surrounding circumstances, confers exclusive possession on the occupiers, then as long as the other elements of 'tenancy' are present and the liability of the occupiers for the rent is joint, they will be joint tenants. Otherwise they will hold under separate licences.

In the *AG Securities* v *Vaughan* appeal, agreements were held to confer separate licences on the occupiers rather than a joint tenancy. The landlord company entered into four separate written agreements with four separate individuals between 1982 and 1985 for the occupation of a large flat which consisted of four bedrooms, a sitting room, a lounge, a kitchen, and a bathroom. The agreements were independent, each individual having entered his own following separate negotiations with the landlord. Although each agreement was in standard form, the rent payable by each occupier was different, as they had arrived at the flat at different times. When one occupier left the flat, the three remaining would decide whether they wished to change their bedrooms, and the replacement occupier would be offered the room the others did not want.

The House of Lords held that the occupiers were not joint tenants of the flat. The written agreements accurately reflected the flexible relationship between the landlord and the occupiers, and they were not shams. Construing the written agreements, their Lordships held that there was no grant of exclusive possession to the occupiers jointly as, in the event of one of the occupiers leaving, the three remaining could not exclude a fourth person nominated by the landlord. It is significant that the occupiers did not contend that they each had exclusive possession of their bedrooms. Had they been granted an identifiable part of the flat, the tenancy having been granted on or after 15 January 1989, they would be able to argue that their tenancy was assured by virtue of the HA 1988, s. 3 (see 2.5.5 below, and also Lord Oliver in *AG Securities* at 471).

2.3.7 For a term

A tenancy must be sufficiently certain. This will rarely be a difficulty with residential lettings. The landlord may let on a fixed term or on periodic tenancy. In *Prudential Assurance Plc* v *London Residuary Body* [1992] 2 AC 386, the London County Council had in 1930 purported to lease a strip of land to predecessors in title of the plaintiff 'until the said land is required by the Council for the purposes of the widening' of the adjacent road. The House of Lords held that these words were not sufficiently certain to comprise a 'term', and whether a lease is for a fixed term or is a periodic tenancy, the requirement of certainty must be satisfied. The duration of a fixed term must be known at the outset. Thus, a provision that the tenancy is for six months, or three years, or will terminate on a given date, will be sufficient. A periodic tenancy (weekly, monthly and so on) is rendered sufficiently certain by the power of landlord and tenant to terminate by giving notice of the appropriate length. Restrictions on the right to terminate (e.g., that one party cannot give notice until a certain length of time has elapsed from the beginning of the lease) are unobjectionable as long as they are clearly prescribed (*Breams Property Investment Co. Ltd* v *Stroulger* [1948] 2 KB 1). In *Centaploy Ltd* v *Matlodge Ltd* [1974] Ch 1, parties purported to create a lease which was determinable by the tenant only. Whitford J held that a term preventing the landlord from terminating a periodic tenancy was repugnant to the nature of such a tenancy. The lease was validated by striking down the offending term.

2.3.8 At a rent

In *Street* v *Mountford*, Lord Templeman appeared to indicate that the existence of rent, in one form or another, was an essential ingredient of a tenancy. This is not consistent with the definition of 'term of years absolute' in the Law of Property Act 1925, s. 205 ('whether or not at a rent'), and in *Ashburn Anstalt* v *Arnold* [1989] Ch 1, the Court of Appeal denied that the reservation of a rent was a requirement. That said, in the protective codes it has been usual to exempt rent-free tenancies, and a tenancy for which no rent is payable cannot be an assured tenancy (HA 1988, Sch. 1, para. 3).

2.4 DWELLING-HOUSE

A dwelling-house may be a house or a part of a house, such as a flat (HA 1988, s. 45(1)), and an assured tenant has the same degree of protection whether his property is a house or a flat (which may be a single bedsitting room: e.g., *Street* v *Mountford*). Little is likely to turn on whether a particular house or flat is a dwelling, that is a house which is capable of being inhabited, as the tenant will be assured only where he occupies the house as his only or principal home, and if he does so occupy it, it is surely inevitable that it is a dwelling so called. The proper interpretation of 'house' is more problematical. In *R* v *Nottingham Rent Officer, ex parte Allen* (1985) 17 HLR 481, the Divisional Court held that a caravan was capable of being a dwelling-house. The question was one of fact and degree, the dominant factor being the extent to which the caravan could be moved. If, unlike the facts in *ex parte Allen*, the caravan was completely immobile, it was more likely to come within the term 'dwelling-house'. Although never judicially considered, it seems that in the light of this authority that tenancies of house-boats, or, more particularly, their moorings, could not be assured.

One possible line of attack, albeit rarely pursued, is to claim that the subject matter of the tenancy does not include the house. In *Elitestone Ltd* v *Morris* [1997] 1 WLR 687, landlords contended that the tenancy was of a vacant plot of land. Although the tenants had erected and occupied a wooden bungalow on the plot, it was not attached to the land, but merely rested on concrete foundation blocks. It was nothing more than a chattel, the tenancy could not therefore be said to be of a 'dwelling-house', and it was outside Rent Act protection. The House of Lords rejected these contentions, finding that, in the circumstances of the case (in particular the degree and object of the annexation), the bungalow was 'part and parcel of the land'.

The assured tenancy is not restricted to the physical structure of the dwelling-house the subject of the lease. If, under the terms of the lease, the dwelling-house is let together with other land (e.g., a garden, outhouses, or even a small paddock) that land will also be let on assured tenancy, if and so long as the main purpose of the letting is the provision of a home for the tenant (or one of joint tenants) (HA 1988, s. 2(1)). The question of 'main purpose' will involve balancing the various purposes of the letting concerned. In *Feyereisel* v *Turnidge* [1952] 2 QB 29, a camp site was let to the tenant, as well as a bungalow for his personal occupation. It was held that the main purpose of the letting was the use of the site for the tenant's business of camp-site proprietor. In such circumstances, not only the land but also the house is excluded from assured tenancy status. However, where the other land consists of agricultural land exceeding two acres, the tenancy cannot be an assured tenancy (HA 1988, Sch.1, para.6).

2.5   LET AS A SEPARATE DWELLING

The dwelling-house must be let as a dwelling, not, by inference, a shop or an office. Mixed lettings, such as shops with flats over, will be business tenancies and excluded from assured tenancy status by para. 4 of Sch. 1 to the 1988 Act. Schedule 1 excludes no less than four types of potentially mixed letting (see chapter 3 below).

2.5.1   Use of the property

The requirement that the dwelling-house be a separate dwelling means that it must be a coherent unit of occupation where the 'essential operations of living' go on (*per* Jenkins LJ in *Wimbush* v *Cibulia* [1949] 2 KB 564). 'The right to retain possession is dependent on the tenant establishing that the premises are used by him as a home' (*per* Sir John Arnold P in *Kavanagh* v *Lyroudias* [1985] 1 All ER 560). It is the use of the property as contemplated at the time of the letting which is material. As Eveleigh LJ stated in *St Catherine's College, Oxford* v *Dorling* [1980] 1 WLR 66, at 68:

> ... one has to consider the terms of the lease and the surrounding circumstances at the time that the lease was granted. It may be that in some cases assistance can be obtained from the subsequent user of the premises. In my opinion generally speaking such assistance will be found to be a matter of last resort.

If all the tenant does in the property is sleep, it is not let as a separate dwelling, as he will presumably cook, eat, wash and so forth elsewhere

(*Curl* v *Angelo* [1948] 2 All ER 189). Likewise if the tenant does everything there except sleep (*Wimbush* v *Cibulia*). Thus sleeping appears to be essential but not sufficient. In *Kavanagh* v *Lyroudias*, the tenant was granted at different times tenancies of adjoining houses. The house of which possession was sought was used by the tenant for sleeping in, and occasionally doing work which he brought home. The house had no hot water, and the tenant never cooked or ate there; he would do those things in the adjoining house. The Court of Appeal held that the house was not let as a separate dwelling, clearly evidenced by the fact that the tenant did not occupy it as a complete home.

2.5.2   Two units as one dwelling

A landlord may let two physically separate living units to the tenant, the intention being that the tenant will occupy them as a single dwelling. Despite the reference in the statutory provisions to 'a' dwelling, the courts have held that a dwelling-house need not be in one location only. In *Langford Property Co. Ltd* v *Goldrich* [1949] 1 KB 511, two flats on the same floor, although not structurally connected or even adjacent, were let 'as a separate dwelling' to the tenant and his family: see also *Whitty* v *Scott-Russell* [1950] 2 KB 32. In *Hampstead Way Investments Ltd* v *Lewis-Weare* [1985] 1 WLR 164, the House of Lords criticised the failure of the Court of Appeal in *Kavanagh* v *Lyroudias* [1985] 1 All ER 560 to consider

> whether the defendant tenant occupied [the two houses] as a combined or composite home of the kind contemplated in *Wimbush* v *Cibulia*, bearing in mind that the leases of both houses had originally been granted to the tenant by a person who was the owner of both, and that it was only subsequently that the reversions of the two houses passed into different hands.

It was not apparently conclusive that the landlord's interests in the two adjoining houses no longer belonged to the same person.

2.5.3   Tenancy comprising units separately occupied

In *Horford Investments Ltd* v *Lambert* [1976] Ch 39, the tenant converted two houses let to him by the same landlord into a number of 'accommodation units'. The Court of Appeal held that neither house could in consequence be said to be let as a separate dwelling. A similar conclusion was reached in *St Catherine's College, Oxford* v *Dorling* (above), where the landlord let a house to a college on the understanding (supported by a covenant by the college to like effect) that the house was to be occupied by undergraduates of the college, each student having the use of a room as a study bedroom, and sharing with the others the kitchen and the bathroom. The Court of Appeal held that the college did not have a protected tenancy of the house, as it was not let as a separate dwelling to the college, but as a building for multiple occupation in various units.

2.5.4 Business tenancy construction

In *Groveside Properties Ltd* v *Westminster Medical School* (1983) 47 P & CR 507, the Court of Appeal, on similar facts to *St Catherine's College, Oxford* v *Dorling*, construed an agreement between a landlord and a medical school as giving rise not to a protected tenancy but to a business tenancy within Part II of the Landlord and Tenant Act 1954. The medical school occupied the premises for the purposes of an 'activity' it carried on, namely the provision of residential accommodation for its student body (see the 1954 Act, s. 23). The possibility of such a finding makes schemes of this kind rather less attractive to the landlord, although it does depend on the tenant exercising sufficient control over the property in the way it provides for its students or other residents as to comprise 'occupation' within the 1954 Act (on which concept the leading case is *Graysim Ltd* v *P & O Property Holdings Ltd* [1996] AC 329).

2.5.5 Tenants sharing accommodation

The requirement that the property must be let as a separate dwelling implies that those tenants who share some part of their living accommodation with others cannot be assured: 'the occupier must have the exclusive use of the essential living rooms of a separate dwelling-house' (*per* Mackinnon LJ in *Cole* v *Harris* [1945] KB 474, at 479). Thus, in *Cole* v *Harris,* a tenant who had exclusive use of a living room, bedroom and kitchen, but joint use with the landlord of a bathroom, WC, and the garden, was a protected tenant under the Rent Acts as the property was let as a separate dwelling. However, in *Neale* v *del Soto* [1945] KB 144, sharing the kitchen with the landlord took the letting outside the protection of the Acts. In *Goodrich* v *Paisner* [1957] AC 65, where the House of Lords approved the distinction between the above two decisions of the Court of Appeal, Lord Morton of Henryton considered that a kitchen, a dining room, a bedroom, and a sitting room were all living accommodation, the sharing of which would negative a protected tenancy, whereas a bathroom and WC were not. However, the HA 1988 (as the RA 1977 did) provides some protection for those who share their accommodation with other occupiers but not with the landlord.

2.5.5.1 Sharing with the landlord

An occupier who shares living accommodation with his landlord (whether alone, or in conjunction with other occupiers) is unlikely to be an assured tenant on one of three grounds:

(a) the landlord's use of the accommodation is so extensive that it denies the occupier exclusive possession, and so he is not a tenant; or

(b) the property of which the occupier is tenant is not 'let as a separate dwelling'; or

(c) the 'resident landlord exception' applies (see further 3.10 below).

2.5.5.2 Sharing with other occupiers

Where the tenant shares with other occupiers (whether tenants or licensees), not including his landlord, ss. 3 and 10 of the HA 1988 must be carefully examined. A common sharing arrangement is one where individual tenants are given a room of their own, where they sleep, but they share common facilities such as the kitchen, living room, bathroom and so on with other tenants. A tenant could not without more claim that the room let to him under such an arrangement was 'let as a separate dwelling'. Nor could it be argued successfully that the tenants had together a joint tenancy of the whole house: they do not have a joint right of exclusive possession to the bedrooms. However, s. 3 deems certain units to be let on assured tenancy. The tenancy of the 'separate accommodation' (i.e. the bedroom in the above example) will be deemed to be an assured tenancy if the following conditions are satisfied:

(a) the tenant has exclusive occupation of the separate accommodation (*cf.* the arrangement in *AG Securities* v *Vaughan*, at 2.3.6 above, where no occupier had exclusive rights to his bedroom);

(b) the terms on which he holds that room include the use of the other accommodation (i.e. the kitchen, living room etc.) in common with others, not the landlord;

(c) the letting of the bedroom must not be excluded from assured tenancy status by any provision other than HA 1988, s. 1 itself.

Although the tenant does not obtain an assured tenancy of the accommodation which is shared, the same effect is achieved, as the statute prohibits the court from making an order for possession of that shared accommodation while the tenant remains in possession of the separate accommodation. Only when the court makes, or has made, a possession order relating to the separate accommodation will it have the necessary jurisdiction to order that possession of the shared accommodation be given up. As the separate accommodation is held on assured tenancy, the landlord who seeks possession will have to prove grounds (see chapter 4).

Any term of the tenancy terminating or modifying the tenant's right to use the shared accommodation, or allowing the landlord so to terminate or modify, is of no effect while the tenant remains in possession of his separate accommodation (HA 1988, s. 3(3)). The landlord who seeks to prevent the tenant from using common rooms without authority in the tenancy agreement would be acting in breach of contract, and a tenant could apply for an injunction restraining the landlord's conduct. For a recent example of a living arrangement which fell within the analogous provisions in the RA 1977, see *Gray v Brown* [1993] 1 EGLR 119.

Certain actions are, however, open to the landlord:

(a) He may invoke a term in the lease allowing him to terminate or modify the tenant's right to use shared accommodation in so far as that accommodation is not 'living accommodation' (HA 1988, s. 3(3)). 'Living accommodation' is 'accommodation of such a nature that the fact that it constitutes or is included in the shared accommodation is sufficient, apart from this section, to prevent the tenancy from constituting an assured tenancy of a dwelling-house' (HA 1988, s. 3(5)). In other words, it is accommodation the exclusion of which from the lease itself prevents the dwelling-house being 'let as a separate dwelling', as required by HA 1988, s. 1(1).

(b) If, under the lease, the landlord is entitled to increase the number of persons with whom the tenant has to share, he will be free to invoke such a term, despite the fact that by increasing the number of sharers the landlord will be to some extent modifying the use of the shared accommodation by the existing tenants (HA 1988, s. 3(4)).

The landlord is entitled to apply to the court to enforce the above contractual rights, and on such application the court may make such order as it thinks just (HA 1988, s. 10(3)).

2.5.5.3 *Sharing with sub-tenant(s)*

Where a tenant sub-lets part, but not the whole, of the dwelling-house let, then no part of the dwelling-house is to be treated as excluded from being a dwelling-house let on assured tenancy by reason only that the terms on which the sub-tenant holds include the use of accommodation in common with other persons (HA 1988, s. 4). Thus the tenant may still be an assured tenant although the accommodation is being shared in part with a sub-tenant. The landlord cannot contend that the dwelling-house is not, as a result, let as a separate dwelling. Where a tenant sub-lets the whole of the dwelling-house let to him, he will thereupon cease to be an assured tenant as he will not satisfy the residence condition (for a recent example, see *Ujima Housing Association v Ansah* (1997) 30 HLR 831).

2.6 INDIVIDUAL

A tenancy is assured only if and so long as the tenant, or in the case of joint tenancy, each of the joint tenants, is an individual. This provision is intended to prevent companies or other institutions from holding on an assured tenancy, although it is arguably unnecessary as it has been held in the context of the Rent Acts that a company or other artificial person cannot occupy a dwelling-house as its residence (*Hillier v United Dairies Ltd* [1934] 1 KB 57).

2.6.1 Company lets

Landlords have on occasion let residential property to companies rather than individuals, in the certain knowledge that the company would allow an individual into occupation. This 'company let' arrangement has the benefit of avoiding the protective legislation, at least in so far as it is not struck down as a sham or an artificial device. The letting to the individual would be outside the assured tenancy provisions either because it was a licence (difficult since *Street v Mountford*), or because the individual paid no rent. Most schemes involved a company which had a pre-existing connection with the individual concerned (*Firstcross Ltd v East West (Export/Import) Ltd* (1981) 41 P & CR 145), and in such a case, Stocker LJ stated:

> I would not wish to express any view ... as to what the situation might be under the Rent Acts where there is a letting in which the company does not perform genuinely the obligations under the lease and in which a company had been put in as tenant solely as a cloak to avoid the operation of the Rent Acts which would otherwise apply. (*Estavest Investments Ltd v Commercial Express Travel Ltd* [1988] 2 EGLR 91, at 93)

Nevertheless, the company let scheme has proved surprisingly successful at avoiding protective legislation. Schemes have been upheld where the landlord has required the intending occupier to purchase a company 'off the shelf', that company then becoming the tenant. In *Hilton v Plustitle Ltd*

[1989] 1 WLR 149, the Court of Appeal considered that as a company let was the intention of both parties, and they had full knowledge of what this involved, the written agreement was effective and not a sham. In *Kaye v Massbetter Ltd* [1991] 2 EGLR 97, the individual was guarantor of the rent payable by the company purchased 'off the shelf'. The Court of Appeal placed the onus of proving that the written documents were sham firmly on the occupier, who, according to Nicholls LJ, 'has to establish that, contrary to the terms of the document, the common intention of himself and [the landlord] was that the company ... was not to be subject to an obligation in law to pay rent or to perform the obligations imposed by the agreement on the tenant'.

The decline and fall of the company let is however inevitable. Landlords of residential property obtain most practical advantages they can hope for with the assured shorthold tenancy, a mode of letting with express Parliamentary approval and without the risk inherent in using a mere device.

2.6.2 Children

Registered social landlords (in particular) may wish to accommodate individuals below the age of 18, and the question then arises whether it is legally possible to grant an assured tenancy to a minor. Although a legal estate (including a term of years absolute) cannot be held by a minor (Law of Property Act 1925, s. 1(6)), the problem is more apparent than real. Part I of the HA 1988 defines 'tenancy' as including an agreement for a tenancy, thereby permitting equitable leases to take effect as assured tenancies (s. 45(1)). A contract to enter into an assured tenancy between a landlord and a minor will take effect in equity, and will be effective as an assured tenancy. It will be enforceable against the minor, being excluded from the general rule of unenforceability as a contract for a 'necessary'. Support for this reasoning can be found in the decision of the Court of Appeal in *Kingston Upon Thames Borough Council v Prince* [1999] 1 FLR 593, holding that a minor can succeed to a secure tenancy under the Housing Act 1985. Registered social landlords have been issued with guidance regarding tenancies for 16 and 17 year olds (see Housing Corporation Guidance Circular R3-05/96), which requires that they should normally grant assured shorthold tenancies to persons who are not yet 18, granting them an assured periodic tenancy following their eighteenth birthday.

2.7 OCCUPATION AS ONLY OR PRINCIPAL HOME

A tenancy will be assured only if and so long as the tenant, or one of joint tenants, occupies the dwelling-house as his only or principal home. This terminology is identical to that used for secure tenancies, but differs significantly from the residence condition for Rent Act statutory tenants, who are required to occupy the dwelling in question 'as a residence'. There is no significant distinction between 'home' and 'residence' (see *Hampstead Way Investments Ltd* v *Lewis-Weare* [1985] 1 WLR 164, at 169). In imposing the requirement for an assured tenancy that the dwelling be the tenant's only or principal home, Parliament has set out to prevent privileged tenants who have two or more residences claiming security of tenure in a property which is not in fact their main home. Thus, in construing the residence condition for assured tenancies, considerable care must be taken in using Rent Act authorities, as the question being asked is subtly different. As the Court of Appeal has itself noted, the test for the tenant claiming an assured tenancy is stricter (*Ujima Housing Association* v *Ansah* (1997) 30 HLR 831, 843).

2.7.1 Occupation a question of fact

Whether a tenant occupies the dwelling as his only or principal home is a question of fact for the first instance judge (see, e.g., *Gofor Investments Ltd* v *Roberts* (1975) 29 P & CR 366). The question being one of fact, the Court of Appeal will not reverse the decision of a first instance judge who has asked himself the right question unless his findings on the evidence are 'so unreasonable as to be perverse' (*per* Lawton LJ in *Gofor Investments Ltd* v *Roberts*, at 375). It should not be thought that simply because the Court of Appeal has upheld the decision of a county court judge that a tenant is or is not in occupation, the judges in the Court of Appeal would necessarily have come to the same conclusion themselves, or that a subsequent county court judge will do so on similar facts.

2.7.2 Continuity of occupation and absentee tenants

The leading authority here is *Brown* v *Brash & Ambrose* [1948] 2 KB 247, the leading judgment that of Asquith LJ. The obvious point was made that no tenant can be expected to remain inside his house 24 hours a day, 365 days a year, in order to 'occupy' it. A tenant will inevitably leave the property, sometimes overnight, sometimes for weeks on end, on business, holiday, and so forth, and absences of this kind should not lead to a cessation of his occupation. However, where the absence is so prolonged or uninterrupted as to compel the *prima facie* inference that the tenant has ceased to occupy, he will then, in the event of a claim for possession being made, have the burden of proving that he had not ceased to occupy. To do this, he will have to show:

(a)   that this property remains his residence; and

(b)   that he intends to return to the property after his absence, having left some physical manifestation of that intention behind him. To use the everyday Latin, he must prove an *animus possidendi* and a *corpus possessionis*.

2.7.2.1   *Intention to return*

The intention to return need not be immediate, and it may even be conditional. In *Gofor Investments Ltd v Roberts* (see 2.7.1), the Court of Appeal upheld a decision of a judge who found *animus possidendi* where the tenant did not intend to return for eight to ten years from the date of her departure (although two years from the date of the hearing). In *Tickner v Hearn* [1960] 1 WLR 1406, a tenant had been a patient in a mental home for over six years, and was very unlikely to leave hospital. The Court of Appeal considered that sufficient intention to return was proved, emphasising that there had to be 'a real hope [of return] coupled with the practical possibility of its fulfilment within a reasonable time'. In *Brickfield Properties Ltd v Hughes* (1987) 20 HLR 108, a tenant, now aged 74, was absent from a London flat from 1978 until 1987, excepting two brief visits. His children lived in the flat, while he lived in a cottage in Lancashire with his wife. The Court of Appeal upheld the decision of the judge that the tenant still occupied the London flat: he intended to return to London if his wife predeceased him, or if they found living alone too difficult, and this was enough.

On the other side of the line are the following decisions of the Court of Appeal. In *Duke v Porter* [1986] 2 EGLR 101, the tenant left the cottage in 1975 to live with his children in a flat above his work place following the death of his wife. Although he visited the cottage frequently, and claimed that he intended to return to live there (and did in fact go back following the commencement of proceedings), he no longer occupied it as his residence. In *D.J. Crocker Securities (Portsmouth) Ltd v Johal* [1989] 2 EGLR 102, the tenant left the flat in 1977, returning to his native Malaysia where he established a thriving practice as a lawyer. On proceedings being commenced in 1985, the tenant claimed an intention to return to live in the London flat, but this was summarily rejected by the Court of Appeal: it was an 'abuse of language' to describe him as occupying the flat as his home. In *Robert Thackray's Estates v Kaye* [1989] 1 EGLR 127, the tenant left her flat at the request of the landlord as he wished to carry out repairs. When she refused to return to the flat unless the landlord did further works, she was held to have thereby lost her statutory tenancy: her *animus possidendi* had been relinquished.

It is important that the tenant intends to live in the dwelling. It is not enough that he merely wishes to use it intermittently for storage purposes, or otherwise for his personal convenience (see, e.g., *Regalian Securities Ltd v Scheuer* (1982) 47 P & CR 362, following *Beck v Scholz* [1953] 1 QB 570). Where the tenant has himself sub-let, even for a relatively short time, he will find it very difficult to assert that continuity of occupation has been preserved (*Ujima Housing Association v Ansah* (1997) 30 HLR 831).

2.7.2.2 Visible sign of continued occupation

In *Brown v Brash & Ambrose* [1948] 2 KB 247, the Court of Appeal stressed the importance of the tenant leaving some physical manifestation of his intention to return on the property, a *corpus possessionis*. The tenant was sentenced to two years' imprisonment for stealing tea. He intended at all times to return to the property when he was free to do so. For the first six months of his incarceration, his common law wife and children carried on living there. They comprised the necessary *corpus*, being 'some visible state of affairs in which the *animus possidendi* finds expression'. The mistress was in a sense a 'caretaker' (using the word in its widest sense), charged with the function of preserving the premises for the tenant's homecoming. When the family left the property, however, the tenant ceased in law to occupy, as there was no longer a 'symbol of continued occupation'. Later cases have been more generous to the tenant, holding that even the presence of furniture on the property may be enough to satisfy this element (*Gofor Investments Ltd v Roberts* (1975) 29 P & CR 366; *Hoggett v Hoggett* (1980) 39 P & CR 121). Thus, the departure of the caretaker, or even the removal of furniture by a third party (but presumably not the landlord), can deprive the tenant of his statutory status even though he does not know that this has occurred, and still intends to return to the property. The presence of furniture in the premises will not of itself be sufficient if the tenant is unable to show that it was indicative of his intention to return. Mere use of the premises for storage is not enough (see, e.g., resident landlord case of *Jackson v Pekic* [1989] 2 EGLR 104).

2.7.2.3 Time to ask question

In *Gofor Investments Ltd v Roberts* (1975) 29 P & CR 366, the Court of Appeal differed as to the date at which the residential qualification has to be assessed. Mackenna J stated that the tenant's intention and other similar matters must be considered at the date when her right to continue as a statutory tenant is challenged. Cairns LJ believed that if at any time between the ending of the contractual tenancy and the hearing the tenant ceased to occupy the dwelling as her residence, then she could not be a statutory tenant. The latter view accords more closely with the wording of the statute, which preserves a statutory tenancy if and so long as the tenant occupies the dwelling as his residence. It certainly cannot be the case that a tenant who is physically absent from the dwelling (and has in law ceased to occupy) can on receipt of the summons return to the property and claim that at the date of the hearing he is in occupation.

2.7.3 Husband and wife

Part IV of the Family Law Act 1996 (FLA 1996) makes important qualifications to the requirement of occupation where a husband and wife are concerned. Where one spouse only is assured tenant of the property, the other will have 'matrimonial home rights', comprising:

(a) if in occupation, the right not to be evicted or excluded from the dwelling-house or any part of it by the other spouse except with the leave of the court given by an order under FLA 1996, s. 33;

(b) if not in occupation, the right with the leave of the court under FLA 1996, s. 33 to enter into and occupy the dwelling-house (FLA 1996, s. 30(2)).

Matrimonial home rights are not conferred where the dwelling-house has at no time been, and was at no time intended by the spouses to be, a matrimonial home of theirs (FLA 1996, s. 30(7)). Thus, if a husband provides his estranged wife with a rented property to live in following their separation, it is unlikely that she will have matrimonial home rights in it (see *Hall* v *King* [1988] 1 FLR 376, although note that the then legislation was more restricted).

A spouse's occupation by virtue of the FLA 1996, s. 30 is treated, for the purposes of Part I of the HA 1988, as occupation by the tenant spouse (FLA 1996, s. 30(4)). Thus, if the tenant spouse (for ease of exposition, let us say the husband, although the provisions are gender neutral) leaves the wife, not intending to return, her occupation will be enough for his assured tenancy to persist. She will be entitled to make payments of rent and other outgoings herself (FLA 1996, s. 30(3)), and would be well advised to do so in the event of her husband defaulting, as the landlord may otherwise have grounds for possession.

The operation of these provisions in the FLA 1996 depends upon the parties being married. No protection is provided in the form of 'quasi-matrimonial home rights' for 'common law spouses' (see, on the previous legislation, *Colin Smith Music Ltd* v *Ridge* [1975] 1 WLR 463), and a deserted unmarried partner of an assured tenant has no right to remain as against the landlord under the HA 1988. If the parties have been married but are no longer, the same principle will usually prevail, as the matrimonial home rights continue only so long as the marriage subsists (FLA 1996, s. 30(8)). However, the spouse may apply, during the marriage (i.e. before decree absolute or the divorce order), for an order providing that the matrimonial home rights are not to be brought to an end by the termination of the marriage (FLA 1996, s. 33(5)). This is an important and useful extension of the pre-existing law. The spouse may achieve longer-term relief by seeking an order transferring the tenancy into her name (FLA 1996, s. 53, Sch. 7, a remedy which is available to cohabitants and former cohabitants, as well as to spouses). Where the spouses are joint tenants of the matrimonial home problems of this nature should not arise, as in such a case the tenancy will remain assured as long as one of them occupies the dwelling as his or her only or principal home (HA 1988, s. 1(1)(b)). See further 4.2 below and Bridge [1998] Fam Law 26.

CHAPTER THREE

Exclusions from Assured Tenancies

A tenancy cannot be an assured tenancy, or, by definition, an assured shorthold tenancy, 'if and so long as' it falls within any paragraph of Sch. 1 to the HA 1988. These will now be dealt with in turn.

3.1 TENANCIES PRE-DATING THE HOUSING ACT 1988

It was the policy of the 1988 Act to retain Rent Act status for protected or statutory tenancies existing at the time the Housing Act came into force. The 1988 Act was not (with one or two exceptions) retrospective in nature. Thus, as a general rule, tenancies (whether or not Rent Act regulated) entered into before 15 January 1989, or pursuant to a contract made before that date, cannot be assured tenancies (Sch. 1, para. 1).

3.1.1 Transfers to the private sector

An important exception to this general rule is found in the HA 1988, s. 38. By this provision, a tenant of a 'public body' (e.g., a local authority, a new town corporation, an urban development corporation, a housing action trust: see s. 38(5) for full definition) whose tenancy was entered into before 15 January 1989, or pursuant to a contract made before that date, and whose landlord subsequently alienates its interest to a non-public body, thereupon becomes an assured tenant of that new landlord, if in all other respects the conditions necessary for an assured tenancy are fulfilled. The broad effect can be summarised by stating that tenants who move from the public to the private sector become assured tenants on transfer irrespective of the dates their tenancies were entered into.

Example

In 1988, district council L let a house on secure tenancy to T. In 1990, L sold the house to P, which is not a 'public body' within s. 38(5). On the date of completion T ceased to be a secure tenant, as the 'landlord condition' of HA 1985, s. 80, was no longer satisfied. T's tenancy will have become assured, as long as it fulfils the usual conditions, although it was entered into before the commencement of the 1988 Act.

There are special provisions concerning new town corporations (see HA 1988, s. 38(4), as amended by the Local Government and Housing Act 1989, s. 194(1), Sch. 11) and, of wider relevance, housing associations.

3.2 HIGH VALUE PROPERTIES

The abolition of the domestic rating system led to considerable complexity in ascertaining whether a property was within the scope of the HA 1988. Amendments were made to the Act, in consequence of the replacement of rates by the community charge, by the References to Rating (Housing) Regulations 1990 (SI 1990, No. 434).

Under Sch. 1, para. 2A, if the tenancy was entered into before, or pursuant to a contract made before, 1 April 1990, then the test refers to the rateable value of the dwelling-house on 31 March 1990. If in Greater London this exceeded £1,500, or elsewhere £750, the tenancy cannot be assured.

Under Sch. 1, para. 2, if the tenancy was entered into after 1 April 1990, or the dwelling-house had no rateable value on 31 March 1990, then the test is the rent payable. If this exceeds £25,000 a year 'for the time being', the tenancy cannot be assured. For the purposes of para. 2 (and also para. 3 below), 'rent' does not include sums payable by the tenant which are expressed to be payable in respect of rates, services, management, repairs, maintenance or insurance, unless they could not have been regarded by the parties as sums so payable (Sch. 1, para. 2(2)). 'Rent' has been held not to include the value of services rendered by the tenant for the benefit of the landlord (*Barnes* v *Barratt* [1970] 2 QB 657). Where a tenant was employed by his landlord and occupied rent-free accommodation, receiving a smaller wage as a result, it was held proper to quantify the rent by reference to the reduction in wages (*Montagu* v *Browning* [1954] 1 WLR 1039).

If during the tenancy the annual rent is increased to a level in excess of £25,000, the tenancy will cease to be an assured tenancy. This may occur where the landlord invokes rent review provisions in the tenancy agreement, or where the landlord serves notice of increase on an assured periodic tenant pursuant to the HA 1988, s. 13. A rent assessment committee has jurisdiction to determine a rent for an assured tenancy in excess of £25,000 per annum (*R v London Rent Assessment Panel, ex parte Cadogan Estates Ltd* [1997] 2 EGLR 134).

3.3   TENANCIES AT A LOW RENT

There is no prohibition as such on 'long tenancies' (where the tenant obtains a lease exceeding 21 years, probably for a substantial premium) being assured tenancies. However, many will be caught by para. 3 of Sch. 1. As with para. 2 above, complexities have arisen from the abolition of domestic rates: see again for relevant amendments SI 1990, No. 434.

If the tenancy is entered into before 1 April 1990, or in pursuance of a contract made before that date, then it cannot be assured if the rent for the time being payable is less than two-thirds of the rateable value of the dwelling-house on 31 March 1990 (Sch. 1, para. 3B). If the tenancy was entered into on or after 1 April 1990, or the dwelling-house did not have a rateable value on that date, the tenancy cannot be assured if the rent for the time being is payable at a rate of £1,000 or less per year in Greater London, £250 or less per year elsewhere (Sch. 1, para. 3A). It follows (but is also expressly stated in Sch. 1, para. 3) that a tenancy under which for the time being no rent is payable cannot be an assured tenancy.

A landlord may seek to avoid the creation of an assured tenancy by charging a rent below these limits, but combining it with a high premium at the commencement of the lease. Under the RA 1977, the courts were known to strike down premiums which were essentially a capitalised pre-payment of rent (*Samrose Properties Ltd v Gibbard* [1958] 1 WLR 235), premiums being in any case restricted in relation to protected or statutory tenancies. However, it is perfectly lawful to charge a premium as consideration for an assured tenancy, and it may be more difficult for the courts to rationalise intervention where assured tenancies are concerned.

3.4   BUSINESS TENANCIES

A tenancy to which Part II of the Landlord and Tenant Act 1954 applies (i.e. a 'business tenancy') cannot be an assured tenancy (Sch. 1, para. 4). The definition of business tenancy is:

any tenancy where the property comprised in the tenancy is or includes premises which are occupied by the tenant and are so occupied for the purposes of a business carried on by him or for those or other purposes. (Landlord and Tenant Act 1954, s. 23(1))

'Business' is in turn widely defined, so as to include a trade, profession or employment, and it 'includes any activity carried on by a body of persons, whether corporate or unincorporate' (Landlord and Tenant Act 1954, s. 23(2)). There has been much reported litigation on the interpretation of these provisions.

3.4.1 Mixed user

The definition in s. 23(1) of the 1954 Act is wide, including as it does property which 'includes premises' which are occupied for business 'and other purposes'. A small but significant amount of business user of a dwelling-house will be enough to make the tenancy a business tenancy, and thereby take it outside the provisions of the HA 1988. Thus, a doctor who uses a room in his rented house as a consulting room will occupy the premises for the purposes of his business (i.e. 'profession'). A shopkeeper who holds under his lease a shop with a flat above will be a business tenant. However, the business user must be a significant purpose of the occupation, and not merely incidental to occupation as a residence, for the tenancy to fall within the 1954 Act. Essentially, this is a question of degree. In *Royal Life Saving Society* v *Page* [1978] 1 WLR 1329, a doctor rented a maisonette as his home. With the landlords' consent, he saw the occasional patient at his home in an emergency, and he used the telephone in the flat for professional purposes. The business user was not significant enough for the tenancy to be a business tenancy. Geoffrey Lane LJ said (at 1339):

The businessman ... who takes work home in the evening which he does in a study set aside for the purpose may very well be using the premises partly for carrying thereat a business, but he could scarcely be said to be occupying the premises for the purposes of a business, any more than the person who watches the television regularly every evening can be said to be occupying his house for the purpose of watching television. It is only if the activity is part of the reason for, part of his aim and object in occupying the house that the section will apply.

The test contained in the final sentence was approved by the Court of Appeal in *Gurton* v *Parrot* (1990) 23 HLR 418, holding that a tenant who used her property for the grooming, breeding, and kenneling of dogs 'as a hobby which provided her with some money to help with living expenses and upkeep of the property' was not occupying the premises for that purpose.

3.4.2 Change of user: from residence to business

In *Cheryl Investments Ltd* v *Saldanha* [1978] 1 WLR 1329 (consolidated with *Royal Life Saving Society* v *Page* in the Court of Appeal), a protected tenant equipped his flat with a telephone, a work table and printed notepaper, and commenced to carry on a seafood importing business from the flat. He had no other place of work. Lord Denning MR held that the tenancy was a business tenancy under Part II of the 1954 Act rather than a Rent Act protected tenancy. The change of use effected a change in the status of the tenancy once it could be said that the premises were being occupied for the purposes of a business. It was immaterial that the landlord did not know about the business use being carried on.

3.4.3 Change of user: from business to residence

In *Pulleng* v *Curran* (1980) 44 P & CR 58, a tenant attempted to argue that his tenancy, which he acknowledged had started life as a business tenancy, had become protected under the RA 1977 by virtue of his cessation of trading. The premises comprised a grocer's and dairyman's shop, with rooms at the rear and living accommodation above. The tenant contended that he had ceased to trade in 1965, and thereupon the tenancy became protected under the Rent Acts. The Court of Appeal, while refusing to subvert the judge's finding of fact that significant business use had continued up to the date of the relevant proceedings, denied the basic premise of the tenant's argument that a cessation of business use would automatically lead to premises which were being lived in becoming protected under the Rent Acts, following *Wolfe* v *Hogan* [1949] 2 KB 194.

The HA 1988 (and the RA 1977) in setting the criteria for an assured (or, as the case may be, protected) tenancy requires the court to examine the agreement between the parties ('let as a dwelling': HA 1988, s. 1(1)). Part II of the Landlord and Tenant Act 1954 requires the court to look at the purpose of the occupation at the given time ('occupied for the purposes of a business'). The effect is that while a tenancy may change from being a residential tenancy to being a business tenancy without the knowledge, actual or assumed, of the landlord, the converse is not the case. The issue received its closest analysis in *Russell* v *Booker* (1982) 263 EG 513, where the Court of Appeal was asked to decide whether on termination of agricultural use a property, originally let as an agricultural holding, which included a dwelling-house, became a protected tenancy. Slade LJ stated:

> If a tenant changes the user of the premises and the fact of change is fully known to, and accepted by, the landlord, it may be possible for the court to infer a subsequent contract to let them 'a separate dwelling-house', although this would be a contract different in essentials from the original tenancy agreement ... However, unless a contract of the last-mentioned nature can be spelt out, a mere unilateral change of user will not enable a tenant to claim the protection of the Rent Acts in a case where the terms of the tenancy agreement itself provide for and contemplate the use of the premises for some particular purpose which does not attract the protection of the Acts – for example as a shop or agricultural holding ... Where the tenancy agreement does not provide or contemplate the use of the premises for any particular purpose, actual subsequent user has to be looked at in determining whether a house is 'let as a separate dwelling-house', so as to attract the protection of the Rent Acts.

The above passage has equal application to a possible transformation from a business or agricultural tenancy to an assured tenancy, replacing 'Rent Acts' with 'Housing Act 1988' where necessary.

3.4.4 Tenant tactics

While the above case law, decided on the equivalent provisions in the RA 1977, proceeds on the rational assumption that a tenant is better off as a Rent Act regulated tenant (enjoying as he does the benefit of rent control) rather than as a business tenant (whose tenancy will not have a controlled rent), it may not always be in the tenant's interests to argue that he is an assured tenant rather than a business tenant. The procedure for obtaining possession of property let on a business tenancy is highly technical and fraught with pitfalls, and the tenant may on advice see himself in a stronger bargaining position as a business tenant. This will nowhere more clearly be the case than where the landlord has initiated proceedings on the basis that the defendant is an assured tenant, as the landlord will clearly be unable to succeed in such an action if the tenant can establish that his tenancy is protected by Part II of the Landlord and Tenant Act 1954.

3.5   LICENSED PREMISES

A tenancy under which the dwelling-house consists of or comprises premises licensed for the sale of intoxicating liquors for consumption on the premises cannot be an assured tenancy (Sch. 1, para. 5). This exclusion largely affects public houses. Since 11 July 1992, such tenancies have been brought within the business tenancy code contained in Part II of the Landlord and Tenant Act 1954 (see Landlord and Tenant (Licensed Premises) Act 1990), and so most of these tenancies will now be denied assured status anyway by para. 4 above. Most tenancies of 'off-licences' will be business tenancies under Part II of the 1954 Act.

3.6   TENANCIES OF AGRICULTURAL LAND

A tenancy under which 'agricultural land' (as defined in the General Rate Act 1967, s. 26(3)(a)), exceeding two acres, is let together with the dwelling-house cannot be an assured tenancy (Sch. 1, para. 6). If not more than two acres of agricultural land is let with the dwelling (or any amount of non-agricultural land), that other land is to be treated as part of the dwelling-house as long as the 'main purpose' of the letting is the provision of a home for the tenant, or for one of two or more joint tenants (HA 1988, s. 2).

3.7   TENANCIES OF AGRICULTURAL HOLDINGS ETC.

The Agricultural Tenancies Act 1995 made radical changes to the law relating to the letting of agricultural land, and provided a new structure for agricultural tenancies. The 1995 Act deregulated the landlord and tenant relationship, creating a new form of tenure known as the farm business tenancy, whereby the parties' agreement was to be respected and enforced, with a minimum amount of statutory interference. However, the Act did not affect agreements entered into before 1 September 1995, many of. which would attract security of tenure pursuant to the Agricultural Holdings Act 1986. Tenancies of agricultural holdings have always been excluded from the HA 1988 (and, before that, the RA 1977). The Agricultural Tenancies Act 1995 amended the 1988 Act so that farm business tenancies are similarly excluded. It is impossible to do justice to the complexity of the underlying definitions of 'agricultural holdings' and 'farm business tenancies' in this book. Reference should be made to one of the specialist texts on agricultural tenancies, such as Scammell & Densham, *Law of Agricultural Holdings*, 8th ed., 1997.

By para. 7 of Sch. 1 to the HA 1988, a tenancy under which the dwelling-house is comprised in an agricultural holding and is occupied by the person responsible for the control (whether as tenant, or as servant or agent of the tenant) of the farming of the holding cannot be an assured tenancy. Likewise, a tenancy under which the dwelling-house is comprised in the holding held under a farm business tenancy and is occupied by the person responsible for the control (whether as tenant or as agent or servant of the tenant) of the management of the holding cannot be an assured tenancy.

A property which is initially let as a dwelling-house, with no, or purely subsidiary, use for agriculture, may be converted from being an assured tenancy to a tenancy within the Agricultural Holdings Act 1986 or the Agricultural Tenancies Act 1995 by a change of use. However, although a dwelling-house which is initially let as part of an agricultural holding or pursuant to a farm business tenancy may, on a cesser of agricultural use, no longer be within the 1986 Act or the 1995 Act, it does not follow that it will thereupon convert into an assured tenancy as a matter of course. To qualify as an assured tenancy, the property must be 'let as a dwelling' (HA 1988, s. 1(1)), and the tenant must therefore prove that a new contract has been made, either on the parties' express agreement or by inference from the landlord's tacit acceptance of the position (*Russell* v *Booker* (1982) 263 EG 513: see 3.4.3 above).

3.8 LETTINGS TO STUDENTS

Despite this heading in Sch. 1, para. 8, by no means all lettings to students are excluded from protection as assured tenancies. The identity of the landlord is the determining factor. Paragraph 8 excludes tenancies which are granted to students by a 'specified educational institution or body of persons'. The institution must have been specified by the Secretary of State by statutory instrument. The current instrument is the Assured and Protected Tenancies (Lettings to Students) Regulations 1998 (SI 1998 No. 1967), which can be found in Appendix C. It lists universities, university colleges, other publicly-funded further or higher education institutions, registered housing associations, and various named bodies. The student need not be full-time: he or she must be merely pursuing, or intending to pursue, a course of study at a specified educational institution. If an educational institution is specified by regulation, any tenancy it grants to a student cannot be assured, even if it is desired by the institution. For several years many such institutions established business expansion ('B.E.S.') schemes, under which fiscal advantages were obtained provided that lettings to students were on assured tenancy. Under such schemes (which have ceased to be available), the landlord was the B.E.S. company, not itself a specified institution, and so no difficulty with para. 8 resulted. Vacation lettings of student accommodation to other persons are not covered by para. 8. However, the landlord has the opportunity of availing himself of a mandatory ground for possession on termination of such a fixed-term tenancy (HA 1988, Sch. 2, Ground 4).

3.9   HOLIDAY LETTINGS

Tenancies the purpose of which is to confer on the tenant the right to occupy the dwelling-house for a holiday are excluded from assured tenancy status (Sch. 1, para. 9). In *Buchmann v May* [1978] 2 All ER 993, 'holiday' was defined as 'a period of cessation of work or a period of recreation'. A dancer from New Zealand had been the tenant of a dwelling-house for two years when she signed a new agreement which stated that 'the letting hereby made is solely for the purpose of the tenant's holiday'. The Court of Appeal, holding that the onus was on the tenant to displace this *prima facie* evidence of the parties' true purpose, decided that she had failed to do this, and the tenancy was accordingly unprotected. In the light of *Street v Mountford*, where Lord Templeman adverted to the need to detect shams and other artificial devices intended to avoid the application of protective statutes, *Buchmann v May* should be treated with caution. In *R v Camden Rent Officer, ex parte Plant* (1980) 257 EG 713, Glidewell J, sitting in the Divisional Court, took a more sanguine view of a purported 'holiday let'. The landlord let to four student nurses, the written agreement stating that the letting was for the purposes of a holiday. As there was clear evidence that the landlord knew that his tenants were nurses and that they were not occupying for the purposes of a holiday, Glidewell J held that the tenancy was not excluded from protection.

3.10   RESIDENT LANDLORDS

The resident landlord exception, based upon the 'social embarrassment' which would arise from involuntary 'close proximity' of landlord and tenant (*Bardrick v Haycock* (1976) 31 P & CR 420, at 424), was long established in relation to Rent Act protected tenancies. However, whereas tenants of resident landlords would normally hold restricted contracts under the Rent Acts, this is not the case with lettings entered into on or after 15 January 1989. If a resident landlord shares 'accommodation' with such a tenant, the tenant will not even enjoy the most basic protection of a statutory minimum period of notice (Protection from Eviction Act 1977, ss. 3, 3A(2), 5, as amended by the HA 1988, ss. 30, 31).

Three conditions (which we will refer to as the 'Rules') must be fulfilled before the resident landlord exception in Sch. 1, para. 10 is established. The way in which the Rules operate depends on whether or not the dwelling let to the tenant forms part of a 'purpose-built block of flats', as defined by the HA 1988, Sch. 1, para. 22. The building must as constructed contain two or more 'flats'. (A 'flat' is a dwelling-house which forms part only of a building which is separated horizontally from another dwelling-house forming part of the same building.) As 'purpose-built' implies, it cannot include buildings which are converted from their former use, perhaps as a single dwelling-house, into self-contained flats. In *Barnes* v *Gorsuch* (1981) 43 P & CR 294, an attempt was made to argue that a Victorian house which was in 1959 divided into three flats, and then subsequently sub-divided so as to make six flats in all, was nevertheless a 'purpose-built block of flats'. O'Connor LJ rejected this argument, holding that the ordinary meaning of the statutory words ('as constructed') referred to 'the building as it was originally designed and built'. The only circumstances in which later works could have a bearing would be where the works were so extensive that the building changed its character and became a different building altogether.

3.10.1 Where the building is a purpose-built block of flats

Rule A: The dwelling-house let to the tenant must form part of one of the flats.

Rule B: The person who granted the tenancy (the first landlord) must have been an individual (i.e. not a company), and he must have occupied another dwelling-house in the same flat as his only or principal home.

Rule C: Subject to the various qualifications below, at all times each of the later landlords must have been an individual and have occupied another dwelling-house in the flat as his only or principal home.

3.10.2 Where the building is not a purpose-built block of flats

Rule A: The dwelling-house let to the tenant must form part only of the building.

Rule B: The first landlord must have been an individual and he must have occupied another dwelling-house in the same building as his only or principal home.

Rule C: Subject to the various qualifications below, at all times each of the later landlords must have been an individual and have occupied another dwelling-house in the same building as his only or principal home.

3.10.3 Part of the building (or flat)

Whether the dwelling let to the tenant forms part of the same building or flat as the dwelling occupied by the landlord is a question of fact and degree. In *Bardrick v Haycock* (1976) 31 P & CR 420, a substantial house was converted into six flats, which were then let to and occupied by tenants. The landlord lived in a two-storey extension which, although physically attached to the house, did not have any internal means of communication to it. The Court of Appeal upheld the decision of the county court judge that the landlord did not occupy a dwelling-house forming part of the same building as that of which the tenants' dwellings formed part, and the resident landlord exception did not apply. Scarman LJ stated:

> The English word 'building' covers an immense range of all sorts of structures. It is an ordinary English word, and its meaning must therefore be a question of fact, always assuming that the court directs itself correctly as to the intention and meaning of the statute which uses it. As a matter of law, to give a defined or precise meaning to the word 'building' is an impossibility. It is beyond the capacity of even the most consummate master of the English language to do so. This itself is, in my judgment, an indication that Parliament is leaving the question of fact to the judge.

3.10.4 Occupation by the landlord

The landlord must occupy a dwelling-house in the same building or flat as the tenant's dwelling, and must do so as his only or principal home. This test is the same which must be satisfied for a tenant to be assured (HA 1988, s. 1(1)(b): see 2.7 above). It is essentially a question of fact, but the mere retention of a sparsely furnished room in the building, which the landlord sleeps in only occasionally, will not be sufficient. As landlords may frequently have more than one home, it is important to check what other residences, if any, the landlord has, and, if he has, whether this is his principal home.

3.10.5 Joint landlords

Where the landlord's interest is held by more than one person, the occupation of one will suffice to fuel the resident landlord exception. As long as at least one of those holding the landlord's interest is an individual, and that individual or one of them is occupying at the relevant times, it is immaterial that a company, or an institution, is a joint owner of that interest (HA 1988, Sch. 1, para. 10(2)).

3.10.6 ˙ Occupation throughout the tenancy

It can be seen from the above statement of the basic Rules, in particular Rule C, that where the tenant has had different landlords, the evaluation of whether the tenancy is excluded from assured tenancy status by reason of the resident landlord exception may involve a close analysis of the way in which the landlord's interest has been passed on, and the residence of each and every subsequent landlord. One must not lose sight also that the first landlord must have been in occupation at the time of the tenancy agreement (i.e. Rule B), although there appears to be a certain amount of latitude for landlords where they move property together with their tenants. In *Barnett* v *O'Sullivan* [1995] 1 EGLR 93, the tenant had lived in premises let by the resident landlords since 1960. In 1984, both landlords and the tenant moved to a different property in the same street. The tenant moved one week before the landlords, and subsequently contended that resident landlord status was thereby lost, as neither landlord had been in occupation at the date of the grant of the new tenancy. The Court of Appeal held that where there was a move by landlord and tenant from one building to another by mutual consent, it was wholly artificial to split up the coordinated transfer into separate stages, nor was it appropriate to consider 'fine matters of timing'. The resident landlord exception continued to apply.

Circumstances may arise in which it becomes difficult, perhaps through no fault of the landlord, to continue to satisfy the residence condition. Schedule 1 to the 1988 Act makes provision for such an eventuality by stipulating that in certain circumstances, Rule C will be 'deemed to be fulfilled', and that in others, a 'period of disregard' will intervene. Where Rule C is deemed to be fulfilled, the resident landlord exception applies, and the landlord will be able to bring proceedings to recover possession on the basis that the tenancy is not an assured tenancy. During a period of disregard, the landlord's right to recover possession without proof of grounds for possession is suspended, but on Rule C being once more satisfied (e.g., the landlord goes back into residence) the resident landlord exception will apply again.

3.10.7 Rule C 'deemed to be fulfilled'

The effect of Rule C being deemed to be fulfilled in one of the instances set out below is that, if Rules A and B are also satisfied, the tenancy will not be assured. Nor will the tenancy be a restricted contract, having been entered into on or after 15 January 1989, and the landlord will be able to obtain possession by any common law method of terminating the tenancy (forfeiture, notice, expiry of fixed term, etc.), subject only to compliance with the Protection from Eviction Act 1977.

Rule C will be deemed to be fulfilled in three instances:

    (a)   where the landlord's interest is vested in trustees on trust for a beneficiary or beneficiaries, at least one of whom occupies a dwelling-house which is part of the building (or flat) as his only or principal home (HA 1988, Sch. 1, para. 18);

    (b)   where the landlord's interest has been so vested in trustees, and the tenancy has come to an end, during the full duration of any new tenancy of the same (or substantially the same) dwelling-house which the trustees grant to the sitting tenant (para. 19);

    (c)   for a period, not exceeding two years, throughout which the landlord's interest is vested in personal representatives (i.e. the persons who, following the death of the resident landlord, have his estate vested in them by his will or on his intestacy) (para. 20).

Example

A house is settled on trust by settlor S, the beneficiaries being A, B and C. C occupies a room in the house (which is not a purpose-built block of flats) as his principal home, and has done so ever since the other rooms in the house were let in 1990. The tenants of those rooms will not be assured tenants as long as C continues to reside, and the trustees will be able to obtain possession of any of the rooms by giving the tenants the notice to which they are entitled under the terms of their tenancy agreements. (The tenants would be entitled to a minimum of four weeks' notice in writing, unless the tenancy is an 'excluded tenancy': Protection from Eviction Act 1977, s. 5(1).)

3.10.8   Periods of disregard

A 'period of disregard' is a period of grace where for a specific reason the landlord may find it difficult to satisfy the condition of residence. The period of disregard will end on the residence condition being once more fulfilled, whether by the individual owning the landlord's interest commencing to occupy the dwelling as his only or principal home, or by activation of the deeming provisions above. During a period of disregard, no order for possession of the dwelling-house shall be made other than an order which might be made were the tenancy an assured tenancy (HA 1988, Sch. 1, para. 21). However, although possession cannot be ordered during a period of disregard, the tenancy may be terminated by any of the common law methods of termination which may be available (e.g., by giving notice in relation to a periodic tenancy). If the tenancy is so terminated, possession can be obtained when the period of disregard ends. The tenancy does not temporarily become an assured tenancy during the period of disregard (if it did, it could not be terminated by the landlord: HA 1988, s. 5(1)).

The fact that the landlord's occupation condition is not for the time being fulfilled will be disregarded in four instances:

(a) for a period of 28 days following the vesting of the landlord's interest in an individual who does not occupy the dwelling-house as his only or principal home (e.g., the landlord sells his interest to a purchaser) (Sch. 1, para. 17(1)(a));

(b) for a further period of six months following the vesting of the landlord's interest in such an individual, provided that the individual has notified the tenant in writing of his intention to occupy the dwelling-house as his only or principal home during the initial 28-day period above. The six months runs from the date the landlord's interest was vested in the individual concerned (not the date of the written notice) (Sch. 1, para. 17(1)(b));

(c) a period of two years following the vesting of the landlord's interest in trustees or the Probate Judge (i.e. on death intestate) (Sch. 1, para. 17(1)(c));

(d) a period of two years following the death of a beneficiary behind a trust whose occupation of the dwelling-house has until then caused condition (c) to be fulfilled (Sch. 1, para. 18(2)).

In *Landau v Sloane* [1982] AC 490, Lord Fraser of Tullybelton explained (at 502):

> where a tenancy ... comes to an end during the period of disregard, the tenant, or more properly now the ex-tenant, is left with no relevant rights under the Act except the right not to have an order for possession made against him during the disregard period. It seems inappropriate to describe a person in that position as a trespasser, but I see no alternative.

Landau v Sloane concerned the period of disregard which then applied (for the purposes of the RA 1977) where the landlord's interest was vested in personal representatives of a deceased person. Under both the 1988 Act and the RA 1977 (as amended by the HA 1980, s. 65, which was enacted in consequence of the Court of Appeal decision in *Landau v Sloane*), the landlord's occupation condition is in such circumstances now 'deemed to be fulfilled' for a period of two years. Despite this, the decision of the House of Lords remains the leading authority on the effect of a period of disregard (i.e. the meaning of HA 1988, Sch. 1, para. 21, and RA 1977, Sch. 2, para. 3). The clear position is that during the period of disregard, the tenant's contractual tenancy can be terminated if the agreement so permits, and then, on expiry of that period, a possession order sought from the court.

Example: purchasing the resident landlord's interest

L, the landlord, lives in a basement flat of a house of which he owns the freehold and which has been converted into several one-bedroom flats. T lives in the ground-floor flat which was let to him under a weekly tenancy on 1 January 1994. L has satisfied the condition of residence throughout the period of T's tenancy. On 1 January 1998, L sells the freehold in the house to P, who thereupon becomes T's landlord. On 21 January 1998, P serves written notice on T stating that he intends to occupy the basement flat within the six-month period which commenced on 1 January 1998. Until he goes into occupation, P cannot obtain possession of T's flat unless he can show that were T an assured tenant an order for possession would be made. However, following *Landau v Sloane*, P can terminate the weekly tenancy by giving notice of the appropriate length (four weeks': Protection from Eviction Act 1977, s. 5(1), unless the agreement falls within s. 3A thereof). If, however, P does not terminate the tenancy, and does not go into occupation until after 30 June 1998, he will fail to satisfy Rule C, the resident landlord exception will cease to apply, and T will become a fully fledged assured tenant. The result will be the same if P neither goes into occupation nor serves written notice stating his intention to do so before 29 January 1998.

3.10.9 Re-grants

A landlord may be tempted to sidestep the horribly complicated residence conditions by the simple expedient of granting his tenants new tenancies. Thus, he could argue, at the time of grant, and at all times thereafter, Rules B and C have been satisfied. It would be an effective method of wiping the slate clean. However, this tactic is countered by para. 10(3) of Sch. 1 to the 1988 Act. The resident landlord exception will not apply if the tenancy is granted to a person (alone, or jointly) who, immediately before it was granted, was a tenant under an assured tenancy of the same dwelling-house or of another dwelling-house which forms part of the building in question, and the landlord under the old and the new tenancy is the same person or, if either of the tenancies was granted by two or more persons jointly, the same person is the landlord or one of the landlords under each tenancy.

While this provision will be effective in most simple cases, it is not by any means watertight. The new tenancy must be granted to someone who immediately before the grant was an assured tenant of the landlord. A landlord may seek to engineer a brief lapse of time between the ending of the old tenancy and the commencement of the new. Nor does the provision appear to take account of the landlord who sells his interest and, contemporaneously with that sale, obtains a surrender of the old assured tenancies, the incoming resident landlord then offering the new tenancies.

3.11   CROWN TENANCIES

A tenancy under which the landlord's interest belongs to Her Majesty in right of the Crown (save where it is under the management of the Crown Estate Commissioners) or to a government department or is held in trust for Her Majesty for the purposes of a government department cannot be an assured tenancy (Sch. 1, para. 11). If the landlord's interest is assigned to or from one of these bodies during the existence of the tenancy, the tenancy will cease to be, or become, an assured tenancy, as the case may be.

3.12   LOCAL AUTHORITY TENANCIES ETC.

A tenancy under which the landlord's interest belongs to a local authority (as defined in Sch. 1, para. 12(2)), the Commission for New Towns, the Development Board for Rural Wales, an urban development corporation, a development corporation, a waste disposal authority, a residuary body, a fully mutual housing association (the only kind of housing association to be so excluded), or a housing action trust, cannot be an assured tenancy (Sch. 1, para. 12). Many of these 'public' bodies will let on secure tenancy.

3.13   TRANSITIONAL CASES

A tenancy which is a protected tenancy, a housing association tenancy, a secure tenancy or a tenancy by virtue of which a protected occupier under the Rent (Agriculture) Act 1976 occupies a dwelling-house, cannot be an assured tenancy (Sch. 1, para. 13). These are not all, as the title to the paragraph indicates, purely 'transitional' cases. Secure tenancies are not being phased out as a result of the HA 1988, and there will be protected tenancies and Rent (Agriculture) Act protected occupancies for many years to come.

It is important to realise that 'housing association tenancy' has a very limited meaning in this context. It means a tenancy to which Part VI of the RA 1977 applies: a tenancy where the landlord's interest belongs to a housing association or housing trust or the Housing Corporation, and the tenancy would be a protected tenancy but for s. 15 or s. 16 of the RA 1977 (which excluded from protected status tenancies where the landlord was, for the time being, a certain type of housing association or housing cooperative). It can be seen that this is an essentially transitional exclusion, as it applies almost exclusively to tenancies granted before 15 January 1989 (see HA 1988, s. 35). It must now have very little practical significance.

3.14 ACCOMMODATION FOR HOMELESS PERSONS

Where accommodation is provided in pursuance of statutory obligations to house the homeless, a local authority may use its own housing stock, or (as is becoming more frequent as the public housing stock declines) use accommodation provided by others, particularly registered social landlords which are under a duty to cooperate with local authorities in the discharge of their homelessness functions (HA 1996, s. 213). Where housing is provided by a private landlord (meaning a landlord which cannot let on secure tenancy: see HA 1985, s. 79) pursuant to such arrangements, the tenancy will not normally be an assured tenancy for a period of 12 months beginning with the date on which the applicant for housing was notified of the authority's decision or of any review or the date on which any appeal was finally determined (HA 1996, s. 209(2)). However, if, before or during that period, the private landlord notifies the tenant that the tenancy is to be an assured tenancy, the tenancy will be assured. Where the private landlord is a registered social landlord, any such tenancy must be an assured shorthold tenancy (HA 1996, s. 209(3)).

Where the private landlord does not serve any notice rendering the occupier an assured tenant during the 12-month period, the question may arise what happens at the end of that period if the person continues to occupy. The landlord is unlikely to succeed in an argument that, the accommodation being essentially of a temporary nature, the occupier is a licensee rather than a tenant (*Eastleigh Borough Council* v *Walsh* [1985] 1 WLR 525). It should be noted, however, that certain agreements between local authorities and homeless persons may not evince an intention to grant exclusive possession on the part of the landlord, when that intention is construed against the appropriate background of statutory duties and obligations (see, e.g., *Ogwr Borough Council* v *Dykes* [1989] 1 WLR 295; *Westminster City Council* v *Clarke* [1992] 2 AC 288).

CHAPTER FOUR

Recovery of Possession

4.1 INTRODUCTION

As long as the tenant is an assured tenant, the landlord will be able to recover possession of the dwelling-house only by obtaining a possession order from the court. Unless the tenant is an assured shortholder, the court has jurisdiction to make a possession order only where grounds for possession set out in the HA 1988 are made out. In this chapter, we shall consider how the landlord can recover possession, and in doing so explain the extent of security which the assured tenant enjoys. In the following chapter, we shall examine the means of recovery of possession available where the tenant is an assured shorthold tenant.

It is important to realise, however, that in the event of the tenant ceasing to be an assured tenant, the landlord's powers to recover possession are no longer circumscribed by the 1988 Act; and, further, that the assured tenant may be vulnerable to the exercise of powers by public bodies which enable them to obtain possession of the property, or to the exercise of a mortgagee's power to repossess the leasehold interest. Before considering the means whereby the landlord can regain possession by seeking an order of the court, we should elaborate briefly upon these other options.

4.2 TENANT CEASES TO BE AN ASSURED TENANT

4.2.1 Termination of tenancy by tenant

Nothing in the HA 1988 prevents the assured tenant from exercising any contractual right he may have to terminate the lease. Thus, he can give notice to quit of whatever length the lease demands of him (subject to the statutory minimum of four weeks: Protection from Eviction Act 1977, s. 5(1)). He can terminate the lease by invoking a break clause. He can surrender the lease by agreement with the landlord, or there may be a surrender by operation of law. In each of these cases, the action of the tenant, if effective to terminate the tenancy (in itself dependent on its terms), will result in the occupier ceasing to be an assured tenant. If, following termination of the tenancy, he remains in occupation, the landlord will be entitled to repossess, although in order to recover possession an order must be sought from the court.

Where the dwelling-house is let to joint tenants, the service of notice of the appropriate length by one joint tenant on the landlord (perhaps following the breakdown of their relationship with the other joint tenant) will thereby terminate the contractual tenancy between landlord and tenants (see *Hammersmith & Fulham LBC v Monk* [1992] 1 AC 478). The effect is that the remaining tenant (or tenants) would cease to be an assured tenant, as there would be no tenancy to which assured status could adhere.

4.2.2 Tenancy ceases to be assured

Another possibility is that the occupier remains a tenant, but ceases for some reason to be an assured tenant. For example, he may cease to occupy the dwelling-house as his only or principal home, having recently bought another property closer to his workplace, but wishing to spend the occasional weekend at the dwelling-house. The landlord will not in these circumstances be entitled to immediate possession. He must terminate the tenancy first, complying with its terms and the provisions of the Protection from Eviction Act 1977 (in particular ss. 3 and 5). However, as the tenancy is no longer assured, the landlord will not be required to prove grounds for possession under the HA 1988.

4.2.3 Anti-avoidance

An agreement at or before the time of the lease that the assured tenant will give up possession on a particular future date will be unenforceable. The

HA 1988, s. 5(5) is an anti-avoidance provision. Where on or before the date the tenancy is entered into, a tenant enters into an obligation to do any act which will cause the tenancy to come to an end at a time when it is an assured tenancy, or executes, signs or gives any surrender, notice to quit or other document which has the effect of bringing an assured tenancy to an end, that obligation, surrender, notice to quit or other document will be of no effect. A landlord seeking to enforce such an agreement would therefore fail.

4.3 EXERCISE OF STATUTORY POWERS

The HA 1985 contains many of the statutory duties owed by local authorities with regard to housing, and it is provided by s. 612 of that Act that where in the exercise of their powers 'under any enactment in relation to housing' possession is required, nothing in Part I of the 1988 Act will prevent possession being obtained. Further specific provisions are contained in the HA 1985 exempting the assured tenant's security in the event of:

(a) enforcement of an undertaking that premises will not be used for human habitation (s. 264(5));
(b) a demolition order (s. 270(3));
(c) a closing order (s. 276);
(d) an obstructive building order (s. 286(3));
(e) exercise of a power to secure that part of a house is not used for human habitation to provide means of escape from fire (s. 368).

4.4 ACTION BY MORTGAGEE OF THE TENANT

The HA 1988 does not restrict the rights of a mortgagee of the assured tenant's leasehold interest who has lent money on the security of the tenancy to bring proceedings for possession (HA 1988, s. 7(1)).

4.5 RECOVERY OF POSSESSION BY THE LANDLORD

Part I of the HA 1988 seriously restricts the availability to the landlord of the normal methods of termination of tenancies (such as forfeiture for breach of covenant, and notice) where the property is let on assured tenancy. The provisions are complex, and have caused much confusion. It is important to establish first whether the dwelling of which possession is sought is held on fixed-term or periodic tenancy.

4.5.1 Types of tenancy

An assured tenancy can take one of three forms: fixed-term, 'contractual' periodic or statutory periodic. Of these, the first two are created by the agreement of the parties, whereas the third is created by operation of law. A *fixed-term tenancy* arises where the landlord and tenant agree that the tenancy will terminate on a fixed date. Thus a tenancy 'until 31 December 1999' or 'for three years' is a fixed-term tenancy. It is essential to satisfy the condition of certainty that it is possible to state the maximum duration of the lease at its commencement. It is perfectly possible, and indeed usual, for the lease to provide for earlier termination, either as a result of the tenant's breach of covenant (forfeiture) or by the giving of a notice of the length prescribed by the parties (a break clause). However, it should not be thought that such terms in a fixed-term assured tenancy will operate so as to entitle the landlord who invokes them to recovery of possession.

A *periodic tenancy* derives conceptual certainty from the ability of either party to terminate the lease by giving notice to quit. It is not possible to state from the beginning of the tenancy how long the tenant will be in possession, other than to say that he is entitled to be there for the duration of the first 'period'. But unless landlord or tenant serves notice on the other to expire at that time, the tenancy will continue. A periodic tenancy may be created by express agreement of the parties, the lease stating that the tenancy is 'weekly', 'monthly', 'quarterly' or 'yearly' as the case may be. It may also be created by implication from the parties' conduct, the tenant being let into possession and paying rent to the landlord on a periodic basis. In these circumstances, the period of the tenancy will be ascertained according to the period with reference to which rent is calculated. A periodic tenancy is under the general law (outside the HA 1988) terminable by notice given by either party, but unless and until notice is given the tenancy will continue from period to period. Although an assured periodic tenancy may be terminated by the tenant (see 4.2.1 above), termination by a landlord's notice to quit is not, however, possible.

The *statutory periodic tenancy* is part of the machinery of security provided by Part I of the HA 1988. When a fixed-term assured tenancy comes to an end by effluxion of time, and the tenant under the fixed-term tenancy is not expressly granted another tenancy of the same, or substantially the same, dwelling-house, a statutory periodic tenancy will arise (HA 1988, s. 5(2), (4)). The terms of the statutory periodic tenancy will be based on the terms of the fixed-term tenancy which it succeeds, the periods of the tenancy being the same as those for which rent was last payable under the fixed-term (see HA 1988, s. 5(3), and further 6.4.1 below). A statutory periodic tenancy will not arise if the fixed-term tenancy comes to an end by the tenant's own action (such as giving notice to quit, or surrendering the lease) or by an order of the court (HA 1988, s. 5(2)). The statutory periodic tenancy, which need not be an assured tenancy itself (although it usually will be), cannot be terminated by landlord's notice to quit.

4.5.2 Security of tenure

The security of tenure of assured tenants is firmly based upon a statutory prohibition on termination of the tenancy by the landlord, contained in the HA 1988, s. 5(1), and a statutory requirement of recovery of possession by court order, contained in s. 7(1) of the Act.

Where the tenancy is *fixed-term*, s. 5(1) permits the landlord to end that term by exercising a 'power to determine' the lease which is contained in the tenancy agreement. However, it does not entitle landlords to end the fixed term by forfeiture (see *Artesian Residential Developments Ltd v Beck* [1999] ECGS 46). Section 45(4) declares 'for the avoidance of doubt' that any reference in Part I of the Act (in which s. 5(1) is included) to 'a power for a landlord to determine a tenancy does not include a reference to a power of re-entry or forfeiture for breach of any term or condition of the tenancy'. The 'power to determine' referred to in s. 5(1) is a power to give notice, possibly at certain defined times during the term by invoking a 'break clause', or by serving notice on the tenant. Termination of an assured fixed term in this way does not entitle the landlord to repossess, as on termination a statutory periodic tenancy will arise by operation of law (HA 1988, s. 5(2)). An order of the court will still be necessary to recover possession from him.

Where the assured tenancy is periodic, whether contractual periodic or statutory periodic, the position is more straightforward. Section 5(1) permits of no exceptions. The landlord cannot unilaterally bring such tenancy to an end, and the final clause confirms the already apparent: service of a notice to quit is of no effect. The landlord must take the tenant to court, and establish a ground of possession.

4.5.3 Summary

(a) *Fixed-term tenancy* Where the tenant holds under a fixed-term tenancy which has not expired, the landlord may:

    (i)   terminate the fixed-term by giving the tenant notice pursuant to a right to do so reserved by the lease. This will almost certainly result in the tenant holding over as a statutory periodic tenant. Termination of the fixed-term will not in itself entitle the landlord to recover possession; or

(ii) seek a possession order from the court *on any of Grounds 2, 8, 10 to 15 inclusive, or 17*, as contained in Sch. 2 to the Act. He can do this only if the lease expressly provides for termination on the particular ground relied upon.

The landlord cannot forfeit the fixed-term pursuant to a right reserved in the lease. If he wishes to recover possession to prevent future breaches of covenant, he must seek a possession order as under (ii) above.

(b) *Periodic tenancy* Where the tenant holds pursuant to a periodic tenancy (whether statutory or 'contractual'), the landlord may seek a possession order from the court *on any of the grounds set out in Sch. 2 to the Act*. No other method of termination is open to him. In particular, service of a notice to quit will be of no effect.

4.6 GOING TO COURT

Section 7(1) of the 1988 Act restricts the jurisdiction of the court to make an order for possession of a dwelling-house let on assured tenancy. No order for possession may be made unless one or more of the grounds set out in Sch. 2 to the Act is established. Grounds 1 to 8 are 'mandatory', on proof of which the court is obliged to make an order for possession. Grounds 9 to 17 are 'discretionary', conferring jurisdiction on the court to make a possession order where it considers that it is reasonable to do so. Where the assured tenancy is a periodic tenancy, any of the grounds may be invoked by the landlord. But where the assured tenancy is for a fixed term the grounds which may be invoked are limited to Grounds 2, 8, 10 to 15 inclusive and 17. Furthermore, the tenancy must contain 'provision for it to be brought to an end' on the particular ground on which possession is being sought. This provision may 'take the form of a provision for re-entry, for forfeiture, for determination by notice or otherwise' (HA 1988, s. 7(6)(b)). Although a landlord cannot terminate an assured fixed term by forfeiture, the presence of something akin to a forfeiture clause in the lease is essential, as without it he has no effective remedy in terms of regaining possession where a tenant holding pursuant to a fixed term is in default. This is an essential ingredient which must be included in any fixed-term lease.

4.6.1 Notice before action

Before the landlord commences proceedings, he should serve on the tenant a notice seeking possession (HA 1988, s. 8). This notice must be in prescribed form (SI 1997 No. 194, Form 3), and must inform the tenant:

(a) that the landlord intends to begin proceedings for possession of the dwelling-house on one or more grounds specified in the notice;

(b) that those proceedings will not begin earlier than a date specified in the notice;

(c) that proceedings will begin not later than 12 months from the date the notice was served.

Although the s. 8 notice must be in the prescribed form, strict adherence is not necessary. By reg. 2 of the instrument, service of a completed form 'substantially to the same effect' as Form 3 will suffice.

In *Mountain* v *Hastings* (1993) 25 HLR 427, Ralph Gibson LJ stated (at 433):

> ... the ground in Schedule 2 may validly be 'specified in the notice' as required by Parliament, in words different from those in which the ground is set out in the Schedule, provided that the words used set out fully the substance of the ground so that the notice is adequate to achieve the legislative purpose of the provision. That purpose, in my judgment, is to give to the tenant the information which the provision requires to be given in the notice to enable the tenant to consider what she should do and, with or without advice, to do that which is in her power and which will best protect her against the loss of her home.

The landlord, who was seeking possession under Ground 8, responded to the invocation in Form 3 to 'give the full text of each ground which is being relied on' by stating 'At least three months rent is unpaid'. The Court of Appeal held that this was not an adequate notice on which the landlord could proceed, as it made no reference to the requirements that the rent be 'lawfully due' and that it be in arrear both at the date of the notice and at the date of the hearing. The safest policy for the landlord to adopt is to repeat the ground on which reliance is placed *verbatim* from the HA 1988.

4.6.2 Alteration of or addition to grounds in notice

By s. 8(2) of the 1988 Act, the grounds specified in a s. 8 notice may be altered or added to with the leave of the court. If, however, the notice is initially defective, the notice may be invalid and not susceptible to amendment by the court. This occurred in *Mountain v Hastings* (above), where the Court of Appeal denied that the court had jurisdiction to add Ground 8 subsequently once it had been improperly and invalidly specified.

4.6.3 Dispensation power

The court has power to dispense with the requirement of a s. 8 notice (where it considers it 'just and equitable to do so') in all cases save where possession is sought under Ground 8 (HA 1988, s. 8(1)(b), (5)). In *Kelsey Housing Association v King* (1995) 28 HLR 270, the Court of Appeal held that in exercising this power, the court must take all the circumstances into account, from the point of view of both landlord and tenant. Even if the failure to give the notice creates prejudice, that is not conclusive. Each case depends on its own facts, and the court must make its decision on all the facts which are known at the date of the hearing.

4.6.4 Proceedings for possession

Once notice has been served under s. 8, the landlord will commence his possession action in the county court, which is given statutory jurisdiction by the HA 1988, s. 40. Account must be taken of the Civil Procedure Rules, in force since 26 April 1999. Unless use is being made of the accelerated possession procedure (applicable only where the tenancy is an assured shorthold, or possession is being sought on one of Grounds 1, 3, 4 or 5, on which see 4.7.4 and 5.4), proceedings will commence by the landlord completing claim form N5 (possession summons), which can be obtained from the county court service. Once issued, the claim form is served on the defendant, together with a reply form (N11), which must be completed and returned to the court within 14 days. Particulars of claim must be served with, or within 14 days of, the claim form.

Order 6, r. 3 of the County Court Rules is preserved in Sch. 2 to the Civil Procedure Rules. The particulars of claim must identify the land in question, indicate that the claim relates to residential premises, state whether the rateable value or rent limits of the RA 1977 are exceeded, (if for non-payment of rent) give full details of the history of non–payment, give details of the tenancy (stating when it was determined and the rent payable), and state the ground on which possession is claimed (CPR, PD 16, para. 6). See further Appendix B, which provides some assistance in drafting particulars.

4.7 GROUNDS FOR POSSESSION

The grounds for possession are either mandatory (on proof of which the court must order possession) or discretionary (on proof of which the court may order possession if it considers it reasonable to do so). The mandatory grounds are Grounds 1 to 8 in Sch. 2 to the 1988 Act; the discretionary grounds are Grounds 9 to 17.

4.7.1 Mandatory grounds

Where the landlord satisfies the court that one or another of the mandatory grounds is established, the court must order possession. Moreover, the order must take effect within 14 days, unless it appears to the county court that exceptional hardship would be caused by the imposition of such a requirement. In a case of exceptional hardship, the delivery up of possession can be postponed for a maximum of six weeks (see generally HA 1980, s. 89.) The extended power to adjourn proceedings (etc.) (contained in HA 1988, s. 9) does not apply where the court is satisfied that the landlord is entitled to possession by virtue of a mandatory ground (s. 9(6)). However, until the court is satisfied of this, its general power to adjourn 'to control and direct the conduct of the trial' may be exercised (*Mountain* v *Hastings* (1993) 25 HLR 427, at 438.)

4.7.2 Grounds 1 to 5: notice in writing

Grounds 1 to 5 all require the giving of a written notice to the tenant not later than the beginning of the tenancy. No forms are prescribed for these notices: the landlord is simply required to give a notice in writing that possession might be recovered on this ground. If such notice is given, the landlord has a 'cast iron' ground for possession, and the tenant's security is from the outset highly precarious. Indeed, where Grounds 1, 3, 4 or 5 (but not 2) are invoked by a landlord, he may be able to make use of an accelerated possession procedure. The lesser security afforded by assured tenancies granted subject to these grounds is acknowledged by the refusal to accept that accommodation on such terms can be 'suitable alternative accommodation' where a landlord is seeking possession of a dwelling-house let under an assured tenancy (see HA 1988, Sch. 2, Part III, para. 2).

4.7.3 Dispensing with the requirement of notice

Grounds 1 and 2 expressly provide for the court dispensing with the notice requirement where it is satisfied that 'it is just and equitable' to dispense with it. Grounds 3 to 5 do not. It appears, therefore, that a failure to give notice at the relevant time will be fatal where these latter grounds are concerned.

With Grounds 1 and 2, it is necessary to consider when the court will use its dispensation power. The court may be invited to use its discretion to dispense with notice in all kinds of circumstances. The landlord, ignorant of the finer points of the 1988 Act and rushing off abroad on business for a few months, may tell the tenant that the property he is about to rent is his home, but not put the information in writing. The landlord may send the tenant written notice, but it is delayed in the post and arrives after he has gone into possession. Or the landlord may not think about recovering the house at all at the time of the initial letting, but two years later when he wants to reclaim possession so that he can live there he reads Ground 1 and regales the court with tales of the hardship he is now under.

On a literal reading of Grounds 1 and 2, the discretion appears to be unfettered. When the Court of Appeal had to consider a dispensation power which was couched in identical terms (Case 11 of the RA 1977), it held that the judge must look at all the circumstances of the case:

> Those would embrace the circumstances affecting the landlord, or his successors in title, the circumstances of the tenant and, of course, the circumstances in which the failure to give written notice arose. It is only if, having considered all those circumstances, the court considers that it would be just and equitable to give possession that it should do so, because it must be borne in mind that, by failing to give the written notice, the tenant may well have been led into a wholly false position. (*per* Griffiths LJ in *Bradshaw* v *Baldwin-Wiseman* (1985) 49 P & CR 382, at 388)

To return to our hypotheses, the landlord who gives the tenant oral notice and the landlord whose notice is delayed in the post may argue strongly, and possibly with some success, that the dispensation power should be exercised in their favour: see *Fernandes* v *Parvardin* (1982) 5 HLR 33 and *Minay* v *Sentongo* (1983) 45 P & CR 190. Where the landlord did not at the outset envisage that recovery of possession could be attained by the use of these grounds, however, the tenant can argue powerfully that the court should take a strong line and refuse to dispense with the notice requirement. In *Bradshaw* v *Baldwin-Wiseman* (above), Griffiths LJ stated that it could not be 'just and equitable' to dispense with notice where there was no initial intention (in that context to create a 'Case 11 tenancy' under the RA 1977), and the same could be said in relation to Grounds 1 and 2 of the 1988 Act.

In *Boyle* v *Verrall* [1997] 1 EGLR 25, the plaintiff acquired a London flat, intending to use it as a base when she and her husband visited the capital. She intended to let the flat to the defendant on assured shorthold tenancy, but omitted to serve a notice under s. 20 of the HA 1988 on the defendant prior to grant of the tenancy. Although the plaintiff did not discuss with the defendant her future intention to occupy the flat herself, he (as a housing officer, married to a solicitor) was aware that she wished to grant an assured shorthold, and had not taken any steps to inform her of the error she was making. The defendant's behaviour was 'uncooperative and obstructive', and he was persistently late in paying the rent. All of these circumstances could be taken into account by the court in the exercise of its discretion, and the Court of Appeal held that it was just and equitable to dispense with the notice requirement. The plaintiff obtained an order for possession pursuant to Ground 1.

4.7.4   Grounds 1, 3, 4 and 5: accelerated possession procedure

The attraction of these grounds has been enhanced by the introduction for landlords of a 'fast track' to repossession by amendment to the County Court Rules which took effect on 1 November 1993 (County Court (Amendment No. 3) Rules, SI 1993 No. 2175) and which has been retained in slightly modified form in the Civil Procedure Rules (CPR, Sch. 2; CCR Ord. 49, r. 6). It is not available merely by satisfying the usual conditions for the application of the ground in question. The following conditions must all be satisfied:

(a)   the tenancy or any agreement for the tenancy was entered into on or after 15 January 1989;

(b)   the proceedings are brought on one of Grounds 1, 3, 4, or 5;

(c)   the only purpose of the proceedings is to recover possession, and no other claim (e.g., for rent arrears) is being made;

(d)   the assured tenancy is the subject of a written agreement, or is a statutory periodic tenancy on the same terms (save as to rent) as such a tenancy, or relates to the same or substantially the same premises which were let to the same tenant, and is on the same terms (save as to rent and/or duration) as such a tenancy;

(e)   the proceedings are brought against the tenant to whom written notice was given (i.e. there has been no assignment);

(f)   the tenant was given written notice, not later than the beginning of the tenancy (thus the procedure is not available where the landlord wishes to invoke the court's dispensation power);

(g)   the tenant was given notice of the proceedings in accordance with s. 8.

These conditions being satisfied, the landlord may bring proceedings for possession under the rule. Application must be in prescribed form (Form N5B; see Appendix B) and must contain information and attach copies of documents as listed in detail in the rules (CPR, Sch. 2; Ord. 49, r. 6(6) as amended). Statements must be verified on oath. Should the application be opposed, the defendant must within 14 days of its service on him deliver at the court office the form of reply which was attached to the application. The application and any reply are then referred to the judge, who may either make an order for possession 'without delay' and 'without requiring the attendance of the parties' (CPR, Sch. 2; Ord. 49, r. 6(15)), or (only where he is not satisfied that the prior notice was served before the tenancy, or that a notice was served in accordance with s. 8, or that service of the application was duly effected, or that the claimant has established he is entitled to recover possession under the ground relied upon against the defendant) fix a hearing date and give directions. In the event of an order for possession being made under this expedited procedure, the court has discretion to set aside, vary, or confirm it on application being made on notice within 14 days of the order, or of its own initiative (CPR, Sch. 2; Ord. 49, r. 6(17)).

There are many potential pitfalls where a landlord seeks to invoke the accelerated possession procedure, but it has clear advantages in terms of speed (and therefore cost) to those who take care to satisfy its requirements.

4.7.5 Discretionary grounds

Grounds 9 to 17 inclusive are discretionary. Where a discretionary ground is proved, the court may order possession to be given up if it considers it reasonable to make the order. The burden of proof is on the plaintiff seeking possession to show that it is reasonable to make the order. According to Lord Greene MR in *Cumming v Danson* [1942] 2 All ER 653, at 655:

> The duty of the judge is to take into account all relevant circumstances as they exist at the date of the hearing. That he must do in what I venture to call a broad commonsense way giving weight as he thinks right to the various factors in the situation. Some factors may have little or no weight: others may be decisive.

By virtue of s. 9 of the 1988 Act, the court has an extended discretion to adjourn proceedings 'for such period or periods as it thinks fit', and on making an order for possession or at any time before execution it may stay or suspend execution of the order, or postpone the date of possession, for such period as it thinks just. On exercise of these powers, the court must impose conditions with regard to the payment of rent arrears (if any) or other payments in respect of occupation after the termination of the tenancy, unless it considers that to do so would cause exceptional hardship to the tenant or would otherwise be unreasonable. It may impose such other conditions as it thinks fit. The flexibility of these provisions is in part to enable the court to use its powers to make the tenant pay the rent, or comply with the other obligations of the tenancy, and to allow the tenant to remain in possession if that is possible.

4.8 THE STATUTORY GROUNDS

As discussed in 4.7 above Grounds 1 to 8 in the HA 1988, Sch. 2 are mandatory; Grounds 9 to 17 are discretionary.

4.8.1 Ground 1: Past or future occupation by landlord

Not later than the beginning of the tenancy, and subject to the power of the court (considered at 4.7.3 above), to dispense with the requirement where it is just and equitable to do so, the landlord must have given written notice to the tenant that possession might be recovered on this ground. The landlord will obtain possession as of right if he can prove one of two alternatives.

Alternative (a) requires that the landlord seeking possession occupied the dwelling-house as his only or principal home (see 2.7 above) at some time before the beginning of the tenancy. Past occupation must be proved. It is not necessary that the landlord occupied immediately before the assured tenancy was granted. Nor is it necessary that the landlord now requires the dwelling-house again for his occupation. It is perfectly in order for the landlord to invoke this part of Ground 1 to recover possession with a view to selling his interest with vacant possession.

Alternative (b) is wholly distinct. It does not require the landlord to have occupied at all prior to the grant of the assured tenancy. He must have been sufficiently perspicacious to have given the tenant notice under this ground before the tenancy was entered into, and then be able to establish that he requires the dwelling-house for his occupation or for that of his spouse (making resort to this ground useful in the event of the landlord's divorce or separation). There is no need for the requirement to occupy to be reasonable, although it must, obviously, be genuine. While he may rely on a written notice served by an earlier landlord, neither he nor any predecessor of his must have acquired the interest he now has 'for money or money's worth'. Thus the Act seeks to prevent abuse of the ground by persons buying reversions simply in order to repossess by virtue of a relatively short-term intention to occupy. Where a person has acquired a reversion by gift (perhaps by will or on intestacy following the death of the previous landlord), Ground 1 can still be invoked.

4.8.2 Ground 2: mortgagee seeking possession

The dwelling-house is subject to a mortgage granted before the beginning of the tenancy, and three further conditions are satisfied, namely:

(a) the mortgagee is entitled to exercise a power of sale conferred on him by the mortgage or by s. 101 of the Law of Property Act 1925; and

(b) the mortgagee requires possession of the dwelling-house for the purpose of disposing of it with vacant possession in exercise of that power; and

(c) either notice was given as mentioned in Ground 1 above or the court is satisfied that it is just and equitable to dispense with the requirement of notice.

This ground is ancillary to Ground 1. It contemplates the situation where the landlord lets his house, over which there is a pre-existing mortgage, to an assured tenant, serving prior to the tenancy a notice reserving his rights under Ground 1, probably because he intends to occupy at a future date (alternative (b) rather than alternative (a)). The landlord then defaults on the mortgage. The mortgagee wishes to realise its security. The landlord cannot viably argue in these circumstances that he intends to occupy the property as his only or principal home, as once possession is recovered the mortgagee will insist on sale. However, he will be able to utilise Ground 2.

But Ground 2 may not be applicable. The mortgage may have been granted after the beginning of the tenancy. No Ground 1 notice may have been served, and the court may refuse to dispense with the notice requirement. Is there any route whereby the mortgagee could recover possession in such circumstances? Such case law as there is concerns the Rent Acts, but it would seem to be applicable to assured tenants as well. Recovery of possession cannot be obtained by a 'landlord' except by obtaining an order of the court on the grounds set out in Sch. 2, and 'landlord' is defined in s. 45(1) to include persons deriving title under the original landlord, and those who would be entitled to possession but for the existence of the assured tenancy. This is the same definition, for practical purposes, as that in RA 1977, s. 152.

Under the doctrine of 'title paramount', a mortgagee's rights of possession have been held to prevail over the rights of both protected and statutory tenants, where the tenancy in question was granted by the mortgagor subsequent to the mortgage, in breach of the terms contained in the mortgage deed (*Dudley & District Benefit Building Society* v *Emerson* [1949] Ch 707; *Britannia Building Society* v *Earl* [1990] 1 WLR 422). This doctrine could therefore be used by a mortgagee in place of Ground 2 where no notice under Ground 1 had been served, and the court refused to dispense with the requirement of notice. But it would not avail a mortgagee where the tenancy pre-dated the mortgage, or the tenancy was not in breach of the mortgage deed. In *Woolwich Building Society* v *Dickman* [1996] 3 All ER 204, a protected tenancy was in existence at the date of the creation of the mortgage of the landlord's interest. Even though the tenants had given written consent to the mortgage, their rights bound the mortgagee by virtue of the Land Registration Act 1925, s. 70(1)(g), in the absence of any provision rendering their rights subordinate being expressed on the register. The expeditious registration of the charge by the mortgagee is essential, as a failure to register prior to a tenancy being granted, even in breach of the terms of the mortgage, by the mortgagor, can lead to the tenant's statutory rights being accorded priority over the contractual rights of the mortgagee (*Barclays Bank plc* v *Zaroovabli* [1997] 2 All ER 19). The mortgagee must also be aware of the dangers of allowing the tenant to occupy the property once they have repossessed. In *Mann* v *Nijar* (1999) April 1999, Legal Action 14, the bank sold the reversion to purchasers following repossession, informing the purchasers that vacant possession could not be obtained in view of the assured tenancy which existed. The Court of Appeal held that a new tenancy, binding on the purchasers of the reversion, had arisen between the bank and the tenant of the mortgagor.

Where a mortgage is secured on the leasehold interest of an assured tenant, Part I of the 1988 Act does not restrict the rights of the mortgagee to recover possession pursuant to the mortgage agreement (see proviso to HA 1988, s. 7(1), and 4.4 above).

4.8.3   Ground 3: off-season holiday lets

By the HA 1988, Sch. 1, para. 9, holiday lets are excluded from assured tenancy status. If at some time within the period of 12 months prior to the commencement of the tenancy, the dwelling-house has been occupied under a right to occupy it for a holiday, then a tenancy for a fixed term not exceeding eight months will, although an assured tenancy, carry with it a mandatory ground for possession. However, the landlord must have given notice in writing to the tenant no later than the beginning of the tenancy that Ground 3 was applicable. The landlord will not be able to obtain possession under Ground 3 until the fixed term has expired, but once it has, on proper application the court must order possession. Although it is convenient to think of these as off-season lettings of holiday accommodation, the provisions are not so limited in their terms.

4.8.4 Ground 4: vacation lets of student accommodation

As with off-season lettings of holiday accommodation, so with vacation lettings of student accommodation. Within the 12 months prior to the tenancy, the dwelling must have been let on a tenancy falling within the HA 1988, Sch. 1, para. 8. The present tenancy must be a fixed-term tenancy not exceeding 12 months, and the landlord must have given notice in writing to the tenant no later than the beginning of the tenancy that Ground 4 was applicable. Although it will normally be the case, it is not necessary that the tenancy is granted by a 'specified educational institution'. The landlord will not be able to recover possession pursuant to Ground 4 until the fixed term has expired.

4.8.5 Ground 5: residence of minister of religion

The dwelling-house must be held for the purpose of being made available for occupation by a minister of religion as a residence from which to perform the duties of his office, and the court is satisfied that the dwelling-house is now required for occupation by a minister of religion as such a residence. Notice in writing must have been given to the tenant by the landlord at the beginning of the tenancy that Ground 5 was applicable. The ground enables lettings of ministers' residences without significant statutory security both to the ministers themselves and to others.

4.8.6 Ground 6: intention to demolish etc.

Ground 6 is complex. The landlord who is seeking possession must intend to demolish or reconstruct the whole or a substantial part of the dwelling-house, or carry out substantial works on the dwelling-house or any part thereof, or on any building of which it forms part, three conditions being fulfilled:

(a) the work cannot be carried out without the tenant giving up possession, for one of four stated reasons (the tenant is not willing to agree to variation of the terms of the lease; the nature of the work

67

is such that no such variation is practicable; the tenant is not willing to accept an assured tenancy of part of the dwelling-house; the nature of the work is such that such a tenancy is not practicable);

(b) since the grant of the tenancy, no person holding the landlord's interest has acquired it for money or money's worth;

(c) the assured tenancy did not arise by succession to a Rent Act protected or statutory tenancy (or if an assured agricultural occupancy, did not arise by succession to a Rent (Agriculture) Act 1976 tenancy).

Although Ground 6 was an innovation in private sector housing law, there has been a similar ground in relation to secure tenancies since 1980 and the analogous provision in the business tenancy code (Landlord and Tenant Act 1954, s. 30(1)(f)) has given rise to much litigation. One particular difficulty which the courts have had to face in relation to the latter has been the proof of intention. In relation to Ground 6, it is the intention of the landlord which is material save where the landlord is a registered social landlord or charitable housing trust, in which case the intention of a superior landlord may suffice. In *Cunliffe* v *Goodman* [1950] 2 KB 237, Asquith LJ stated: 'An "intention" ... connotes a state of affairs which the party "intending" ... does more than merely contemplate: it connotes a state of affairs which, on the contrary, he decides, so far as in him lies, to bring about, by his own act of volition.' Denning LJ in *Fisher* v *Taylors Furnishing Stores Ltd* [1956] 2 QB 78, at 84 stated that:

> ... the court must be satisfied that the intention to reconstruct is genuine and not colourable; that it is a firm and settled intention, not likely to be changed, that the reconstruction is of a substantial part of the premises, indeed so substantial that it cannot be thought to be a device to get possession; that the work is so extensive that it is necessary to get possession of the holding in order to do it; and that it is intended to do the work at once and not after a time.

In seeking to prove intention, the landlord should come to court armed with any planning permission which might be necessary, proof of ability to finance the operation and sufficient details of the intended works to convince the court that the plan is not merely colourable. If the landlord is a company, its intention is best shown by a resolution of the directors as recorded in the minutes or, if the matter is beyond their powers, by a resolution of the company in general meeting. The landlord may undertake to the court that it will take the requisite steps, and this has been considered an effective course of action in relation to business tenancies (*Espresso Coffee Machine Co. Ltd* v *Guardian Assurance Co. Ltd* [1959] 1 WLR 250).

Landlords 'by purchase' are excluded from Ground 6 by condition (b) referred to above. This is designed to prevent property developers from buying up the reversions of dwelling-houses let on assured tenancy, and then using Ground 6 as a means of obtaining vacant possession. It would be particularly easy for such landlords to offer attractive new tenancies to the sitting tenants, and then argue Ground 6 on the basis that they have not acquired the interest as landlord since the date of the tenancy. This abuse is, however, obviated by the second paragraph of Ground 6. If, immediately before the grant of the tenancy, the tenant (or any one of joint tenants) was the tenant under an earlier assured tenancy, then the landlord must not have acquired his interest for money or money's worth since the grant of that earlier tenancy.

Where the court makes an order for possession by virtue of Ground 6, the landlord must pay the tenant his reasonable removal expenses (HA 1988, s. 11). The landlord who obtains a possession order by misrepresenting or concealing material facts may be ordered by the court to pay compensation to his former tenant (HA 1988, s. 12). While this latter provision has general application to assured tenancies, it may have particular use in relation to Ground 6, where landlords may be tempted to disguise their true intentions in the interests of obtaining a possession order.

4.8.7   Ground 7: death of periodic tenant

Assured periodic tenancies cannot be terminated by notice to quit (HA 1988, s. 5(1)). On the death of the assured periodic tenant, his interest will vest in his spouse (or person living with him as his spouse), subject to the various exceptions and qualifications of s. 17 of the 1988 Act, irrespective of the operation of his will or the rules of intestacy. In these circumstances, Ground 7 has no application. If, however, the tenant does not leave a surviving spouse, or for some other reason s. 17 does not apply, the periodic tenancy will devolve in accordance with the tenant's will or the intestacy rules. The effect could well be that the landlord is left with a tenant whom he does not want.

Ground 7 gives the landlord a 12-month period of grace following the death of a periodic tenant to assess the character and financial viability of the person who has inherited the tenancy under the general law. If the landlord does not wish him or her to remain tenant, he need not justify his decision to seek possession, as if proceedings are commenced within the 12-month period the court must make the order sought. Where the landlord did not immediately become aware of the tenant's death, the court has a discretion to calculate the 12 months from the date the landlord did become aware of it. However, the landlord would be safer in proceeding, if he can, in the 12-month period beginning with the tenant's death, as he is not then reliant on the exercise of discretion in his favour.

If the court were to imply that a new periodic tenancy had been created during the 12-month period from the tender and acceptance of rent, the policy of Ground 7 would be frustrated. The tenancy would not any longer be the periodic tenancy which had devolved under the will or intestacy of the former tenant, and Ground 7 would not apply. A rider therefore provides that the court must not make such an implication, unless the landlord agrees in writing to a change 'in the amount of the rent, the period of the tenancy, the premises which are let or any other term of the tenancy'. However, a tenant could argue in an appropriate case that a new periodic tenancy had been expressly orally agreed with the landlord, and was not merely inferred from tender and acceptance of rent. Such a contention, if established on the evidence, would prevent the landlord from claiming possession by virtue of Ground 7.

4.8.8 Ground 8: non-payment of rent

Ground 8 is particularly attractive to landlords seeking possession. It is a mandatory ground, and so if the landlord can establish the requisite amount of rent outstanding, both at the date of the service of the s. 8 notice and at the date of the hearing, the court must grant him possession, and cannot, for example, allow the tenant time to pay. Ground 8 can be used even though the assured tenant is holding under a fixed-term tenancy (see further 4.5, 4.6 above). The amount of rent arrears required to trigger Ground 8 was reduced (in relation to tenancies where the rent is payable weekly, fortnightly or monthly) by HA 1996, s. 101.

Where the landlord is seeking to rely upon Ground 8, he must serve a s. 8 notice prior to commencing proceedings. The court has no power to dispense with service (HA 1988, s. 8(5)). At the date of service of that notice, there must be the appropriate amount of rent due. The tenant then has the opportunity to pay off a sufficient amount to ward off the threat of repossession. As the landlord has to prove that at the date of the hearing there is still the requisite amount of rent due, the tenant who pays enough rent to take the level below that for possession to be granted under Ground 8 will probably frustrate the landlord's proceedings. Although a prudent landlord will have particularised Grounds 10 and 11 as alternatives in his s. 8 notice (see 4.8.10 and 4.8.11 below), they are discretionary, and if the tenant has shown a recent ability and willingness to pay the rent, the court is unlikely to make an immediate order for possession against him. It is particularly important that the landlord proceeding under Ground 8 gets his s. 8 notice right, as the court has no power to dispense with service of a valid notice. However, the Court of Appeal has not welcomed technical arguments alleging invalidity where the tenant was clearly not prejudiced by a deficiency in the notice. In *Marath v MacGillivray* (1996) 28 HLR 484, the landlord served a s. 8 notice alleging that at a meeting over three months previously, a sum of arrears had been agreed by the parties, and that that sum had not been paid. No further particulars were given, but the court held that the notice was valid. It was sufficient for the notice to make clear (i) that the landlord was alleging that more than three months' rent (as was then required) was at that date unpaid and due, and (ii) how much, or how the tenant could ascertain how much, was alleged to be due.

The landlord must also ensure that any particulars of claim he might serve in the court proceedings comply with CPR, PD 16, para. 6(4) (see 4.6.4 and Appendix B).

The tenant may defend proceedings under Ground 8 on the basis that the rent is not due, or that he would have a defence to an action by the landlord for the rent itself. He may argue, for instance, that the landlord is in breach of his repairing covenant (perhaps under the Landlord and Tenant Act 1985, s. 11) and he (the tenant) either has a counterclaim for damages which he can set off against the entirety of the landlord's claim (*British Anzani (Felixstowe) v International Marine Management (UK) Ltd* [1980] QB 637; *Televantos v McCulloch* [1991] 1 EGLR 123) or has had to pay for repairs which the landlord had failed to perform out of the rent moneys (*Lee Parker v Izzet* [1971] 1 WLR 1688).

It is not a defence to a rent action that the tenant has not been able to obtain, or has had difficulties obtaining, housing benefit. Where housing benefit is being paid, it may be paid directly to the tenant, or to the landlord on the tenant's behalf. In *Marath v MacGillivray* (1996) 28 HLR 484, at 496, Sir Iain Glidewell considered that a deliberate attempt by or on behalf of the landlord to delay the receipt of housing benefit (until after the date of the court hearing so that the necessary amount of arrears would remain due) would incur the disapproval of the court, which would in consequence be unwilling to make a possession order against the tenant. It was not made clear on what basis the court would be acting, as the words of the statute do not appear to give it any discretion in such matters. However, it has been made clear that a landlord is under no obligation to accept tenders of rent made by or on behalf of any other person than the tenant, unless he is aware that the person is acting as agent for the tenant (*Bessa Plus plc v Lancaster* (1997) 30 HLR 48).

4.8.9   Ground 9: suitable alternative accommodation

'Suitable alternative accommodation' is defined in Part III of Sch. 2 to the 1988 Act. The landlord has two main options open to him in establishing this ground. He may produce a certificate of the local housing authority stating that the authority will provide suitable alternative accommodation, and such a certificate will be conclusive evidence that such accommodation will be provided by the date there specified. However, local authority certificates are hard to come by, as local authorities have diminishing (and sometimes no) housing stock, and the needs of a person who already holds an assured tenancy are not pressing.

Alternatively, the landlord may suggest some accommodation which he, or some other landlord, can provide is suitable. It will be deemed to be suitable if it satisfies two requirements, one concerning the security of tenure of the premises, the other concerning the suitability of the accommodation itself. The premises must be let on assured tenancy, or alternatively on terms affording 'reasonably equivalent' security to that offered by an assured tenancy. A public sector letting to the tenant might suffice, if the tenancy was secure and therefore within Part IV of the HA 1985. However, the letting must not be an assured shorthold tenancy, nor must it be on assured tenancy where the landlord has given notices pursuant to Grounds 1 to 5. The accommodation offered must in any case be reasonably suitable to the needs of the tenant and his family as regards proximity to place of work, and must either satisfy the comparison with local authority accommodation in the area which is provided for persons with similar needs to the tenant and his family as regards extent, or be otherwise reasonably suitable to their needs as regards extent and character. The 'character' of the accommodation is significant only if the accommodation is not being compared with the local authority accommodation. 'Character' may include the physical environs of the property concerned (*Redspring* v *Francis* [1973] 1 WLR 134), but not the provision of on-site recreations (e.g., a pony: *Hill* v *Rochard* [1983] 1 WLR 478). The accommodation must be furnished if that under the assured tenancy was furnished, and the furniture provided must be either similar to that in the present house or reasonably suitable to the needs of the tenant and his family. There is no reason why part of the dwelling-house presently let to the tenant should not constitute suitable alternative accommodation in an appropriate case (see, e.g., *Mykolyshin* v *Noah* [1970] 1 WLR 1271).

The court must determine the question whether it is reasonable to order possession independently of the question whether the accommodation offered is suitable (*Battlespring Ltd* v *Gates* (1983) 268 EG 355). Where the landlord obtains an order for possession under Ground 9, the tenant is entitled to his reasonable removal expenses from the landlord, and can sue the landlord if he fails to pay them (HA 1988, s. 11).

4.8.10   Ground 10: non-payment of rent

It is not necessary for proof of this ground that any rent remain unpaid at the date of the hearing. However, there must have been some rent due at the date of the commencement of proceedings, and at the date of service of the s. 8 notice. The court may dispense with service of the s. 8 notice in relation to this ground (unlike Ground 8), and in such circumstances, rent due at the commencement of proceedings will suffice for proof of the ground. Particulars of claim must comply with CPR, PD 16, para. 6(4) (see 4.6.4 and Appendix B). On proof of Ground 10, the court is much more likely to make a suspended order for possession, imposing conditions for the payment of rent arrears by the tenant (HA 1988, s. 9).

4.8.11   Ground 11: persistent delay in paying the rent

The landlord need not show that rent is or has been in arrears at any particular time. He will, however, have to show 'persistent delay'. It is essential, to comply with the rules of procedure, that a detailed history of the tenant's rent payments (as well as 'relevant information' about the tenant's circumstances) is provided in the particulars of claim (CPR, PD 16, para. 6(4); see 4.6.4 and Appendix B). Even if the landlord establishes Ground 11, the court may be reluctant to order possession in the exercise of its discretion when the landlord has been paid all the rent which is then due to him.

4.8.12   Ground 12: breach of obligation

Any breach of obligation (save for one relating to the payment of rent) will suffice for this ground. However, the landlord is likely to obtain possession only if the breach is serious and/or continuing despite requests to remedy. In *City of Bristol* v *Mousah* (1997) 30 HLR 32, the premises (let on a secure tenancy by a local authority landlord) had been used for the supply of crack cocaine, in breach of a covenant in the lease that drugs should not be supplied from the property. The Court of Appeal allowed the local authority landlord's appeal against the dismissal of its claim for possession. The breach of covenant had involved the commission of a serious criminal offence over a period of some months, and it would only be in exceptional cases that it could be said that it was not reasonable to make an order.

4.8.13   Ground 13: deterioration of dwelling-house

Ground 13 does not require proof of a breach of a covenant or obligation of the tenancy by the tenant. It does require proof of deterioration of the condition of the dwelling-house or the common parts owing to acts of waste, or the neglect or default of the tenant (or any person residing in the dwelling-house). An act of 'waste' is any act which alters the nature of the land let to the tenant (see Megarry & Wade, *Law of Real Property*, 5th ed., 1984, p. 96); the expression here is intended to cover the tenant whose action, as opposed to inaction ('neglect') causes the condition of the dwelling-house to deteriorate. In *Holloway* v *Povey* (1984) 15 HLR 104, a failure to attend to the garden (which is part of the premises let on the assured tenancy: HA 1988, s. 2(1)) fell within the similar ground in the RA 1977. Where the act of waste, or neglect or default, is that of a person lodging with the tenant or of a sub-tenant of his, the landlord must also prove that the tenant has not taken such steps as he ought reasonably to have taken for the removal of the lodger or sub-tenant in question.

4.8.14   Ground 14: tenant misconduct or conviction

Ground 14 was substantially widened by amendment in the HA 1996. The landlord must prove either misconduct or a criminal conviction on the part of the tenant or any person residing in or visiting the dwelling-house (one presumes lawfully). If he alleges misconduct, it must have caused (or been likely to cause) a nuisance or annoyance to anyone residing (etc.) in the locality – a considerable extension from the previous 'adjoining occupiers' (defined in *Cobstone Investments Ltd* v *Maxim* [1985] QB 140; see now *Northampton BC* v *Lovatt* (1997) 30 HLR 875). 'Nuisance' is given its ordinary, everyday, non-technical meaning; 'annoyance' has been held to be something which 'reasonably troubles the mind and pleasure, not of a fanciful person ... but of the ordinary sensible [English] inhabitant of a house' (*Tod-Heatley* v *Benham* (1888) 40 ChD 80, at 98).

If the landlord bases his claim on a conviction, it is necessary for him to show either that the conviction relates to use of the dwelling-house for immoral or illegal purposes, or that it is for an arrestable offence committed in (or in the locality of) the dwelling-house. Thus, it is no longer necessary to establish that the dwelling-house has been used in the commission of an offence if that offence is arrestable. There is no need for the use to be continuous, frequent or repeated (*Schneiders & Sons Ltd* v *Abrahams* [1925] 1 KB 301, at 307).

The premises will have been used for immoral purposes where the conviction relates to an offence involving unlawful sexual intercourse, such as living on the earnings of prostitution or keeping a brothel (Sexual Offences Act 1956, ss. 30 and 33). Using the premises for immoral purposes may in itself cause nuisance or annoyance to those in the locality, and in those circumstances a conviction will not be necessary. The occupation of a dwelling by two unmarried adults is not to be considered 'immoral' (*Heglibiston Establishment* v *Heyman* (1977) 36 P & CR 351).

4.8.15   Ground 14A: domestic violence

This ground, added by the HA 1996, s. 149, is only available to landlords who are registered social landlords or charitable housing trusts. The dwelling-house must have been occupied by a married couple or a couple living together as husband and wife (hence they must have been of the opposite sex: *Fitzpatrick* v *Sterling Housing Association* [1998] Ch 304). One or both of them must have been the tenant, and one must have left the dwelling-house because of violence or threats of violence by the other towards them, or towards another member of their family. If the court is satisfied that the partner who has left is unlikely to return, it may, if it considers it reasonable to do so, make an order for possession against the partner who remains (and anyone else who is continuing to occupy the dwelling-house). While this would enable the landlord to enter into a new tenancy agreement with the partner who has left the premises as a result of the violence, there is no need for the landlord to establish that this is their intention in bringing proceedings.

4.8.16   Ground 15: deterioration of furniture

Ground 15 is similar to Ground 13, save that the deterioration is in the condition of furniture rather than the dwelling-house itself.

4.8.17   Ground 16: termination of employee-tenant's employment

It is not necessary for proof of Ground 16 for the landlord to show that he has a need for possession of the dwelling (perhaps because the tenant's replacement as employee wishes to occupy the dwelling-house). However, such evidence would be useful to the landlord as he attempts to convince the court that it is reasonable to order possession against the tenant. Ground 16 is not available as a ground for possession of dwelling-houses let on assured agricultural occupancies.

4.8.18   Ground 17: False statement made by tenant

This ground was added by the HA 1996, s. 102. It requires the landlord to establish that he was induced to grant the tenancy by a false statement made knowingly or recklessly by the tenant, or by a person acting at the tenant's instigation. It follows that the tenant must have been the person, or one of the persons, to whom the tenancy was granted. There has been a similar ground for many years in the secure tenancy regime. An example of its operation can be found in *Rushcliffe Borough Council* v *Watson* (1991) 24 HLR 124. A secure tenant made an application for housing to the landlords indicating that she was currently 'sharing with family or friends', a statement found by the judge to be knowingly false. The Court of Appeal upheld the possession order made. In doing so, they accepted the need for the courts to balance the interests of the tenant in being housed with the public interest in discouraging deceitful applications for housing. It is likely that Ground 17 will be most frequently invoked by registered social landlords, but it is not so restricted.

4.9   SUB-LEASES

4.9.1   Effect of sub-letting

By the HA 1988, s. 15, sub-letting of the whole or part of premises let on assured periodic tenancy without the landlord's consent is prohibited (see further 6.2.4 below). Where the landlord is himself a tenant of the property, termination of the landlord's interest will result in the assured (sub-) tenant holding directly on assured tenancy from the former landlord's landlord, provided that the assured tenancy is lawful and that the new landlord can grant an assured tenancy (i.e. the tenancy is not now excluded from the HA 1988 by Sch. 1 to the 1988 Act).

Example
An assured tenant (S) holds under a periodic tenancy from his landlord (T). T's ten-year fixed-term tenancy, held of L, expires. S will now hold as assured periodic tenant from L, provided that his tenancy from T was lawful (i.e. was not in breach of covenant) and that L is not, for example, the Crown or some other landlord which cannot grant assured tenancies.

4.9.2   Lawfully let

The sub-letting will not be lawful if it is in breach of a covenant against sub-letting in the head lease (*Maley* v *Fearn* [1946] 2 All ER 583). If the immediate landlord is himself an assured tenant, the sub-letting is very likely to be in breach of such a covenant, in view of the HA 1988, s. 15, above. However, a sub-letting which is at the outset unlawful may become lawful if the landlord waives the breach.

4.9.3   Reversionary leases and assured tenancies

If a landlord grants a fixed-term assured tenancy, and then subsequently grants a lease of his reversion, the assured tenant will take priority over the reversionary leaseholder, and can assert possession against him. On expiry of the fixed term, the assured tenant holding over as statutory periodic tenant, that tenancy will continue to bind the leaseholder (see HA 1988, s. 18(3), (4)).

CHAPTER FIVE

Assured Shorthold Tenancies

5.1 INTRODUCTION

Part I of the HA 1988 first enabled landlords to grant assured shorthold
tenancies. They provided a means whereby the landlord could let
residential property without according any security of tenure to the
tenant, as they were intended to give an incentive to investors to enter the
market and increase the number of dwellings available for accommodation. There were certain restrictions on the property which could be let (for
example, a landlord could not, by entering into new agreements with his
tenants, unilaterally transform them from Rent Act regulated tenants, or
even assured non-shorthold tenants, into assured shortholders; there was
a statutory minimum term of six months, during which the landlord's
powers were very limited, and the tenant had to be made aware, before
entering into the tenancy, what the nature of the arrangement was by
service of a notice in writing). Moreover, the assured shorthold tenant was
given the statutory right, denied to assured non-shorthold tenants, of a
market rent, as he could ask a rent assessment committee to determine
what rent it was reasonable to expect an assured shorthold tenant to pay.
But despite these drawbacks, assured shorthold tenancies proved very
popular.

The HA 1996 makes the assured shorthold tenancy the default mode of
letting in the private residential sector. Most assured tenancies entered
into on or after 28 February 1997 (the date the relevant provisions of the

1996 Act came into force) will be assured shorthold tenancies, irrespective of any notice being given and whether they are granted for a fixed term or are periodic tenancies. This has resulted in a greater erosion into tenant security, but it is intended to lead to a larger supply of properties for letting.

The attraction to landlords of assured shorthold tenancies is the relative ease with which possession can be recovered. Not only is the court obliged to make an order for possession when the requisite steps have been taken by the landlord, but there is also a fast track route to repossession. However, it must be realised that if and so long as a shorthold is a fixed-term tenancy, the tenant is entitled to the same security as any other assured tenant who holds a fixed term. Once the first six months of the tenancy have expired, the landlord may be able to terminate the fixed term by invoking a break clause contained in the lease, and then instigate possession procedures against the statutory periodic tenant. Failing this, the only route to possession will be by obtaining an order of the court pursuant to the HA 1988, s. 7(6).

This chapter deals with the identification and creation of assured shorthold tenancies, and recovery of possession from assured shorthold tenants. The duty of landlords to provide their assured shorthold tenants with a statement of their contractual terms, together with the right of shortholders to challenge the level of their rent, are dealt with in chapter 6.

5.2 DEFINITION

The date on which the assured tenancy is entered into is crucial. If it is before 28 February 1997, the assured tenancy will be a shorthold only if it satisfies the conditions set out in the HA 1988, s. 20. If it is entered into on or after 28 February 1997, otherwise than pursuant to a contract made before that date, it will be a shorthold although those statutory conditions are not satisfied, unless it is excluded from shorthold status by the HA 1988, Sch. 2A (see HA 1988, s. 19A, inserted by the HA 1996, s. 96). There are certain differences of substance between these types of assured shorthold tenancies.

5.2.1 Assured tenancy entered into before 28 February 1997: '1988 Act shortholds'

By s. 20(1) of the HA 1988 (as substituted by the HA 1996, Sch. 8, para. 2(3)):

Subject to subsection (3) below, an assured tenancy which is not one to which section 19A above applies is an assured shorthold tenancy if—

(a)   it is a fixed term tenancy granted for a term certain of not less than six months;

(b)   there is no power for the landlord to determine the tenancy at any time earlier than six months from the beginning of the tenancy, and

(c)   a notice in respect of it is served as mentioned in subsection (2) below.

The tenancy must be an assured tenancy. It must fall within the statutory definition of 'assured tenancy', and must not be excluded by virtue of Sch. 1 to the 1988 Act or any other provision (see further chapters 2 and 3 above). It must initially be for a fixed term of not less than six months. Despite the terminology ('shorthold'), there is no maximum duration, and the term need not be short. The prohibition on the reservation by the landlord of a 'power to determine' the tenancy in its first six months is deceptive. It has always been perfectly in order, and indeed highly advisable, for landlords to reserve a right of re-entry for breach of covenant and so forth which is exercisable during the first six months. By s. 45(4) of the HA 1988, 'any reference in [Part I] of this Act (however expressed) to a power for a landlord to determine a tenancy does not include a reference to a power of re-entry or forfeiture for breach of any term or condition of the tenancy'. Not only is the reservation of a right of re-entry consistent with the grant of an assured shorthold tenancy, failure to make such a reservation will leave the landlord powerless to deal effectively with tenant default while the fixed term is current.

But if the landlord has reserved the right to give notice during the first six months of an assured tenancy entered into before 28 February 1997, the tenancy will not be a shorthold. Section 20(1)(b) will not be satisfied. A power to give notice once the first six months has elapsed will not, however, prevent the tenancy from being a shorthold. In *Aylward v Fawaz* (1996) 29 HLR 408, a clause provided that 'The landlord or the tenant may determine the tenancy hereby created at or at any time after the end of the first six months of the tenancy provided one month's prior notice in writing of such desire is given to the other party'. This did not prevent the tenancy, granted in June 1995, being an assured shorthold tenancy.

The s. 20(2) notice must be in the prescribed form, be served before the assured tenancy is entered into by the person who is to be landlord on the person who is to be tenant, and must state that the assured tenancy to which it relates is to be a shorthold tenancy. The form is contained in the Assured Tenancies and Agricultural Occupancies (Forms) Regulations 1988, SI 1988 No. 2203, as amended by SI 1990 No. 1532 (Form 7). There is no power in the court to dispense with the requirement for such a notice, and if none is served, or it is served late, the tenancy will take effect as a standard assured tenancy. For an imaginative recourse to the dispensation power relevant to Ground 1, see *Boyle v Verrall* [1997] 1 EGLR 25 (at 4.7.3 above).

Minor inaccuracies in a s. 20 notice may be excused, as the rules provide that a notice 'substantially to the same effect' as that in the prescribed form will suffice (SI 1988 No. 2203, reg. 2). In *York v Casey* [1998] 2 EGLR 25, Peter Gibson LJ explained the scope of the court's power to excuse errors, as being akin to the approach advocated by the House of Lords in *Mannai Investment Co. Ltd v Eagle Star Life Assurance Co. Ltd* [1997] AC 749:

> ... [W]hat the court must do is to see whether the error in the notice was obvious or evident and, second, whether notwithstanding that error the notice read in its context is sufficiently clear to leave a reasonable recipient in no reasonable doubt as to the terms of the notice.

In *York v Casey*, the Court of Appeal upheld a notice which gave a date for termination of the tenancy which pre-dated its grant, and which gave the names of two persons as landlords where the tenancy itself had only one. The Court followed *Andrews v Brewer* (1997) 30 HLR 203, where the notice provided that the tenancy would commence on 29 May 1993 and end on 28 May 1993, on its face the day before it commenced, an obvious clerical error which did not detract from the validity of the notice. See also *R v London Borough of Newham, ex parte Ugbo* (1993) 26 HLR 263, where a notice which gave the wrong address was upheld.

However, in *Panayi v Roberts* (1993) 25 HLR 421, approved by the Court of Appeal in *York v Casey*, a tenancy was granted for a one-year fixed term from 7 November 1990, prior notice being served on the tenant indicating that the tenancy terminated on 6 May 1991. This was a material perplexity, the notice was invalid, and in consequence the tenancy was not an assured shorthold. Omission of the date of service of the notice (*Patel v Rodrigo* (1997) June 1997, Legal Action 20), the name, address and telephone number of the landlord (*Stevens v Lamb* (1996) March 1996, Legal Action 12), and the landlord's signature (coupled with a misspelling of the landlord's name *Symons v Warren* (1995) December 1995, Legal Action 8) have all led to the notice being declared invlaid by county courts. However, these latter decisions must be treated with some caution, as the more recent and more authoritative *York v Casey* is probably indicative of a new approach prompting the courts towards validity of notices which marginally transgress the rules.

In certain circumstances, a s. 20 notice is not required for the tenancy, although entered into before 28 February 1997, to be an assured shorthold tenancy:

(a) Where an assured shorthold tenancy (or a shorthold tenancy which was, but no longer is, assured) comes to an end, a new tenancy of the same, or substantially the same, premises under which the landlord and the tenant are the same as under the shorthold will be an assured shorthold tenancy if and so long as the tenancy remains assured. This will be so irrespective of the length of the term (if it is a fixed term) and any reservation by the landlord of rights to terminate, and there is no need for a s. 20 notice to be served. If, however, the landlord served notice on the tenant, before the tenancy is entered into, that the tenancy is not to be an assured shorthold, then it will not be an assured shorthold tenancy (HA 1988, s. 20(5)). These provisions cover not only the situation where the landlord expressly grants a new tenancy to his assured shorthold tenant, but also the situation where the tenant holds over following expiry of the fixed term. He will be holding over as statutory periodic tenant by virtue of the HA 1988, s. 5(2), and that statutory periodic tenancy will itself be an assured shorthold.

(b) Amendments to the Rent Act 1977 in the early 1980s provided for a letting by way of protected shorthold tenancy, under which the protected tenant received a lesser security of tenure. If a protected shorthold tenant obtained a new tenancy from his landlord on or after 15 January 1989, that tenancy would be an assured shorthold tenancy unless the landlord served notice to the contrary (even though the usual conditions contained in the HA 1988, s. 20, were not satisfied) (see HA 1988, s. 34(2)). Normally the grant of a new tenancy to an existing Rent Act protected or statutory tenant subsequent to the coming into force of the 1988 Act is not effective to grant an assured tenancy, and the new tenancy will remain regulated under the RA 1977. But the legislative policy was to deprive protected shorthold tenants of this advantage, on the basis that their security was recognised as inferior to other protected tenants, and the 1988 Act therefore facilitates the conversion of protected shorthold tenancies into assured shorthold tenancies.

(c) Similar provision is made for succession on death to a protected shorthold tenancy (see HA 1988, s. 39(7)).

Section 20(3) of the HA 1988 operates to protect acquired rights of assured tenants who are not shortholders. The grant of a new tenancy to a person who immediately before its grant was a standard assured tenant by the landlord who was landlord under the assured tenancy could not take effect as an assured shorthold. Thus, landlords were not able, by the simple expedient of granting new fixed-term tenancies of the appropriate length, with the appropriate notice, to convert existing assured tenants into assured shortholders. However, this situation changed as a result of the HA 1996, which provided that s. 20(3) (and s. 20(4)) of the 1988 Act was not to apply where the tenancy was one to which the new s. 19A applied (see HA 1996, Sch. 8, para. 2(4), inserting HA 1988, s. 20(5A)). Thus, if a landlord grants a new tenancy to an existing assured tenant on or after 28 February 1997 he may grant it as a shorthold. It will not be a shorthold automatically. But if, before the tenancy is entered into, the tenant serves notice on the landlord in the prescribed form (SI 1997 No. 194, Form No. 8: see Appendix C), proposing that the assured tenancy to which it relates is to be a shorthold tenancy, it will be a shorthold (HA 1988, Sch. 2A, para. 7, inserted by HA 1996, Sch. 7). The new tenancy may be for a term certain, or it may be a periodic tenancy. The tenant is under no obligation to serve a notice on his landlord and thereby dilute his statutory security. As long as he is assured tenant, he has security of tenure, and the landlord can recover possession only by obtaining an order for possession on proof of a ground before the court. The form of notice makes this very clear to the tenant: 'You do not have to complete this form even if your landlord has asked you to do so. Your existing security of tenure as an assured tenant will be unaffected if you do not complete it.'

Where an assured tenancy which is not a shorthold comes to an end (e.g., by effluxion of time or by the landlord exercising a contractually reserved right to serve notice), thereby giving rise to a statutory periodic tenancy by virtue of the HA 1988, s. 5, the landlord may not convert that tenancy into an assured shorthold by getting the tenant to serve notice to such effect on him. The use of the word 'grant' in Sch. 2A, para. 7, indicates that a new tenancy, whether fixed-term or periodic, must be created. Furthermore, para. 8 of Sch. 2A excludes from assured shorthold status without any qualification an assured tenancy 'which comes into being by virtue of [HA 1988, s. 5] on the coming to an end of an assured tenancy which is not a shorthold tenancy'.

Example

T was granted an assured tenancy for a fixed term of 12 months in September 1996. No s. 20 notice was served on the tenant prior to the tenancy. It was not, therefore, an assured shorthold tenancy. When the fixed term expired in September 1997, the tenant would hold over as a statutory periodic tenant (HA 1988, s. 5). Service by the tenant of a notice in, say, August 1997, stating that the statutory periodic tenancy was to be an assured shorthold, would be of no effect. No new tenancy was being 'granted' by the landlord. But if the landlord offers, and the tenant accepts, a new tenancy on shorthold terms, that agreement can be made effective by the tenant serving proper notice on the landlord proposing that the new tenancy is a shorthold.

5.2.2 Assured tenancy entered into on or after 28 February 1997: '1996 Act shortholds'

Section 96 of the HA 1996 inserted into the 1988 Act a new s. 19A and a new Sch. 2A. By s. 19A, an assured tenancy entered into on or after 28 February 1997 (otherwise than pursuant to a contract made before that date), or which comes into being on the coming to an end of such an assured tenancy (by virtue of HA 1988, s. 5) is an assured shorthold tenancy unless it falls within any of the paragraphs of Sch. 2A. The effect of these provisions is that the assured shorthold tenancy becomes the default mode of letting.

Schedule 2A excludes from this basic rule:

(a) an assured tenancy in respect of which the landlord has served on the tenant, before the tenancy is entered into, a notice stating that the tenancy is not to be an assured shorthold;

(b) an assured tenancy in respect of which the landlord serves on the tenant, after the tenancy has been entered into, a notice stating that the tenancy is no longer an assured shorthold. The landlord cannot use this as a means to frustrate the tenant's application to a rent assessment committee for a reduction of rent (see HA 1988, s. 22(5A), inserted by HA 1996, Sch. 8, para. 2(6));

(c) an assured tenancy which contains provision to the effect that the tenancy is not an assured shorthold tenancy;

(d) an assured tenancy arising by virtue of the HA 1988, s. 39 (on succession to a Rent Act regulated tenancy);

(e) an assured tenancy which became assured on ceasing to be a secure tenancy (typically where a public sector landlord has assigned the reversion to a private sector purchaser);

(f) an assured tenancy arising by virtue of Sch. 10 to the LGHA 1989 (providing statutory security on the ending of long residential tenancies: see chapter 7 below);

(g) an assured tenancy which is granted to a person who, immediately before the tenancy was granted, was the tenant under an assured tenancy which was not an assured shorthold tenancy, unless the landlord (who must be the same landlord as under the previous tenancy) serves the tenant with a notice in prescribed form, before the tenancy is entered into, stating that the assured tenancy is to be a shorthold tenancy. This provision has been considered above, at 5.2.1.

5.3 SECURITY OF TENURE

Section 21 of the HA 1988 governs recovery of possession from assured shorthold tenants, whether or not the shorthold is a 1988 Act shorthold or a 1996 Act shorthold, albeit with some qualifications in the latter case. The first question to ask when considering the appropriate means of recovering possession from an assured shorthold tenant is whether he is holding under a fixed-term or a periodic tenancy.

5.3.1 Fixed-term tenancies

5.3.1.1 During the currency of the fixed term
An assured shorthold tenancy is an assured tenancy. Thus, it is important to realise that while s. 21 will provide the most effective route to repossession in most cases, it is still open to the landlord to seek possession by s. 7. Where a landlord grants a fixed-term assured shorthold tenancy, and wishes to recover possession during that fixed-term (perhaps owing to tenant default, such as failure to pay the rent), s. 21 will be of no assistance. Instead, the landlord should seek an order for possession from the court pursuant to s. 7, noting the limited number of grounds for possession which are available while the tenancy is a fixed term, and that the tenancy must have made provision for it to be brought to an end on the ground in question (HA 1988, s. 7(6)). Reservation of a right of entry exercisable during the fixed term will usually be necessary to provide an effective sanction for default by the assured shortholder. However, as with any other assured tenancy, the fixed term cannot be forfeited as such (see further 4.5.2).

5.3.1.2 Notice under s. 21(1)
The landlord may seek to serve notice on the shortholder while the fixed term is subsisting, that notice to take effect on expiry or shortly thereafter. Sub-sections (1) to (3) of s. 21 of the 1988 Act deal with this situation. The landlord should realise that although he can initiate proceedings before the fixed term expires, possession will not be recovered until expiry has occurred. The landlord must give to the tenant two months' notice in writing (no form is prescribed), stating that he requires possession of the dwelling-house. That done, the landlord is entitled to a possession order if the court is satisfied that the assured shorthold tenancy has come to an end, and no further assured tenancy is in existence, other than an assured shorthold periodic tenancy (whether statutory or not). Unless the landlord has granted a new fixed-term tenancy to the assured shorthold tenant before the matter comes to court, the court is obliged to make an order for possession in favour of the landlord.

The landlord may have reserved for himself the right to give notice to the tenant during the fixed-term tenancy. Prior to 28 February 1997, the landlord could not reserve such a right exercisable during the first six months of the tenancy (HA 1988, s. 20(1)(b)). However, as occurred in *Aylward* v *Fawaz* (1996) 29 HLR 408, the landlord may have reserved the right to determine the fixed term by giving notice after the first six months have ended. In that case, service of a notice seeking possession under HA 1988, s. 21(1)(b) was held to be sufficient (as a matter of construction) both to determine the fixed term and to comply with the statute.

Example

T is an assured shorthold tenant. He was granted a two-year fixed term on 1 January 1997. L served notice prior to the grant stipulating that the tenancy was to be an assured shorthold. Until the term expires, T is in a relatively strong position. If L wishes to recover possession before 1 January 1999, he will in most cases have to invoke HA 1988, s. 7(6). If, for instance, T has more than eight weeks' rent in arrears, L will be able to seek possession under Ground 8, provided that he has reserved the right to bring the tenancy to an end on the ground in question. L would then serve a notice of proceedings for possession (HA 1988, s. 8) and proceed accordingly. This procedure is, however, cumbersome, and may be frustrated by T paying off the arrears. If the fixed term is coming to an end, it is more sensible for L to serve notice under HA 1988, s. 21(1)(b). L must serve T with no less than two months' written notice on or before the day on which the fixed term expires – so notice can be served at any time during the fixed term (up to and including 31 December 1998). On expiry of that notice, L will be entitled to an order for possession. The court's powers of postponement will be strictly limited (HA 1980, s. 89).

5.3.2 Periodic tenancies

Where the assured tenancy is periodic (either a fixed term has ended and the tenant is holding as a statutory periodic tenant, or the landlord has granted a periodic tenancy) the landlord should use HA 1988, s. 21(4). The landlord will be entitled to an order for possession from the court if he satisfies the following conditions:

(a)   The landlord gives notice to the tenant stating that possession is required by virtue of HA 1988, s. 21(4).
(b)   The notice must expire not less than two months after it is given.
(c)   The notice must specify (as the date after which possession is required) a date which is the last day of a period of the tenancy, and

which is not earlier than the earliest day on which (apart from HA 1988, s. 5(1)) the tenancy could be brought to an end by a notice to quit given by the landlord on the date the s. 21(4) notice is given. In most cases, two months' notice will suffice. But if there is express provision in the lease for a longer period of notice, or if the tenancy is quarterly or yearly (in which case notice of three months and six months respectively is implied), then care needs to be taken.

Example

T is granted a fixed-term assured shorthold in March 1995. It is for six months only, but after its expiry T holds over as statutory periodic tenant pursuant to HA 1988, s. 5(2). Rent having been payable monthly (on the first day of each month) under the shorthold agreement, the statutory periodic tenancy will be a monthly tenancy. L now wishes to recover possession by 1 December 1998. Provided he gives notice by 1 October 1998 stating that he requires possession on 1 December 1998, the court will be obliged to make a possession order in his favour.

5.3.3 Post-1996 Act tenancies: bar on recovery of possession in first six months

The HA 1996 makes the assured shorthold tenancy the default mode of letting, and, as must now be clear, the security it offers is considerably less than that of a non-shorthold assured tenancy. However, the 1996 Act does materially restrict the landlord's rights to repossession during the first six months of the landlord–tenant relationship where the letting is one to which s. 19A applies. Thus, an order for possession may not be made pursuant to HA 1988, s. 21 so as to take effect in that period (HA 1988, s. 21(5)–(7), inserted by HA 1996, s. 99). The period is rather laboriously defined. In effect, the tenant is protected for the first six months of the relationship. If the landlord grants a new tenant a three-month fixed term, or a monthly tenancy, the tenant will nevertheless be entitled to stay in the property for a minimum period of six months. If the tenant is holding pursuant to a 'replacement tenancy', which came into being after the ending of an earlier assured shorthold, the landlord's rights under s. 21 will not be restricted. In any case, the landlord may invoke any ground for possession which might be available on the facts.

Example

(a) A tenancy is granted on 1 April 1997 to a new tenant, T, for a fixed term of six months. During that fixed term, L may invoke HA 1988,

s. 7(6), if a right of entry for breach of condition has been reserved in the lease. L may seek to recover possession on expiry of the fixed term by serving notice under HA 1988, s. 21(1), while the fixed term is current. If no such notice is served then T will, on expiry of the fixed term, hold over as statutory periodic tenant. L may then recover possession under HA 1988, s. 21(4). If L grants T a new three-month fixed term on 1 January 1998, the same principles will apply to this tenancy as to the previous one. It is a replacement tenancy, and so there is no bar on L recovering possession on expiry of the fixed term at the end of March 1998, provided that notice under HA 1988, s. 21(1) is served.

(b) If the tenancy granted on 1 April 1997 to the new tenant is for a fixed term of three months, the court cannot order possession under HA 1988, s. 21, to take effect until 1 October 1997. L will be able to recover possession in that first six-month period only by proof of a ground for possession. During the first three months, L's rights will be governed by HA 1988, s. 7(6); thereafter possession may be recovered by proof of any ground for possession, as HA 1988, s. 7(1) may be invoked.

5.4 ACCELERATED POSSESSION PROCEDURE

5.4.1 Summary

As a result of recommendations made by the Civil Justice Review (Cm. 394), an accelerated possession procedure was introduced with effect from 1 November 1993. This procedure may be invoked by landlords seeking to recover possession of property held on assured shorthold tenancy and on assured tenancy where Grounds 1, 3, 4 or 5 are being relied upon (see 4.8). However, the vast majority of claims under the accelerated possession procedure have concerned assured shorthold tenants. The 'fast track' procedure has the undoubted advantage to landlords of obtaining a possession order expeditiously in cases which are either uncontested or where the tenant has no apparent defence to the proceedings. The order can be made by the district judge without the need for attendance by either party, in what may be little more than 14 days from the date of service of the application on the tenant. However, it is important to realise that not all assured shorthold tenancies can be subjected to the procedure, and that close adherence to the relatively complex rules is necessary. There are numerous pitfalls lying in wait for the unwary.

5.4.2 Conditions to be satisfied

The detail of the procedure is to be found in Ord. 49, r. 6A of the County Court Rules, which has been retained in a modified form in the Civil Procedure Rules (see CPR, Sch. 2). The rule and forms can be found in Appendix B. There are two routes to repossession implicit in r. 6A, which correspond to the two routes available under s. 21 of the 1988 Act. Where the landlord has served notice on the tenant *before or on the day on which a fixed-term assured shorthold expires* (HA 1988, s. 21(1)(b)), reference should be made to r. 6A(3). Where the landlord serves notice *at a time when the assured shorthold tenancy is a periodic tenancy* (HA 1988, s. 21(4), reference should be made to r. 6A(9). In either case, two conditions must be satisfied:

(a) The tenancy and any agreement for the tenancy must have been entered into on or after 15 January 1989. (Thus the procedure cannot be used where the assured shorthold came into being as a result of the operation of the transitional provisions contained in the HA 1988).

(b) The only purpose of the proceedings must be to recover possession of the dwelling-house. The landlord cannot make any other claim in the proceedings (e.g., for rent arrears).

Then certain additional conditions must be satisfied depending on the type of notice which the landlord has served. It is difficult, and dangerous, to generalise here, but it should be noted that the fast track procedure can be used only where the landlord–tenant relationship can be traced back to an initial written agreement to which the current tenant was a party. Furthermore, the notice stating that the landlord requires possession of the dwelling-house must have been in writing. This is now a statutory requirement (following amendments to s. 21 of the HA 1988 effected by s. 98 of the HA 1996).

5.4.2.1 *Claim following s. 21(1) notice*
The following additional conditions must be satisfied:

(a) the tenancy must have been an assured shorthold tenancy;

(b) the tenancy must not have immediately followed a non-shorthold assured tenancy;

(c) the tenancy must have fulfilled the conditions provided by s. 19A or s. 20(1)(a) to (c) of the HA 1988;

(d) the tenancy must have been the subject of a written agreement;

(e) if the tenancy (or agreement for tenancy) was entered into before 28 February 1997, a s. 20(2) notice was served on the tenant against whom the proceedings are now being brought;

(f) a s. 21(1)(b) notice was given to the tenant in writing.

5.4.2.2 Claim following s. 21(4) notice

The following additional conditions must be satisfied:

(a) the tenancy is an assured shorthold tenancy;

(b) the tenancy did not immediately follow a non-shorthold assured tenancy;

(c) the tenancy is the subject of a written agreement, or the tenancy is on the same terms (save possibly rent) as a tenancy which was subject to the written agreement, and it arises by virtue of s. 5 of the HA 1988; or it relates to the same (or substantially the same) premises which were let to the same tenant and is on the same terms (save possibly rent and duration) as a tenancy the subject of a written agreement;

(d) if the tenancy (or agreement for tenancy) was entered into before 28 February 1997, a written s. 20(2) notice was served on the tenant in relation to the first assured shorthold tenancy of the premises, and it is that tenant against whom proceedings are now being brought;

(e) a notice in writing under s. 21(4) was given to the tenant.

5.4.3 Mode of application

Where the above conditions are satisfied, the landlord may bring proceedings for possession under the accelerated procedure instead of making a claim in accordance with Ord. 6, r. 3 of the County Court Rules as preserved by CPR, Sch. 2 (action for recovery of land). Notice of application must be in the prescribed form (Form N5A; see Appendix B), and a copy of the application (with a copy for each defendant) must be filed in the county court for the district in which the dwelling-house is situated. Where the claim is based on a s. 21(1)(b) notice, the application must contain the information and statements listed in CPR, Sch. 2; Ord. 49, r. 6A(6). Where it is based on a s. 21(4) notice, the information and statements listed in Ord. 49, r. 6A(10) must be given. In either case, the documents listed in r. 6A(7), including 'any other documents necessary to prove the claim', must be attached. All statements and documents must be verified by the claimant on oath.

5.4.4 Role of the court

On receipt of the landlord's application for possession, the court should send it, together with attached documents, to the defendant tenant by way of service. The defendant then has 14 days in which to deliver a reply (the form for which must be attached to the claimant's application). If no reply is received within that time limit, the claimant may file a written request for a possession order. If a reply is received, it is referred with the claimant's application to the judge. The judge then, 'without delay', considers the application and any reply, and must do one of two things. He must either order possession or fix a hearing date, and he may do the latter only if he is not satisfied that the appropriate written notices were served or given, that service of the application was duly effected, or that the claimant has established that he is entitled to possession under s. 21 of the HA 1988 against the defendant tenant. Once the conditions for the use of the procedure are satisfied, the presumption is heavily in favour of repossession.

5.4.5 Setting aside

Quite apart from its general jurisdiction (CPR, r. 13), the county court has jurisdiction to set aside, vary or confirm an order made pursuant to the accelerated possession procedure, of its own initiative or on application made to it within 14 days of service of the order.

5.5 ORDERS OF THE COURT

5.5.1 Limited discretion

Where the court makes an order for possession following service of notices under s. 21 of the HA 1988, its discretion to postpone the giving up of possession is severely restricted. It may postpone for a maximum of 14 days, unless it appears that exceptional hardship would be caused by requiring possession to be given up by that date, in which case it may postpone for a period no more than six weeks from the making of the order (HA 1980, s. 89).

5.5.2 Costs

Costs are at the discretion of the court. In a recent case, the court awarded costs against the defendant on an indemnity basis where provision had been made in the tenancy agreement to such effect (*Church Commissioners* v *Ibrahim* [1996] EGCS 25).

CHAPTER SIX

Terms and Obligations of the Assured Tenancy

6.1 INTRODUCTION

6.1.1 The role of contract

As a general rule, the terms contained in the assured tenancy are those agreed by landlord and tenant. The assured tenancy is based on the contract between them, and the courts will enforce the terms which they have agreed. In ascertaining the terms of an assured tenancy, it is a matter of construction of the parties' agreement. The tenancy will frequently be committed to writing, in which case most of the terms will there be found. However, certain terms are implied by law, some of which cannot be excluded even by contrary stipulation, or express words in the written lease.

6.1.2 Assured shortholds: written statement of terms

Where an assured tenancy is entered into on or after 28 February 1997, it is likely to be an assured shorthold tenancy (HA 1988, s. 19A, inserted by HA 1996, s. 96). The tenant of an assured shorthold tenancy which is granted on or after that date (a 1996 Act shorthold) is entitled to be provided by the landlord with a written statement of any terms of the tenancy which are not 'evidenced in writing' (HA 1988, s. 20A, inserted by HA 1996, s. 97). The terms to which he is entitled are the date of commencement, the rent payable, the dates on which the rent is payable, any rent review clauses, and the length of the fixed term (if it is a fixed-term tenancy). The landlord's statement is not conclusive evidence of what was agreed by the parties to the tenancy, and so can be questioned by the tenant in any subsequent proceedings. Failure to provide a written statement 'without reasonable excuse' within 28 days of service of a notice on the landlord is a summary offence punishable on conviction with a fine (s. 20A(4)).

Appendix A contains draft frameworks of assured tenancy agreements. These are not intended to comprise comprehensive tenancy documents, but may be of assistance in guiding the practitioner as to the bare essentials which a tenancy agreement should cover. Clauses which are italicised are intended to be by way of guidance only, and are not set out in full.

6.2 IMPLIED TERMS

6.2.1 Rights to information

There are certain terms which are implied as a matter of law into certain types of tenancies. Thus, for instance, where a tenant has 'the right to occupy premises as a residence in consideration of a rent payable weekly', the landlord is obliged to provide him with a rent book (Landlord and Tenant Act 1985, s. 4). If the landlord's interest under a tenancy of 'premises which consist of or include a dwelling' is assigned, the new landlord must give written notice of the assignment, and of his name and address, within a strict time limit (1985 Act, s. 3). Information must be provided to tenants on demand of the detail of their corporate landlords (1985 Act, s. 4), and the landlord of premises which consist of or include a dwelling (not held under a tenancy to which Part II of the Landlord and Tenant Act 1954 applies) must by notice furnish the tenant with an address in England and Wales at which notices may be served on him by the tenant (Landlord and Tenant Act 1987, s. 48).

6.2.2 Repair

Where the assured tenancy is a lease of a dwelling-house (granted on or after 24 October 1961 – not likely to be a problem) for a term of not less than seven years, there is implied a covenant by the landlord to keep in repair the structure and exterior of the dwelling-house, and to keep in repair and proper working order certain installations for the supply of water, gas and electricity and for sanitation, and the installations for space heating and heating water (Landlord and Tenant Act 1985, s. 11). This well-known and much litigated implied covenant will apply to most assured tenancies (the list of exclusions is limited: see the 1985 Act, s. 14), as contracting out is permitted only with the prior sanction of the county court (1985 Act, s. 12). By Landlord and Tenant Act 1985, s. 11(6), a covenant by the tenant is implied into leases to which that section applies that the landlord, or persons authorised by him in writing, may at reasonable times of the day and on giving 24 hours' notice, enter the premises for the purpose of viewing their condition and state of repair. Assured tenants are under an additional obligation by the HA 1988, s. 16, to allow access and all reasonable facilities to the landlord so that the landlord may execute the repairs himself.

6.2.3 Service charges

The statutory control of service charges effected by ss. 18 to 30 of the Landlord and Tenant Act 1985 (limiting the amount recoverable to charges which are reasonably incurred, in relation to works which are of a reasonable standard) has application to many assured tenancies. The amendments recently introduced by the HA 1996, ss. 83 and 84, effecting a transfer of jurisdiction from the county court to the leasehold valuation tribunal, should be noted.

6.2.4 Assignment

Section 15(1) of the HA 1988, implies a term into all statutory periodic tenancies (which are assured tenancies) that the tenant shall not assign the tenancy, in whole or in part, or sub-let or part with possession of the whole or part of the dwelling-house without the landlord's consent. A similar term is implied into all contractual periodic tenancies unless the parties have themselves expressly prohibited or permitted assignment, or sub-letting or parting with possession in the lease (absolutely or conditionally) or a premium is payable on grant or renewal of the lease (HA 1988, s. 15(3)). No such term is, however, implied into fixed-term assured tenancies. In such cases, the landlord is expected to make appropriate provision in the lease itself.

If a qualified covenant against assignment or sub-letting etc. is implied into a residential lease as a result of the HA 1988, s. 15, the tenant will not be able to complain that the landlord's refusal to consent to a proposed assignment etc. is unreasonable, as the relevant provisions of the Landlord and Tenant Act 1927 (s. 19) are excluded by the HA 1988, s. 15(2). Moreover, as the statutory covenant against alienation is not qualified by a provision that the landlord's consent is not to be unreasonably withheld, the landlord will not be under a statutory duty to make his decision whether or not to consent to alienation within a reasonable time of the tenant's application to him (Landlord and Tenant Act 1988, s. 1). The effect of these provisions is that an assignment or sub-letting by an assured periodic tenant without the landlord's consent will usually be in breach of covenant, and the landlord will be able to institute proceedings for possession based upon Ground 12 (breach of obligation). For recovery of possession of dwellings held on sub-tenancy, see 4.9 above.

6.3   RENTS

There is no control of assured tenancy rents in the way that rents of Rent Act regulated tenancies were (and still are) controlled. Parties to an assured tenancy are free to agree the amount of rent, and to provide for rent reviews if they consider it appropriate. Nor is there any restriction on a landlord charging his tenant a premium as part of the consideration for the grant of the tenancy. However, there are two statutory procedures of which the parties must be aware. An assured shorthold tenant may in certain circumstances apply to a rent assessment committee for a reduction in the rent payable under his tenancy on the basis that it is excessive (HA 1988, s. 22). There is also a statutory procedure for the variation of rents of assured periodic tenancies where no rent review provision is for the time being operative (HA 1988, ss. 13, 14).

6.3.1   Increases of rent under assured periodic tenancies

While a fixed-term tenancy is continuing, the parties will be bound by the terms of the lease. If the tenant has agreed to pay £x per week or month for y years, that is the sum which can be enforced. The landlord cannot claim any more, neither can he increase the rent unilaterally: if he purports to do so, the tenant can simply refuse to pay. The landlord cannot go before a rent assessment committee and ask for an increase in the rent. Neither can the tenant seek a reduction. Both are bound by the lease. There may be a rent review clause in that lease. The timing and frames of reference of the rent review will be as stipulated in the lease: there is nothing in the HA 1988 which has any bearing upon it. Once the fixed term has expired, however, and the assured tenant holds over by force of the statute, it is not unreasonable for the landlord to expect to be able to invoke some machinery whereby the rent can be increased in line with the free market which the 1988 Act is designed to promote. Sections 13 and 14 provide that machinery, which may be used also where the assured tenant has always held as a 'contractual' periodic tenant.

6.3.2 Statutory periodic tenancies

A statutory periodic tenancy arises when an assured fixed-term tenancy comes to an end, generally by expiry of the term (HA 1988, s. 5(2)). Under the tenancy which is imposed by statute, the rent payable will continue at the same level as before (HA 1988, s. 5(3)). However, the landlord now has the right to propose a rent increase. This is justified on the basis that the tenant is holding over by force of statute, and the parties' agreement as such has ended. Without a statutory procedure the landlord would be powerless to increase the rent in view of the tenant's security of tenure, as there would be little effective sanction available to the landlord when faced with a tenant who refused to agree any increase in the rent. Accordingly, the landlord may propose a rent increase at the earliest opportunity following the expiry of the tenant's fixed term, and he has the same right where a tenant has succeeded as assured periodic tenant to a tenancy which was previously Rent Act regulated. These provisions presuppose a rising market, as the tenant has no corresponding right to propose rent reduction. The rent increase provisions apply to all statutory periodic tenancies, even where they are no longer assured tenancies (as long as the landlord's interest does not belong to the Crown or one of the public bodies listed in HA 1988, Sch. 1, paras 11 and 12).

6.3.3 'Contractual' periodic tenancies

Where a periodic tenancy has been created by agreement, express or implied (from payment and acceptance of rent), the landlord would normally seek to obtain a rent increase by threatening notice to quit in the event of the tenant refusing to come to terms. The availability of this course of action is curtailed by the security afforded to assured periodic tenants by the 1988 Act, and thus it is necessary to enable landlords to seek rent increases by some other means. If there is provision in the lease for the rent to be greater (or to be made greater) for a particular, later, period of the tenancy, in other words a rent review clause, then s. 13 cannot be used for as long as such provision is binding on the tenant. Freedom of contract will then prevail.

6.3.4 Rent increase procedure

The landlord serves on the tenant a notice in prescribed form (SI 1997 No. 194, Form No. 4). The notice proposes a new rent and the date it is to take effect. The notice must inform the tenant of his rights in relation to the procedure. If the tenant wishes to contest the rent proposed, he must refer the notice to a rent assessment committee (SI 1997 No. 194, Form No. 6) before the date on which the proposed rent is to take effect. If he fails to do so, the rent as proposed will take effect on the date shown in the notice. The procedure for the increase of rent, which may be initiated only by the landlord, is quite distinct from the procedure whereby the terms of a statutory periodic tenancy may be varied (at the behest of either landlord or tenant). The latter procedure may increase rent only in the sense of 'adjusting' it to take account of the terms which have been determined. The rent increase procedure does not entitle the rent assessment committee to vary any terms other than rent.

As the rent assessment committee is the tribunal in both cases, it is possible that the committee will have two references pending which relate to the same tenancy. The committee is not obliged to hear the two references together, but it would seem to be common sense to do so. If it does, the variation of terms reference should be heard first. Once the terms of the tenancy have been determined, the committee can go on to consider what the appropriate rent should be for an assured tenancy having those terms (HA 1988, s. 14(6)).

The date on which the new rent is proposed to take effect must comply with s. 13(2) and (3), provisions which are at first sight complex, but not difficult in application. Two examples follow, relating to the different kinds of tenancy in relation to which a rent increase may be sought.

Example A

The landlord let a house on a fixed-term tenancy of 12 months, which expired by effluxion of time on 22 April 1998. A statutory periodic tenancy then takes effect, the rent being the same as under the old fixed term, and the periods of the tenancy being those for which the rent was payable (HA 1988, s. 5(2)). As the rent was payable monthly, the new tenancy is a monthly tenancy. The landlord may propose a new rent to take effect on 22 May 1998 (HA 1988, s. 13(3)(c)). It is unclear from the statute whether the landlord may serve notice of increase before the fixed term has expired, to take effect when it has. The cautious landlord will wait until the fixed term has ended, and then serve his notice.

Example B

A landlord let a house on a weekly tenancy (i.e., a contractual periodic tenancy) commencing on 1 July 1998. The earliest date for a rent increase will be 1 July 1999 (the first anniversary of the tenancy: HA 1988, s. 13(2)(b)). If the landlord wishes to propose an increased rent from that date, he must serve his notice no later than one month before (i.e., 1 June 1999), as the period of the tenancy is less than a month (HA 1988, s. 13(3)(b)). If the rent is increased from that date, the landlord will next be able to propose an increase of rent to be effective from 1 July 2000 (HA 1988, s. 13(2)(c)), notice to be served no later than 1 June 2000.

6.3.5 Market rent

The rent assessment committee must determine the rent at which it considers the dwelling-house concerned might reasonably be expected to be let in the open market by a willing landlord under an assured tenancy having the same terms as the tenancy in question (HA 1988, s. 14(1)). In making the determination, the committee must disregard any effect on the rent attributable to the grant of a tenancy to a sitting tenant, any increase in value of the dwelling-house attributable to certain tenants' improvements (defined in s. 14(3)), and any reduction in value of the house attributable to the tenant's breach of covenant (s. 14(2)). 'Rent' is defined for these purposes by s. 14(4). The committee is to assume that rates in respect of the dwelling-house are not borne by the landlord or superior landlord, even if they are (s. 14(5)).

The formula to be applied by rent assessment committees in determining assured tenancy rents is very different from that applicable to the 'fair rents' procedure under the Rent Acts, although, as will be seen, rents under the two regimes are gradually being drawn closer together. The committees determining rents for assured tenancies are expected to consider the local 'market', the number of potential tenants for this particular property, and then assess the sum at which a 'willing landlord', i.e. someone who wants to let, given a reasonable return on his property, being appraised of the market conditions, would reasonably expect the property to be rented for. The committees are not being asked to determine what is a reasonable rent for this tenant to pay, or, indeed, what a reasonable rent for the property would be. Their task is to determine what a landlord's reasonable expectation for the rent for this property should be, if it is let on an assured tenancy with the same terms on which the tenant presently holds.

The rent assessment committee may, in determining the rent, wish to refer to comparable assured tenancy rents in the vicinity, and the president of each rent assessment panel is placed under a duty to keep and make publicly available certain information with respect to rents under assured tenancies (including assured shortholds): by this means there is a ready source of comparables for those appearing before rent assessment committees (HA 1988, s. 42).

6.3.6 Effect of determination

When the rent assessment committee has made its determination of the rent, the rent thus determined will be the rent under the tenancy with effect from the date specified in the landlord's initial notice proposing the increase. Only if the committee forms the view that this would cause undue hardship to the tenant may it specify a later date, and that date may not in any circumstances be later than the date of the committee's determination (HA 1988, s. 14(7)). If there is a substantial delay between the landlord's notice and the decision of the rent assessment committee, and the rent is then increased, the tenant may find himself with a substantial amount of back rent to pay off. At all stages of the proceedings (including after the determination by the rent assessment committee), the parties may come to an agreement about the rent to be charged, and withdraw the reference to the committee or vary the decision which the committee has reached (HA 1988, s. 14(7), (8)).

For the regulations governing the procedure before rent assessment committees, see the Rent Assessment Committees (England and Wales) Regulations 1971, SI 1971 No. 1065, as amended by SI 1988 No. 2200. Appeals from rent assessment committees are governed by the Tribunals and Inquiries Act 1971, s. 13(1): appeal is on a point of law, and is to the High Court. Unlike the Rent Act 'two-tier' system of rent officer and rent assessment committee, neither party may appeal on a question of fact, such as the quantum of the market rent. Only if the committee has misdirected itself in law will an appeal be tenable. For a full treatment of review of the decisions of rent assessment committees, see Megarry, *The Rent Acts*, 11th ed., 1988, chapters 24 and 33.

6.3.7 Rent reduction for assured shorthold tenants

The rent payable under an assured shorthold tenancy may be challenged by the tenant on the basis that it is above the appropriate market rent for the dwelling-house and that the rent should be reduced in consequence. Section 22 of the HA 1988 (as amended) enables an assured shorthold tenant to apply to a rent assessment committee for a determination of the rent which, in the committee's opinion, the landlord might reasonably be expected to obtain under the assured shorthold tenancy. Where the committee makes such a determination, the rent which exceeds the rent so determined will thereafter be irrecoverable from the tenant (HA 1988, s. 22(4)). However, the determination does not bind the property (it does not 'act *in rem*'), and thus on the recovery of possession by the landlord he can let the property to a new tenant at whatever rent that tenant will agree. Application to the rent assessment committee is made in prescribed form (SI 1997 No. 194, Form No. 6: see Appendix C).

6.3.8 Exclusions

Application may not be made:

(a) where the rent payable had previously been determined by a rent assessment committee following application under s. 22. Once the rent has been reduced, it cannot be challenged further;

(b) where the tenancy was entered into on or after 28 February 1997 (and is therefore a tenancy to which s. 19A applies), and the first six months of the landlord–tenant relationship have elapsed;

(c) where an assured shorthold tenancy was entered into before 28 February 1997 (or later, in pursuance of a contract made before that date), and a new tenancy has come into being with the same landlord and tenant. As this terminology covers both the assured shorthold tenant holding over as statutory periodic tenant following expiry of the fixed term, and the assured shorthold tenant who is expressly granted a new tenancy by the landlord on expiry of the old, it appears that pre-1996 Act assured shorthold tenants can seek rent reduction only during their initial fixed term. The rationale for this restriction is that once the initial fixed term has expired, the landlord who has elected not to exercise his right to repossession should not be penalised by having his commercial return diminished.

The committee must determine the rent the landlord might reasonably be expected to obtain under the assured shorthold tenancy. Although there is no express provision to this effect, the inference is that the landlord who lets on assured shorthold tenancy should not reasonably expect to obtain as much as a landlord who lets on an assured tenancy which is not shorthold. The price to the landlord of conferring no security of tenure is a potential return on property somewhat lower than that otherwise obtainable. The committee is expected to consider comparables, and should not make a determination at all unless it considers that there is a sufficient number of similar dwelling-houses in the locality let on assured tenancies (shorthold or not) (HA 1988, s. 22(3)(a)). The committee should not tamper with the agreed rent. Unless it considers the rent the tenant pays is 'significantly higher' than the rent the landlord might reasonably be expected to obtain (having regard to the comparables), the committee should not make a determination at all (HA 1988, s. 22(3)(b)). It has been established that a rent assessment committee has jurisdiction to determine a rent in excess of £25,000 per annum (and must assess the market rent without reference to the £25,000 limit), although the effect of making such a determination is that the tenancy will cease to be an assured tenancy (*R v London Rent Assessment Panel, ex parte Cadogan Estates Ltd* [1997] 2 EGLR 134).

The Secretary of State has powers to order that the rent reduction procedure will not apply in certain areas or in certain circumstances (HA 1988, s. 23). Appeals from rent assessment committees are tenable pursuant to the Tribunals and Inquiries Act 1971, s. 13.

6.3.9 Relationship to increase of rent under assured periodic tenancies

If a determination is made reducing the rent on application by the tenant, the landlord cannot seek to increase the rent until 12 months have elapsed from the date the determination takes effect (HA 1988, s. 22(4)(c)).

6.3.10 Comment

The shortcomings of the rent reduction procedure should be noted. If the tenant wishes to stay in the property for any length of time, he will need to think long and hard whether such an application is advisable. For if the tenant secures a rent reduction, the landlord may simply seek to recover possession at the earliest opportunity, and let the property to a tenant who is ready to pay the rent he wants. The landlord is, at least in a buoyant property market, in a dominant position, and there is little in the legislation which appears to prevent its abuse. The tenant's attempts to secure a market rent are always in danger of being undermined by the landlord's power to recover possession on giving notice.

6.4 FIXING TERMS OF STATUTORY PERIODIC TENANCIES

6.4.1 Statutory periodic tenancy

Although the statutory periodic tenancy is not as such agreed by the parties, its terms will largely derive from the fixed-term tenancy which preceded it. By the HA 1988, s. 5(3), the statutory periodic tenancy:

(a) takes effect in possession immediately the fixed-term tenancy comes to an end;

(b) has as its landlord and tenant those persons who were landlord and tenant under that fixed term;

(c) is of the same dwelling-house as was let under the fixed term;

(d) has as its periods those by which rent was last payable under the fixed term (e.g., if under the fixed term the rent was £2,000 per year payable monthly, the statutory periodic tenancy will be a monthly tenancy);

(e) is one under which the other terms are those of the fixed-term tenancy, with one exception. Any provision in the fixed term for determination by landlord or tenant shall not have effect while the statutory periodic tenancy remains an assured tenancy. This exception is highly significant, placing the matter of termination of the tenancy, and recovery of possession, firmly in the province of the court, which, as will be seen, can order possession only on statutorily prescribed grounds.

6.4.2 Variation of terms

The landlord and tenant to any assured tenancy may agree to vary the terms of the tenancy at any time, with the one qualification that terms providing for determination by either of them will have no effect while a statutory periodic tenancy remains assured. The parties cannot unilaterally vary the terms of a statutory periodic tenancy, but a procedure is provided by the HA 1988, s. 6, whereby a proposal by either party to vary can be made, and a binding determination made by a rent assessment committee in the event of opposition by the other party.

6.4.3 Exclusions

The s. 6 procedure cannot be used:

(a) where the tenancy is not an assured tenancy by virtue of paras 11 or 12 of Sch. 1 to the 1988 Act (i.e., the landlord is the Crown or a listed public body: s. 6(1));

(b) to vary the rent as such. A separate procedure is provided whereby rent increases can be effected (see 6.3 above). The rent assessment committee may, however, make adjustments to the rent to take account of the terms it has determined in the course of a s. 6 reference (HA 1988, s. 6(5)).

6.4.4 Procedure

The s. 6 procedure takes the following course:

(a) The fixed term ends, and a statutory periodic tenancy takes effect.
(b) Not later than the first anniversary of the ending of the fixed term, the landlord (or tenant) serves a notice in prescribed form (SI 1997, No. 194, Form 1) proposing varied terms.
(c) Within three months of notice being served, the tenant (or landlord) refers the notice to the rent assessment committee, again using a form prescribed for the purpose (SI 1997, No. 194, Form 2). If the tenant (or landlord) fails so to refer the notice within the three-month period, the variation, and any adjustment of rent, will take effect.
(d) The committee considers the proposed terms and makes a determination.
(e) The committee specifies an adjustment to the rent to take account of its determination.
(f) The committee directs the date (no earlier than the date specified in the notice proposing variation) from which the terms it has determined shall become terms of the statutory periodic tenancy, and the adjustment in rent, if any, takes effect.

6.4.5 The criteria for variation

The rent assessment committee must determine whether the terms proposed in the notice are such as might reasonably be expected to be found in an assured periodic tenancy of the dwelling-house concerned. This hypothetical tenancy is to be viewed as one beginning on the date of termination of the fixed-term tenancy, granted by a willing landlord, and having the same terms as the statutory periodic tenancy before the committee except for those terms which 'relate to the subject matter of the proposed terms'. In other words, the rent assessment committee should take the lease as it currently stands with the exception of the terms being proposed, and terms which would be closely affected by the variation in question.

6.4.6 Powers of the committee

The rent assessment committee may accept the terms as proposed. It may reject them outright, and refuse any variation. The committee may, if it wishes, devise terms of its own in place of the currently implied terms and the proposed terms, as long as the terms it devises deal with the same subject-matter as the proposal before it. The committee shall, if it considers it appropriate, specify a rent adjustment, even though the initial notice of variation did not propose one. In making its determination and specifying a rent adjustment, the committee must disregard any effect of the terms or rent attributable to the tenancy being granted to a sitting tenant. The rent assessment committee may require the parties to provide such information as it may reasonably require for the performance of its functions, and failure to comply with such a requirement may result in the imposition of a fine in the magistrates' court (HA 1988, s. 41). If there are concurrent applications before a rent assessment committee for variation of the terms of a lease and increase of the rent payable (under HA 1988, s. 13), the committee may 'consolidate' the applications, and should then hear the s. 6 reference first (HA 1988, s. 14(6)). This is common sense. The committee will be able to fix the market rent only when the terms of the tenancy have been properly established.

6.4.7 Appeals

There is no right of appeal from a determination of a rent assessment committee under s. 6 provided by the 1988 Act, but it appears that appeal under the Tribunals and Inquiries Act 1971, s. 13, will be available. Where the committee has misdirected itself in law, there may be a remedy by way of judicial review.

6.5 ASSURED TENANCIES OF REGISTERED SOCIAL LANDLORDS

Where the landlord is a registered social landlord, the freedom to negotiate terms is restricted by the requirement that the landlord comply with guidance issued from time to time by the Housing Corporation. The Corporation has encouraged RSLs to grant long-term security of tenure wherever possible, but at the same time has recognised that assured shorthold tenancies may be appropriate in the case of temporary housing arrangements. The current guidance, issued in October 1996, is at the time of writing the subject of consultation and review, but can be found in Housing Corporation Circular R3-36/96.

6.6 STATUTORY SUCCESSION

6.6.1 Relationship between statute and will etc.

On the death of an assured tenant, the devolution of the tenancy will depend on whether, at the time of death, it is for a fixed term or is periodic.

If it is a fixed-term tenancy, it will pass according to the will of the tenant, or, in the event of no testamentary provision being made which covers the tenancy, in accordance with the rules of intestacy (see Administration of Estates Act 1925, ss. 46–49; Intestates' Estates Act 1952, s. 5, Sch. 2, as variously amended). If the tenancy is periodic, whether 'contractual' periodic or statutory periodic, the tenancy may still devolve according to the will or the intestacy rules, but only if s. 17 of the HA 1988 does not apply. By s. 17(1):

In any case where—
   (a)   the sole tenant under an assured periodic tenancy dies, and
   (b)   immediately before the death, the tenant's spouse was oc-cupying the dwelling-house as his or her only or principal home, and
   (c)   the tenant was not himself a successor, as defined in subsec-tion (2) or subsection (3) below,
then, on the death, the tenancy vests by virtue of this section in the spouse (and, accordingly, does not devolve under the tenant's will or intestacy).

6.6.2   Sole tenant

If at the date of death, there are two (or more) persons holding the tenancy, s. 17 will not apply. Instead, the tenancy will pass by virtue of the right of survivorship to the surviving joint tenant(s). This will then preclude the tenancy passing, on the subsequent death of the survivor, by s. 17 (see s. 17(2)(b)).

6.6.3   Spouse

The ordinary meaning of 'spouse' (of a person lawfully married to the tenant) is extended to include a person who was living with the tenant as his or her wife or husband (s. 17(4)). It has been accepted that this terminology excludes the possibility of the survivor of a homosexual relationship qualifying as a 'spouse' (see, on the similar succession provisions for secure tenancies, *Harrogate Borough Council* v *Simpson* (1984) 17 HLR 205, recently followed in relation to Rent Act regulated tenancies by *Fitzpatrick* v *Sterling Housing Association* [1998] Ch 304). In the unlikely event of there being more than one person who qualifies as a spouse, the successor will be decided by agreement between them, failing which the county court will decide (s. 17(5)).

6.6.4 Occupying the dwelling-house as his or her only or principal home

This is the same test to be applied in determining whether a tenant is assured (HA 1988, s. 1; see 2.7 above). The tenant whom the claimant is seeking to succeed must also have been occupying the dwelling-house as his only or principal home up to the time of death in order to remain assured tenant. There is no express requirement that the tenant was 'living with' the claimant unless they were not lawfully married (see then s. 17(4)). If, therefore, a husband and wife, who were lawfully married, the husband being the assured tenant of their dwelling-house, were living in separate households under the same roof, the wife would succeed on the death of her husband.

6.6.5 Tenant not himself a successor

This is the most important limitation on statutory succession under the 1988 Act. The basic principle which is being promoted is that there should be no more than one succession to a periodic tenancy. Succession is widely defined in s. 17(2) and (3). A tenant will be a successor if he has himself become tenant by virtue of s. 17, or by virtue of survivorship or by succession to a Rent Act regulated tenancy. The grant of a new tenancy to a person who was at the time of grant a successor will not 'wipe the slate clean', as that person will still be deemed a successor if the new tenancy is of the same or substantially the same dwelling-house. Where a successor to an assured tenancy transfers the tenancy to his spouse, or former spouse or cohabitant pursuant to an order under Sch. 7 to the Family Law Act 1996 (transfer of tenancies on divorce or separation of spouses, or separation of cohabitants), the transferee will be deemed to be a successor also, and on her death, no further statutory succession will be possible (FLA 1996, Sch. 7, para. 7(4)).

6.6.6 Devolution under the will or on intestacy

If s. 17 does not apply, for whatever reason, it does not follow that the death of the assured periodic tenant will terminate the tenancy. It will form part of the tenant's estate, and fall to be disposed of under the terms of his will or in accordance with the intestacy rules. However, the landlord has the right to recover possession in the period of 12 months from the date of the death (or, if the court directs, the date of landlord became aware of the tenant's death) by invoking Ground 7, a mandatory ground of possession (see 4.8.7). This provision will be required only where the person entitled to the tenancy goes into occupation: if he does not, the tenancy will cease to be assured, and the landlord will then be free to terminate it by giving notice of the appropriate length.

CHAPTER SEVEN

Long Tenancies at a Low Rent

7.1 INTRODUCTION

Many dwellings in England and Wales are held by the occupiers on long leases, for which a substantial premium has been paid. The arrangements whereby these persons have purchased the leasehold interest in their houses or flats are little different from those involved in the purchase of a freehold. Thus, the premium paid on assignment or grant of a long lease may be similar in amount to prices paid for freeholds in the same vicinity, and the purchasers may be taking a term which is unlikely to expire in their lifetime and may well last for hundreds of years. In short, the long leaseholder has become a very familiar figure in our conveyancing processes. However, recent legislative changes, responding to the difficulties faced by long leaseholders as a result of the depreciating nature of the long lease as an asset, have entitled many leaseholders to purchase outright their landlords' interest and become freeholders themselves – to 'enfranchise'. In due course, a wholly new system of land holding, 'commonhold', is likely to be introduced, which will provide a more effective machinery to enforce covenants between those with similar interests in a building or development, and thereby remove one of the major attractions of granting long leases in the first place.

Security of tenure for long leaseholders is complex. The Rent Acts never directly applied to them, as the vast majority of long leases are at a low rent and thereby excluded from regulation. The HA 1988 has a similar exclusion, and so likewise long leases are not likely to be assured tenancies. However, for many years, protection was afforded by Part I of the Landlord and Tenant Act 1954, granting security to tenants on the termination of a long tenancy at a low rent. The 'qualifying condition' was somewhat artificial, requiring the circumstances to be such that on the coming to an end of the tenancy the tenant would, if the tenancy were not one at a low rent, be entitled by virtue of the Rent Act to retain possession of the whole or part of the property. The hypothesis that the tenancy was not at a low rent was therefore applied. Where a tenancy was within Part I of the 1954 Act, the long tenancy would continue automatically at the end of the term, albeit subject to the landlord converting the tenancy into a statutory tenancy under the Rent Acts or seeking possession by court order on proof of prescribed statutory grounds. Provisions offered the tenant protection against forfeiture during the fixed term as well.

When the HA 1988 came into force, it had an adverse impact on the position of long leaseholders which had been neither anticipated nor appreciated. Where a long tenancy at a low rent was entered into on or after 15 January 1989, merely assuming that the level of the rent did not exclude it from the Rent Acts was not sufficient for it to qualify for Rent Act protection, as by HA 1988, s. 34(1), a tenancy entered into on or after that date cannot (subject to exceptions) be a protected tenancy. It was necessary to enact further legislation to protect long leaseholders whose leases were granted subsequently to the 1988 Act coming into force, and these provisions are to be found in the Local Government and Housing Act 1989 (LGHA 1989), s. 186 and Sch. 10.

The provisions of the LGHA 1989 equate long leaseholders to assured tenants under the HA 1988, and ultimately phase out the 1954 Act with regard to long leaseholders whose tenancies were granted before 15 January 1989. The 1989 Act protects long leaseholders by means of an assured periodic tenancy. An added complexity is that owing to the piecemeal nature of the reforms, it is possible that certain long lease-holders have fallen through the net of protection.

7.2 THE REGIMES OF SECURITY

7.2.1 Tenancies entered into prior to 15 January 1989

A long tenancy at a low rent entered into prior to this date was, on fulfilling the qualifying condition, protected by the statutory code contained in Part I of the 1954 Act. However, any such tenancy which was in existence on 15 January 1999 was transformed into a long tenancy under the 1989 Act unless, before that date, the landlord had initiated the process of recovery of possession by serving a notice under the 1954 Act (s. 4) specifying a date of termination earlier than 15 January 1999 (LGHA 1989, s. 186(3)).

7.2.2   Tenancies entered into on or after 1 April 1990

It is possible that certain tenancies entered into on or after 15 January 1989 were initially governed by Part I of the 1954 Act (subject to 7.2.1 above) where the tenancy would, by reason of the transitional provisions in the HA 1988, be a protected tenancy had it not been at a low rent (for example, a long tenancy is entered into pursuant to a contract made before 15 January 1989). But generally, Part I of the 1954 Act is inapplicable to long tenancies at a low rent entered into on or after that date. On 1 April 1990, the relevant provisions of the LGHA 1989 came into force, whereby Sch. 10 to that Act was applied to long tenancies at a low rent entered into on or after that day (LGHA 1989, s. 186(2)). Thus tenancies entered into on or after 1 April 1990 are capable of protection under the 1989 Act provided they were not entered into pursuant to a contract made before that date.

7.2.3   Tenancies entered into between 15 January 1989 and 30 March 1990

It can be seen that there is a possible hiatus in protection. Part I of the 1954 Act cannot apply to tenancies entered into on or after 15 January 1989 (save in exceptional circumstances) as a tenant holding such a tenancy (assuming it were not at a low rent) would not be entitled on termination at that time to retain possession by virtue of the RA 1977. In short, he would not satisfy the 'qualifying condition' set out in the 1954 Act. Yet the code contained in the LGHA 1989 does not appear to have any retrospective application. It does not apply to tenancies granted before 1 April 1990. Thus it appears that long leaseholders whose tenancy was granted on or after 15 January 1989 but before 1 April 1990 are outside both protective codes.

It has been argued (by Arden and Hunter, *Current Law Statutes Annotated 1989*, 42–276) that long tenancies entered into on or after 15 January 1989 could, by an imaginative interpretation of the 1989 Act, s. 186(3), have come within Sch. 10 to that Act. Section 186(3) transforms long tenancies which were subject to Part I of the 1954 Act as at 15 January 1999 into 1989 Act long tenancies. However, such an interpretation founders, in this author's view, as the third condition imposed for the operation of s. 186(3) is that 'immediately before' 15 January 1999 the tenancy was, or was deemed to be, a long tenancy at a low rent for the purposes of Part I of the 1954 Act. As the tenancy in question was granted after 15 January 1989, this cannot have been the case. Much clearer words were necessary if the statute was to have this retrospective effect.

The issue has not been conclusively determined, and the practical difficulty facing those dealing with leases granted in this period is that landlords will only seek to recover possession on expiry of long tenancies in 2010. It can only be hoped that a landlord or tenant may seek declaratory relief before then in an appropriate case, so that the High Court may have the opportunity to rule on whether either of the statutory codes apply to such tenants.

It is not intended to spend time here explaining the statutory code contained in Part I of the 1954 Act. The tenancies not being assured, they are in any event outside the scope of this book, and the statutory regime has now ceased to be of application.

7.3   1989 ACT: DEFINITIONS

7.3.1   Long tenancy

A long tenancy is a tenancy granted for a term of years certain exceeding 21 years, whether or not subsequently extended by act of the parties or any enactment, but excluding any tenancy which is, or may become, terminable before the end of the term by notice given to the tenant (LGHA 1989, Sch. 10, para. 2(3)). The lease cannot be 'backdated' to make up the necessary length. As Russell LJ stated in *Roberts v Church Commissioners* [1972] 1 QB 278, at 284, '. . . a tenant must at some point in time be, or have been, in a position to say that, subject to options to determine, rights of re-entry and so forth, he is entitled to remain tenant for the next 21 years, whether at law or in equity.' In that case, landlords had granted a lease for 10 and a quarter years in 1950. In 1952, the parties agreed to an extension of the term, the landlords then granting a lease for 21 and a quarter years from March 1950 (when the tenants had first gone in to possession). This was not a grant for a term certain exceeding 21 years within the statutory definition.

Where, on the coming to the end of a long tenancy at a low rent (or a tenancy deemed to be such), the tenant is granted a new tenancy (or becomes by implication of law a new tenant) of the whole or part of the property let under the previous tenancy, then the subsequent tenancy will be deemed to be a long tenancy for the purposes of Sch. 10, irrespective of its terms (LGHA 1989, Sch. 10, para. 16(1)). Where the subsequent tenancy is a tenancy from year to year (or any tenancy other than a term of years certain), then Sch. 10 will take effect subject to certain modifications (LGHA 1989, Sch. 10, para. 16(2)).

7.3.2   At a low rent

If no rent is payable under the tenancy, it will be 'at a low rent'. Otherwise, the rules differ according to the date the tenancy was entered into (see generally LGHA 1989, Sch. 10, para. 2(4)). If it was entered into on or after 1 April 1990, the maximum rent payable at any time must be payable at a rate of £1,000 or less in Greater London, or £250 or less elsewhere. If the tenancy was entered before that date (or subsequently, in pursuance of a contract made before that date, where there was a rateable value for the dwelling-house on 31 March 1990), the maximum rent payable must be payable at a rate which is less than two-thirds of the rateable value of the dwelling-house on 31 March 1990.

7.3.3   'Qualifying condition'

The long tenancy at a low rent must satisfy the 'qualifying condition', in this case 'that the circumstances (as respects the property let under the tenancy, the use of that property and all other relevant matters) are such that, if the tenancy were not at a low rent, it would at that time be an assured tenancy within the meaning of Part I of the HA 1988' (LGHA 1989, Sch. 10, para. 1(1)). For this purpose only, Sch. 1 to the 1988 Act must be read with the omission of para. 1 (the exclusion of tenancies entered into before, or pursuant to contracts made before, 15 January 1989) (LGHA 1989, Sch. 10, para. 1(2)). Paragraph 2 of that schedule (excluding high value dwellings) is also read subject to modifications: for the purpose of determining whether the qualifying condition is fulfilled a complex formula is applied (LGHA 1989, Sch. 10, para. 1(2A)). In determining whether the property was 'let as a separate dwelling', the 'nature' and 'purposes' of the letting are deemed to have been the same at the time of creation of the tenancy as they are at the time the question arises (LGHA 1989, Sch. 10, para. 1(7)).

Several cases on Part I of the 1954 Act remain of importance in determining the purpose to which the property was being put when the long lease expires. In *Haines* v *Herbert* [1963] 1 WLR 1401, the tenant acquired by assignment the 'butt-end' (the final six months) of a 99-year lease of a house which was sub-divided into two large living units, each consisting of two floors. The tenant immediately installed herself in the upper two floors, sleeping there four or five nights a week and cooking some meals there. She slept in the lower two floors for some six nights in total over the six-month period, but that was all. However, she gave evidence (which was believed) that she intended to reconvert the property and occupy it as her dwelling. The Court of Appeal, looking at the state of affairs at the end of the fixed term, held that she occupied the house as her residence, and that it was then let to her as a separate dwelling.

A similar result occurred in *Herbert v Byrne* [1964] 1 WLR 519. It was again a 'butt-end' purchase, the final five months of a 99-year term. When the term expired, the tenant was occupying two of the four floors, the other two being sub-let to protected tenants. These sub-lettings did not deter the Court of Appeal from deciding that the house was let as a separate dwelling at the end of the term.

The tenants in both the above cases were opportunists, seizing the chance of obtaining (at that time) a statutory tenancy by purchasing what was on its face a fast-depreciating asset. However, such a factor should not, according to Salmon LJ in *Herbert v Byrne* (at 529), influence the court, as the tenant's knowledge of the legal position, and hope of obtaining advantage therefrom, cannot affect the true nature of his or her occupation.

In *Crown Lodge (Surbiton) Investments Ltd v Nalecz* [1967] 1 WLR 647, the tenant's house was sufficiently commodious to be outside the Rent Act rateable value limits. The tenant sub-let such parts of the house which he did not occupy personally, and then argued that as the apportioned rateable value of the parts he retained as his dwelling-house was within the relevant limits, he was entitled to statutory protection. The Court of Appeal rejected his claim. In considering whether the qualifying condition applied, the whole property let to the tenant must be examined, and as the extent of the property took it outside the rateable value limits, it could not be brought back in by deeming the part occupied by the tenant to be let to him as a separate dwelling.

In *Regalian Securities Ltd v Ramsden* [1981] 1 WLR 611, the House of Lords re-emphasised the importance of looking at the position between landlord and tenant (as opposed to sub-tenants) in the house as a whole. A penthouse which comprised a maisonette and adjoining flat was let for a term of 42 years in 1936. The term was assigned to the defendant in 1973, following which he occupied the maisonette and sub-let the maisonette for the remainder of the head lease less one day. The sub-tenant did not vacate as required to do, and remained in *de facto* occupation of the flat until after the term date. Despite this, the House of Lords held that on the term date the penthouse was let to the tenant as a separate dwelling, as there had initially been a single letting for residential purposes, and the intention of the tenant to occupy the penthouse as a single home as soon as he could, together with his right to possession of the penthouse as a whole, indicated that this was also the position at the expiry of the lease.

7.3.4 Exclusions

There is no list of exclusions as such, but where a tenancy would be excluded from being an assured tenancy under the 1988 Act it will, subject to what is said above, be outside the protection of the 1989 Act as well. Application may be made to the court within the last 12 months of the fixed term for a declaration that the tenancy is not to be treated as a tenancy to which Sch. 10 applies (LGHA 1989, Sch. 10, para. 1(3)). If the 'qualifying condition' is not fulfilled at the time of the application, the court must go on to consider whether the tenancy is likely to be a tenancy to which Sch. 10 will apply immediately before the term date. If the court is satisfied that it is not likely, it must make a declaration, which has the effect that the tenancy shall not be treated as being a tenancy to which Sch. 10 applies, even though the usual criteria are met by the expiry of the term.

7.4 1989 ACT TENANCIES: SECURITY OF TENURE

Schedule 10 to the LGHA 1989 operates by continuing automatically the long tenancy at the end of the term. The landlord may seek to improve his position by one of two means:

(a) He may seek to convert the long tenancy into an assured tenancy under Part I of the HA 1988, following which the tenant will occupy as any other assured periodic tenant. The landlord may then seek to recover possession by invoking the possession procedure appropriate to such a tenant, proving where necessary a ground for possession under Sch. 2 to the 1988 Act.
(b) He may seek to recover possession at an earlier stage, while the tenancy is still continuing pursuant to the provisions of Sch. 10. In this case, however, the grounds for possession are restricted in number.

7.4.1 Continuation of long tenancy

A long residential tenancy shall not come to an end by expiry of the fixed term. It will terminate only by compliance with the provisions of Sch. 10 (LGHA 1989, Sch. 10, para. 3(1)). The terms of the tenancy after the term date will be the same as those before (LGHA 1989, Sch. 10, para. 3(3)).

7.4.2 Termination of tenancy by tenant

The tenant may bring a long residential tenancy to an end on or after the term date by giving not less than one month's notice in writing (LGHA 1989, Sch. 10, para. 8).

7.4.3 Termination of tenancy by landlord

The landlord may terminate the long residential tenancy on or after the term date by giving notice in the prescribed form to the tenant specifying the date at which the tenancy is to come to an end. It must be served not more than 12 nor less than six months before the date specified (LGHA 1989, Sch. 10, para. 4). The notice must take one of two forms:

(a) a notice proposing an assured periodic tenancy;
(b) a notice to resume possession (LGHA 1989, Sch. 10, para. 4(5)).

7.4.3.1 Notice proposing an assured periodic tenancy
The tenancy must be an assured monthly periodic tenancy, at a rent which is such that the tenancy will not be a tenancy at a low rent (LGHA 1989, Sch. 10, para. 9). There are provisions enabling the tenant to challenge the rent or other terms proposed, and jurisdiction is conferred on rent assessment committees to determine disputes on these matters (LGHA 1989, Sch. 10, paras 10 to 12). While the terms of the assured tenancy are being established, the landlord may apply to a rent assessment committee for an interim rent to be assessed (Sch. 10, paras 6 to 7). Once the assured tenancy has taken effect, the landlord will be able to recover possession only by satisfying the provisions of Part I of the HA 1988. Although the assured tenancy will be granted on or after 28 February 1997, it will not be an assured shorthold tenancy, as assured tenancies arising by virtue of Sch. 10 of the 1989 Act are specifically excluded from being automatically shortholds by HA 1988, Sch. 2A, para. 6 (inserted by HA 1996, s. 96, Sch. 7).

7.4.3.2 Notice to resume possession
The landlord may propose to apply to the court for an order for possession on the following grounds:

(a) Ground 6 of the HA 1988, unless the tenancy was a tenancy under Part I of the 1954 Act (LGHA 1989, Sch. 10, para. 5(2)). Ground 6 may be used here although the assured tenant became so by virtue of the succession provisions of the 1977 or the 1988 Acts;
(b) Grounds 9 to 15 inclusive of the HA 1988;
(c) The landlord (which must be a body to which the Leasehold Reform Act 1967, s. 28 applies: LGHA 1989, Sch. 10, para. 5(4)) proposes to demolish or reconstruct the whole or a substantial part of the premises for the purposes of redevelopment after termination of the tenancy;

(d) The premises or part of them are reasonably required by the landlord for occupation as a residence for himself or any son or daughter of his over 18 years of age or his spouse's father or mother and, if the landlord is not the immediate landlord, he will be at the specified date of termination. This ground may not be used where the landlord's interest was created after 18 February 1966 (see further LGHA 1989, Sch. 10, para. 5(5)).

7.4.4 Failure to obtain possession

The landlord's notice to resume possession will cease to have effect if he fails to apply to the court within the prescribed time limit, or if the court refuses to make an order for possession or if he withdraws his application by serving notice in writing to that effect on the tenant. In the last two cases, provision is made for the landlord to serve a notice proposing an assured tenancy within one month of the proceedings for possession being disposed of, or the withdrawal of the notice to resume possession, as the case may be (see LGHA 1989, Sch. 10, para. 15).

7.5 ENFRANCHISEMENT

Many long tenants at a low rent will have the right to purchase the freehold reversion of their house, or the right to obtain a long lease of their flat, pursuant to the Leasehold Reform Act 1967 and the Leasehold Reform and Urban Development Act 1993. The content of these statutes is beyond the scope of this book. Reference should be made to the standard works, in particular *Hague on Leasehold Enfranchisement* (3rd edn, London: Sweet & Maxwell, 1999).

Precedents for Tenancy Agreements

Note: In the precedents, clauses not set out in full are in italics.

A. ASSURED SHORTHOLD TENANCIES

As a result of the HA 1996, any assured tenancy granted on or after 28 February 1997 will take effect as an assured shorthold tenancy, unless certain exceptions apply (see further chapter 5). The frameworks which follow are intended to facilitate the drafting of an assured shorthold. There is no need for the tenancy to state that it is a shorthold, as this is now the default form of letting. Obviously, the majority of terms will depend on the wishes (and negotiating strengths) of the parties, and these precedents are intended to do no more than sketch the possible terms which may be included.

A1 Fixed-term tenancy

[The tenancy here is for a fixed term, in which case it is essential that the terms of the tenancy make provision for it to be brought to an end on the relevant grounds in Sch. 2 to the 1988 Act (see 4.5.1 above, and cl. 5 in the draft).]

THIS AGREEMENT is made this day [date of agreement]

BETWEEN

[landlord's name] of [landlord's address] (hereafter 'the Landlord')

AND

[tenant's name] of [tenant's address] (hereafter 'the Tenant').

1. DEFINITIONS
'Landlord' includes where the context so admits the person for the time being entitled to the reversion immediately expectant on the determination of the Term.

'Premises' includes the dwelling-house and property known as [address] and further described in the First Schedule hereto.

'Rents' means the rents reserved in clause 3 and shall also include such rent as may be ascertained on review in accordance with the provisions of the Fourth Schedule or agreed by the Landlord and the Tenant from time to time.

'Tenant' includes where the context so admits the Tenant's successors in title.

'Term' means the term granted by clause 2 below.

2. LETTING
The Landlord hereby lets to the Tenant the Premises

TOGETHER WITH the easements and rights set out in the Second Schedule

EXCEPT AND RESERVING as mentioned in the Third Schedule

SUBJECT TO all rights easements and privileges to which the Premises are subject

FOR THE TERM OF [THREE YEARS] FROM [date of commencement]

YIELDING AND PAYING the following rents clear of any deductions whatsoever

(1) the monthly rent of [£   ] to be paid [by bankers order if required by the landlord] [in advance/ in arrear] on the first day of each calendar month the first such payment to be made on [specify date] [or such rent as may for the time being be agreed by the parties or ascertained on review in accordance with the provisions of the Fourth Schedule]

(2) on demand all expenses which the Landlord may incur from time to time in connection with procuring the remedying of any breach of the Tenant's covenants contained herein.

3. TENANT'S COVENANTS
The Tenant COVENANTS throughout the Term
(1)   *to pay the Rents*
(2)   *to pay interest*
(3)   *to pay all existing and future rates etc.*

(4)   to use the Premises in a tenant-like manner
(5)   to permit the Landlord to inspect the Premises
(6)   not to assign or underlet or part with possession of the Premises
(7)   to yield and deliver up the Premises at the end of the Term.

4.   LANDLORD'S COVENANTS
The Landlord COVENANTS
(1)   to give quiet enjoyment of the Premises to the Tenant
(2)   to insure
*(3)   to comply with the provisions of the Landlord and Tenant Act 1985 sections
11 to 15 inclusive.*

5.   PROVISO FOR TERMINATION BY THE LANDLORD
(1)   If at any time during the Term any of Grounds 2 8 10 to 15 inclusive
or 17 set out in Schedule 2 to the Housing Act 1988 apply the Landlord
may thereupon bring the Term to an end and seek an order for possession
of the Premises pursuant to section 7(6) of the Housing Act 1988.
(2)   If at any time during the Term
(i)   the Rent is in arrear for [21 days] (whether formally demanded or
not) or
(ii)   the Tenant fails to observe or perform any covenant contained in this
lease or
(iii)   an application for the appointment of an interim receiver is made or
a bankruptcy order is made in respect of the Tenant or the Tenant enters
into any arrangement for the benefit of his creditors or suffers any distress
or execution to be levied on his assets
the Landlord may re-enter upon the Premises or any part thereof and
forfeit the lease but without prejudice to any other remedy of the Landlord
in respect of any antecedent breach of covenants or conditions in the lease.

[The Landlord may wish to reserve the right to give notice to terminate
following the expiry of the first six months of the tenancy. If this is the case,
a clause on the lines of that upheld in *Aylward* v *Fawaz* (1996) 29 HLR 408
should be included in the agreement: see 5.2.1 above.]

AS WITNESS ETC.

FIRST SCHEDULE
[*The Premises described*]

SECOND SCHEDULE
[The easements and rights granted to the Tenant]

THIRD SCHEDULE
[The exceptions and reservations in favour of the Landlord]

FOURTH SCHEDULE
[The rent review provisions]

A2 Periodic tenancy

[The essential differences are obvious. The demise clause needs to cover the relevant period. There is no need for a landlord termination clause to cover resort to HA 1988, s. 7(6).]

THIS AGREEMENT [as A1 above]

1. DEFINITIONS [as A1 above, although 'Term' is no longer relevant]

2. LETTING
The Landlord hereby lets to the Tenant the Premises
TOGETHER WITH the easements and rights set out in the Second Schedule
EXCEPT AND RESERVING as mentioned in the Third Schedule
SUBJECT TO all rights easements and privileges to which the Premises are subject
ON A [MONTHLY] TENANCY FROM [date of commencement]
YIELDING AND PAYING the following rents clear of any deductions whatsoever
(1) the monthly rent of [£   ] to be paid [by bankers order if required by the landlord] [in advance/ in arrear] on the first day of each calendar month the first such payment to be made on [specify date] [or such rent as may for the time being be agreed by the parties or ascertained on review in accordance with the provisions of the Fourth Schedule]
(2) on demand all expenses which the Landlord may incur from time to time in connection with procuring the remedying of any breach of the Tenant's covenants contained herein

3. TENANT'S COVENANTS [as A1 above]

4. LANDLORD'S COVENANTS [as A1 above]

120

5.   PROVISO FOR TERMINATION BY THE LANDLORD

If at any time:

(i)   the Rent is in arrear for [21 days] (whether formally demanded or not) or

(ii)   the Tenant fails to observe or perform any covenant contained in this lease or

(iii) an application for the appointment of an interim receiver is made or a bankruptcy order is made in respect of the Tenant or the Tenant enters into any arrangement for the benefit of his creditors or suffers any distress or execution to be levied on his assets

the Landlord may re-enter upon the Premises or any part thereof and forfeit the lease but without prejudice to any other remedy of the Landlord in respect of any antecedent breach of covenants or conditions in the lease.

AS WITNESS ETC

SCHEDULES

B.   ASSURED (NON-SHORTHOLD) TENANCIES

Notes

To grant an effective non-shorthold tenancy it is now necessary (in most cases) to make specific provision in (or by notice prior to) the tenancy agreement. This is particularly important to registered social landlords, which are not expected to grant assured shorthold tenancies save in specific circumstances.

The tenancy agreement may follow drafts A1 or A2 above. There should be included at some point in the agreement: 'It is hereby agreed (as permitted by paragraph 3 of Sch. 2A to the Housing Act 1988 as amended) that the tenancy granted is not an assured shorthold tenancy.'

Alternatively, the landlord may have served a notice on the tenant prior to the tenancy agreement being entered into stating that the tenancy is not to be an assured shorthold. In such a case, the agreement should recite, preferably immediately following the description of the parties: 'WHERE-AS the Landlord has served a notice on the Tenant pursuant to paragraph 1 of Schedule 2A to the Housing Act 1988 stating that this tenancy is not to be an assured shorthold tenancy.'

Possession Proceedings

1. INTRODUCTION

On 26 April 1999, the Civil Procedure Rules came into operation. They made considerable changes to the regulation of possession proceedings, and this Appendix both summarises their effect and sets out the rules and forms which are now applicable. It is important to distinguish between the accelerated possession procedure, which is available in two instances, and all other proceedings.

Accelerated possession procedure

The accelerated possession procedure is available:

(a) where the dwelling-house has been let on assured tenancy and possession is now sought on one of Grounds 1, 3, 4 or 5 of the HA 1988 (see 4.7.4 for the detail);

(b) where the dwelling-house has been let on assured shorthold tenancy (see 5.4).

Schedule 2 to the Civil Procedure Rules preserved, with some consequential amendments, the substance of Ord. 49, rr. 6 and 6A of the County Court Rules, and these are included in this Appendix. The provisions are complex, and must be consulted carefully in each case to check that they are applicable. If they are, certain standard claim forms are to be used, as tabulated below, and there is no need to draft separate particulars of claim to accompany the claim. The claim form must, however, be served together with a reply form for the defendant's use.

All other proceedings for recovery of possession from assured tenants

Where the accelerated possession procedure is not available, the claimant landlord will proceed by issuing a standard summons for possession, attaching to it the particulars of the claim, and having it served on the defendant together with a reply form which the defendant must return to the court within 14 days.

Forms and precedents

This Appendix sets out the operative provisions of the Civil Procedure Rules, the published forms (the originals of which can be obtained from any county court office) and some draft particulars of claim for proceedings outside the accelerated possession procedures. The procedures can be tabulated as follows:

Possession Proceedings	Claim Form	Reply Form
Accelerated procedure (Grounds 1, 3, 4, 5) (see CCR Ord. 49, r. 6)	N5A	N11A
Accelerated procedure (assured shortholds) (see CCR Ord. 49, r. 6A)	N5B	N11B
All other assured tenancy possession actions (see CCR Ord. 6, r. 3: particulars of claim necessary)	N5	N11

2. CIVIL PROCEDURE RULES

PD 16 PRACTICE DIRECTION – STATEMENTS OF CASE

MATTERS WHICH MUST BE INCLUDED IN THE PARTICULARS OF CLAIM IN CERTAIN TYPES OF CLAIM

Recovery of land
6   In a claim for recovery of land the particulars of claim must:
(1)   identify the land sought to be recovered,
(2)   state whether the claim relates to residential premises,

(3) if the claim relates to residential premises, state whether the rateable value of the premises on every day specified by section 4(2) of the Rent Act 1977 in relation to the premises exceeds the sum so specified or whether the rent for the time being payable in respect of the premises exceeds the sum specified in section 4(4)(b) of the Act,

(4) where the claim relates to residential premises and is for non-payment of rent, state—

   (a) the amount due at the start of the proceedings,

   (b) details of all payments which have been missed,

   (c) details of any history of late or under-payment,

   (d) any previous steps taken to recover the arrears of rent with full details of any court proceedings, and

   (e) any relevant information about the defendant's circumstances, in particular whether any payments are made on his behalf directly to the claimant under the Social Security Contributions and Benefits Act 1992,

(5) give details about the agreement or tenancy, if any, under which the land was held, stating when it determined and the amount of money payable by way of rent or licence fee,

(6) in a case to which section 138 of the County Courts Act 1984 applies (forfeiture for non-payment of rent), state the daily rate at which the rent in arrear is to be calculated,

(7) state the ground on which possession is claimed whether statutory or otherwise, and

(8) in a case where the claimant knows of any person entitled to claim relief against forfeiture as underlessee (including a mortgagee) under section 146(4) of the Law of Property Act 1925 (or in accordance with section 38 of the Supreme Court Act 1981), give the name and address of that person. (See also further rules about recovery of land in RSC Orders 88 and 113 (Schedule 1 to the CPR) and CCR Orders 6 and 24 (Schedule 2 to the CPR).

SCHEDULE 2

COUNTY COURT RULES
ORDER 6

Rule 3 RECOVERY OF LAND

(1) In a claim for recovery of land the particulars of claim shall—

   (a) identify the land sought to be recovered;

   (b) state whether the land consists of or includes a dwelling-house;

   (c) give details about the agreement or tenancy, if any, under which the land is held, stating when it commenced and the amount of money payable by way of rent or licence fee;

(d)   in a case to which section 138 of the Act applies (forfeiture for non-payment of rent), state the daily rate at which the rent in arrear is to be calculated; and

(e)   state the ground on which possession is claimed, whether statutory or otherwise.

(2)   In proceedings for forfeiture where the claimant knows of any person entitled to claim relief against forfeiture as underlessee (including a mortgagee) under section 146(4) of the Law of Property Act 1925 or under section 138(9C) of the County Courts Act 1984, the particulars of claim shall give the name and address of that person and the claimant shall file a copy of the particulars of claim for service on him.

(3)   Where possession of land which consists of or includes a dwelling house is claimed because of non-payment of rent, the particulars of claim shall be in the prescribed form and shall also—

(a)   state the amount due at the commencement of the proceedings;

(b)   give—

(i)   (whether by means of a schedule or otherwise) particulars of all the payments which have been missed altogether; and

(ii)   where a history of late or under-payments is relied upon, sufficient details to establish the claimant's case;

(c)   state any previous steps which the claimant has taken to recover arrears of rent and, in the case of court proceedings, state—

(i)   the dates when proceedings were commenced and concluded; and

(ii)   the dates and terms of any orders made;

(d)   give such relevant information as is known by the claimant about the defendant's circumstances and, in particular, whether (and, if so, what) payments on his behalf are made direct to the claimant by or under the Social Security Contributions and Benefits Act 1992; and

(e)   if the claimant intends as part of his case to rely on his own financial or other circumstances, give details of all relevant facts or matters.

Rule 6   HOUSING ACT 1988: ASSURED TENANCIES

(1)   In this rule

'the 1988 Act' means the Housing Act 1988;

'dwelling-house' has the same meaning as in Part I of the 1988 Act;

a Ground referred to by number means the Ground so numbered in Schedule 2 to the 1988 Act;

'the requisite notice' means such a notice as is mentioned in any of those Grounds; and

'the relevant date' means the beginning of the tenancy.

(2)   This rule applies to proceedings brought by a landlord to recover possession of a dwelling-house which has been let on an assured tenancy in a case where all the conditions mentioned in paragraph (3) below are satisfied.

(3)   The conditions referred to in paragraph (2) are these—

(a)   The tenancy and any agreement for the tenancy were entered into on or after 15 January 1989.

(b)   The proceedings are brought—

(i)   on Ground 1 (landlord occupation);

(ii)   on Ground 3 (former holiday occupation);

(iii)   on Ground 4 (former student letting); or

(iv)   on Ground 5 (occupation by a minister of religion).

(c)   The only purpose of the proceedings is to recover possession of the dwelling-house and no other claim is made in the proceedings (such as for arrears of rent).

(d)   The tenancy is an assured tenancy within the meaning of the 1988 Act (and consequently is not a protected, statutory or housing association tenancy under the Rent Act 1977), and—

(i)   is the subject of a written agreement; or

(ii)   is on the same terms (though not necessarily as to rent) as a tenancy which was the subject of a written agreement and arises by virtue of section 5 of the 1988 Act; or

(iii)   relates to the same or substantially the same premises which were let to the same tenant and is on the same terms (though not necessarily as to rent or duration) as a tenancy which was the subject of a written agreement.

Where the tenancy in relation to which the proceedings are brought arises by virtue of section 5 of the 1988 Act but follows a tenancy which was the subject of an oral agreement, the condition mentioned in sub-paragraph (d)(ii) or (iii) above is not satisfied.

(e)   The proceedings are brought against the tenant to whom the requisite notice was given.

(f)   The tenant was given the requisite notice, not later than the relevant date.

(g)   The tenant was given notice in accordance with section 8 of the 1988 Act that proceedings for possession would be brought.

(4)   Where the conditions mentioned in paragraph (3) of this rule are satisfied, the landlord may bring possession proceedings under this rule instead of making a claim in accordance with Order 6, rule 3 (claim for recovery of land by claim form).

(5)   The application must be made in the prescribed form, and a copy of the application, with a copy for each defendant, must be filed in the court for the district in which the dwelling-house is situated.

(6) The application shall include the following information and statements—

(a) a statement identifying the dwelling-house which is the subject matter of the proceedings;

(b) a statement identifying the nature of the tenancy, namely—

(i) whether it is the subject of a written agreement; or

(ii) whether the tenancy arises by virtue of section 5 of the 1988 Act; or

(iii) where it is the subject of an oral agreement whether the tenancy is periodic or for a fixed term and, if for a fixed term, the length of the term and the date of termination;

(c) a statement that the dwelling-house (or another dwelling-house) was not let to the tenant by the landlord (or any of his predecessors) before 15 January 1989;

(d) the date on which and the method by which the requisite notice was given to the tenant;

(e) a statement identifying the Ground on which possession is claimed giving sufficient particulars to substantiate the claimant's claim to be entitled to possession on that Ground;

(f) a statement that a notice was served on the tenant in accordance with section 8 of the 1988 Act—

(i) specifying the date on which and the method by which the notice was served; and

(ii) confirming that the period of notice required by section 8 of the 1988 Act has been given; and

(g) the amount of rent which is currently payable.

(7) Copies of the following documents shall be attached to the application—

(i) the current (or most recent) written tenancy agreement;

(ii) the requisite notice (referred to in paragraph (6)(d) above); and

(iii) the notice served in accordance with section 8 of the 1988 Act, together with any other documents necessary to prove the claim.

(8) The statements made in the application and any documents attached to the application shall be verified by the claimant on oath.

(9) Service of the application and of the attachments shall be effected by an officer of the court sending them by first-class post to the defendant at the address stated in the application and paragraphs (c) and (d) of Order 3, rule 6 (mode of service) and Order 7, rule 15 (service of claim form for recovery of land) shall apply as they apply where service is effected under those rules.

(10) A defendant who wishes to oppose the claimant's application must, within 14 days after the service of the application on him, complete

and deliver at the court office the form of reply which was attached to the application.

(11)   On receipt of the defendant's reply the court shall—

(a)   send a copy of it to the claimant;

(b)   refer the reply and the claimant's application to the judge, and where a reply is received after the period mentioned in paragraph (10) but before a request is filed in accordance with paragraph (12) the reply shall be referred without delay to the judge.

(12)   Where the period mentioned in paragraph (10) has expired without the defendant filing a reply, the claimant may file a written request for an order for possession and the court shall without delay refer the claimant's application to the judge.

(13)   After considering the application and the defendant's reply (if any), the judge shall either—

(a)   make an order for possession under paragraph (15); or

(b)   fix a day for a hearing under paragraph (14) and give directions regarding the steps to be taken before and at the hearing.

(14)   The court shall fix a day for the hearing of the application where the judge is not satisfied as to any of the following—

(a)   that the requisite notice was given before the relevant date;

(b)   that a notice was served in accordance with section 8 of the 1988 Act and that the time limits specified in the 1988 Act have been complied with;

(c)   that service of the application was duly effected; or

(d)   that the claimant has established that he is entitled to recover possession under the Ground relied on against the defendant.

(15)   Except where paragraph (14) applies, the judge shall without delay make an order for possession without requiring the attendance of the parties.

(16)   Where a hearing is fixed under paragraph (14)—

(a)   the court shall give to all parties not less than 14 days' notice of the day fixed;

(b)   the judge may give such directions regarding the steps to be taken before and at the hearing as may appear to him to be necessary or desirable.

(17)   The court may, on application made on notice in accordance with CPR Part 23 within 14 days of service of the order or of its own initiative, set aside, vary or confirm any order made under paragraph (15).

(18)   A district judge shall have power to hear and determine an application to which this rule applies and references in this rule to the judge shall include references to the district judge.

Rule 6A HOUSING ACT 1988: ASSURED SHORTHOLD TENANCIES

(1) In this rule, 'the 1988 Act' means the Housing Act 1988 and 'dwelling-house' has the same meaning as in Part I of the 1988 Act.

(2) This rule applies to proceedings brought by a landlord under section 21 of the 1988 Act to recover possession of a dwelling-house let on an assured shorthold tenancy on the expiry or termination of that tenancy in a case where all the conditions mentioned in paragraph (3) below (or, as the case may be, paragraph (9)) are satisfied.

(3) The conditions referred to in paragraph (2) are these—

(a) The tenancy and any agreement for the tenancy were entered into on or after 15 January 1989.

(b) The only purpose of the proceedings is to recover possession of the dwelling-house and no other claim is made in the proceedings (such as for arrears of rent).

(c) The tenancy—

(i) was an assured shorthold tenancy and not a protected, statutory or housing association tenancy under the Rent Act 1977;

(ii) did not immediately follow an assured tenancy which was not an assured shorthold tenancy;

(iii) fulfilled the conditions provided by section 19A or section 20(1)(a) to (c) of the 1988 Act; and

(iv) was the subject of a written agreement.

(d) Where the tenancy and any agreement for the tenancy were entered into before 28 February 1997, a notice in writing was served on the tenant in accordance with section 20(2) of the 1988 Act and the proceedings are brought against the tenant on whom that notice was served.

(e) A notice in accordance with section 21(1)(b) of the 1988 Act was given to the tenant in writing.

(4) Where the conditions mentioned in paragraph (3) or paragraph (9) of this rule are satisfied, the landlord may bring possession proceedings under this rule instead of making a claim in accordance with Order 6, rule 3 (claim for recovery of land by claim form).

(5) The application must be made in the prescribed form and a copy of the application, with a copy for each defendant, shall be filed in the court for the district in which the dwelling-house is situated.

(6) The application shall include the following information and statements—

(a) A statement identifying the dwelling-house which is the subject matter of the proceedings.

(b) A statement that the dwelling-house (or another dwelling-house) was not let to the tenant by the landlord (or any of his predecessors) before 15 January 1989.

(c)   A statement that possession is claimed on the expiry of an assured shorthold tenancy under section 21 of the 1988 Act giving sufficient particulars to substantiate the claimant's claim to be entitled to possession.

(d)   Where the tenancy and any agreement for the tenancy were entered into before 28 February 1997, a statement that a written notice was served on the tenant in accordance with section 20(2) of the 1988 Act.

(e)   A statement that a notice in writing was given to the tenant in accordance with section 21(1) of the 1988 Act specifying the date on which, and the method by which, the notice was given.

(f)   In a case where the original fixed term tenancy has expired, a statement that no other assured tenancy is in existence other than an assured shorthold periodic tenancy (whether statutory or not).

(g)   A statement confirming that there is no power under the tenancy agreement for the landlord to determine the tenancy (within the meaning given for the purposes of Part I of the 1988 Act by section 45(4) of the 1988 Act) at a time earlier than 6 months from the beginning of the tenancy.

(h)   A statement that no notice under section 20(5) of the 1988 Act has been served.

(7)   Copies of the following documents shall be attached to the application—

(i)   the written tenancy agreement (or, in a case to which paragraph (9) applies, the current (or most recent) written tenancy agreement);

(ii)   where the tenancy and any agreement for the tenancy were entered into before 28 February 1997 the written notice served in accordance with section 20(2) of the 1988 Act; and

(iii)   the notice in writing given in accordance with section 21 of the 1988 Act,

together with any other documents necessary to prove the claim.

(8)   The statement made in the application and any documents attached to the application shall be verified by the claimant on oath.

(9)   Where on the coming to an end of an assured shorthold tenancy (including a tenancy which was an assured shorthold but ceased to be assured before it came to an end) a new assured shorthold tenancy of the same or substantially the same premises (in this paragraph referred to as 'the premises') comes into being under which the landlord and the tenant are the same as at the coming to an end of the earlier tenancy, then the provisions of this rule apply to that tenancy but with the following conditions instead of those in paragraph (3)—

(a)   The tenancy and any agreement for the tenancy were entered into on or after 15 January 1989.

(b)   The only purpose of the proceedings is to recover possession of the dwelling-house and no other claim is made in the proceedings (such as for arrears of rent).

(c)   The tenancy in relation to which the proceedings are brought—

(i)   is an assured shorthold tenancy within the meaning of section 20 of the 1988 Act and consequently is not a protected, statutory or housing association tenancy under the Rent Act 1977;

(ii)   did not immediately follow an assured tenancy which was not an assured shorthold tenancy; and—

(aa)   is the subject of a written agreement; or

(ab)   is on the same terms (though not necessarily as to rent) as a tenancy which was the subject of a written agreement and arises by virtue of section 5 of the 1988 Act; or

(ac)   relates to the same or substantially the same premises which were let to the same tenant and is on the same terms (though not necessarily as to rent or duration) as a tenancy which was the subject of a written agreement.

Where the tenancy in relation to which the proceedings are brought arises by virtue of section 5 of the 1988 Act but follows a tenancy which was the subject of an oral agreement, the conditions mentioned in sub-paragraph (c)(ii)(ab) or (ac) above is not satisfied.

(d)   Where the agreement and any agreement for the tenancy were entered into before 28 February 1997, a written notice was served in accordance with section 20(2) of the 1988 Act on the tenant in relation to the first assured shorthold tenancy of the premises and the proceedings are brought against the tenant on whom that notice was served.

(e)   A notice in writing was given to the tenant in accordance with section 21(4) of the 1988 Act.

(10)   In a case to which paragraph (9) applies, the application shall include the following information and statements—

(a)   A statement identifying the dwelling-house which is the subject matter of the proceedings.

(b)   A statement identifying the nature of the tenancy, namely—

(i)   whether it is the subject of a written agreement;

(ii)   whether the tenancy arises by virtue of section 5 of the 1988 Act; or

(iii)   where it is the subject of an oral agreement, that the tenancy is periodic or for a fixed term, and if for a fixed term, the length of the term and the date of termination.

(c)   A statement that the dwelling-house (or another dwelling-house) was not let to the tenant by the landlord (or any of his predecessors) before 15 January 1989.

(d)   A statement that possession is claimed under section 21 of the 1988 Act giving sufficient particulars to substantiate the claimant's claim to be entitled to possession.

(e)   Where the tenancy and any agreement for the tenancy were entered into before 28 February 1997, a statement that a written notice was served in accordance with section 20(2) of the 1988 Act in relation to the first assured shorthold tenancy of the premises on the tenant against whom the proceedings are brought.

(f)   A statement that a notice in writing was given to the tenant in accordance with section 21(4) of the 1988 Act specifying the date on which, and the method by which, the notice was given.

(g)   In a case where the tenancy is a fixed term tenancy which has expired, a statement that no other assured tenancy is in existence other than an assured shorthold periodic tenancy (whether statutory or not).

(h)   A statement confirming that there was no power under the tenancy agreement for the landlord to determine (within the meaning given for the purposes of Part I of the 1988 Act by section 45(4) of the 1988 Act) the first assured shorthold tenancy of the premises to the tenant against whom the proceedings are brought at a time earlier than 6 months from the beginning of the tenancy.

(i)   A statement that no notice under section 20(5) of the 1988 Act has been served.

(j)   The amount of rent which is currently payable.

(11)   Service of the application and of the attachments shall be effected by an officer of the court sending them by first-class post to the defendant at the address stated in the application and paragraphs (c) and (d) of Order 3, rule 6 (mode of service) and Order 7, rule 15 (service of claim form for recovery of land) shall apply as they apply where service is effected under those rules.

(12)   A defendant who wishes to oppose the claimant's application must, within 14 days after the service of the application on him, complete and deliver at the court office the form of reply which was attached to the application.

(13)   On receipt of the defendant's reply the court shall—

(a)   send a copy of it to the claimant;

(b)   refer the reply and the claimant's application to the judge and where a reply is received after the period mentioned in paragraph (12) but before a request is filed in accordance with paragraph (14) the reply shall be referred without delay to the judge.

(14)   Where the period mentioned in paragraph (12) has expired without the defendant filing a reply, the claimant may file a written request for an order for possession and the court shall without delay refer any such request to the judge.

(15) After considering the application and the defendant's reply (if any), the judge shall either—

(a) make an order for possession under paragraph (17); or

(b) fix a day for a hearing under paragraph (16) and give directions regarding the steps to be taken before and at the hearing.

(16) The court shall fix a day for the hearing of the application where the judge is not satisfied as to any of the following—

(a) where the tenancy and any agreement for the tenancy were entered into before 28 February 1997 that a written notice was served in accordance with section 20 of the 1988 Act;

(b) that a written notice was given in accordance with section 21 of the 1988 Act;

(c) that service of the application was duly effected; or

(d) that the claimant has established that he is entitled to recover possession under section 21 of the 1988 Act against the defendant.

(17) Except where paragraph (16) applies, the judge shall without delay make an order for possession without requiring the attendance of the parties.

(18) Where a hearing is fixed under paragraph (16)—

(a) the court shall give to all parties not less than 14 days' notice of the day so fixed;

(b) the judge may give such direction regarding the steps to be taken before and at the hearing as may appear to him to be necessary or desirable.

(19) The court may, on application made on notice in accordance with CPR Part 23 within 14 days of service of the order or of its own initiative, set aside, vary or confirm any order made under paragraph (17).

(20) A district judge shall have power to hear and determine an application to which this rule applies and references in this rule to the judge shall include references to the district judge.

3. COURT FORMS

Summons for possession of property

Claim No.	
In the	

County Court

The court office is open from 10 am to 4 pm Monday to Friday

Telephone

Claimant's
full name
address

Name and
address for
service and
payment
(if different
from above)
Ref/Tel No.

seal

Defendant's
full name
(including
title e.g. Mr.
Mrs or Miss)
and address

The claimant (your landlord or mortgage lender) is **claiming possession**

of

for the reasons given in the attached particulars of claim.

The claimant is also making a claim for money.
(details are given in particulars of claim)

Court fee	
Solicitor's costs	
Total amount	
Summons issued on	

WHAT THIS MEANS

- On the date set out below, the court will decide whether or not you have to leave, and if you have to leave, when.

WHAT SHOULD YOU DO

- **Get help and advice immediately** from a solicitor or any of the advice agencies on the attached list.
- Make sure the court knows as much about your circumstances as possible by:
  - **filling in the reply form** attached to this summons, and
  - **coming to the hearing**

(The notes on the back of this form give you more information about what you should do.)

The court will make its decision

on   at   am/pm

at

Important notes to help you

No one can evict you from your home unless the court lets them. The court will not make a decision before the date shown on the front of the form. In certain cases the court can:
- allow you a reasonable time to pay rent arrears or the amount borrowed and let you stay in the property;
- decide not to make a possession order;
- give you time to find somewhere else to live, or
- (for mortgage cases regulated by the Consumer Credit Act only) look at the original loan agreement and decide if it is fair.

But, the court cannot decide any of these things unless it knows about your circumstances. To make sure of this, fill in the reply form **and** come to the hearing, **even if you have reached agreement about repayment with your landlord or mortgage lender since the summons was issued.**

Filling in the reply form

- You must fill in the reply and make sure it reaches the court **within 14 days after the date of service.** The date of service will be 7 days after the court posted the summons to you. The postmark will tell you when this was.
- Fill in the reply form and take or send it to the court even if you cannot come to the hearing.
- If you need help to fill it in you can get it from
  - any county court;
  - any of the advice agencies on the attached list;
  - a solicitor.
- Keep the summons and a copy of your reply form. The court will send a copy of your completed reply to the claimant.

Disagreeing with the claim

- If you disagree with the claim it is even more important that you get help, fill in the reply form and come to the hearing. You may be able to get help with your legal costs. Ask about the legal aid scheme at any firm of solicitors showing the legal aid sign or at any advice agency. A leaflet about legal aid is available from any county court.

Registration of judgments

- If the court orders you to pay money to the claimant (a money judgment) and you do not pay, your name and address may be entered in the Register of County Court Judgments. **This may make it difficult for you to get credit.**
- If the money is paid in full within the time stated on the order, the order **will not be registered.**

- If you do not pay within the time stated on any order, **the order will be registered** when the claimant takes steps to enforce payment.

Interest on judgments

- If the money judgment entered against you is for more than £5000, the claimant may be entitled to interest on the total amount.

How to pay

- **PAYMENT(S) MUST BE MADE** to the person named at the address for payment quoting their reference and the court claim number.

- **DO NOT bring or send payments to the court. THEY WILL NOT BE ACCEPTED.**

- You should allow at least 4 days for your payments to reach the claimant or his representative. **Ask for a receipt.**

- Make sure that you keep records and can account for all payments made. Proof may be required if there is any disagreement. It is not safe to send cash unless you use registered post.

- A leaflet giving further advice about payment can be obtained from the court.

- If you need more information you should contact the claimant or his representative.

Certificate of Service

I certify that the summons of which this is a true copy was served by me on

by posting it to the Defendant on

at the address stated on the summons

Officer of the Court

I certify that the summons has not been served for the following reasons:

Officer of the Court

Application for accelerated possession following issue of a notice under section 8 of the Housing Act 1988

Claim No.	
In the	
	County Court

The court office is open from 10am to 4pm Monday to Friday

☎ Telephone

Claimant's full name and address

Name and address for service and payment (if different from above) Ref/Tel no.

Defendant's name (including title, eg Mr, Mrs or Miss) **and address**

seal

The claimant (your landlord) is claiming possession of

WHAT THIS MEANS

- The court will be deciding whether or not you have to leave, and if you have to leave, when.

You must act immediately - there will not normally be a court hearing.

- **Read this application**, the information leaflet enclosed and the affidavit
- **Get advice** from an advice agency (a list of agencies is attached) or a solicitor
- **Fill in the form of reply** and return it to the court office

Court fee	
Solicitor's costs	
Total amount	
Application issued on	

More information about assured tenancies is available in Housing booklet 'Assured and Assured Shorthold Tenancies: A Guide for Tenants'. The booklet is produced by the Department of the Environment. Your local Citizens Advice Bureau will have a copy.

N5A Application for accelerated possession following issue of a notice under section 8 of the Housing Act 1988 (4.99) *Printed on behalf of The Court Service*

Affidavit to support my application for accelerated possession following issue of a notice under section 8 of the Housing Act 1988 *(The notes in the margin tell you when you have to delete part of the paragraph)*

Paragraph 1
Insert full name, address and occupation of person making this affidavit. Give the address of the property and delete words in brackets to show whether property is a house or part of one

[1] I,

make this affidavit to support my application for an order for possession
of

which is a (dwelling house) (part of a dwelling house).

Paragraph 2
Give the date of the first written tenancy agreement. Attach a copy of the agreement to this affidavit. It must contain all the terms of the agreement. Attach also a copy of the latest written agreement

Delete the words in brackets if there was no previous landlord

Delete as appropriate to show whether there is one or more defendant. Give date when tenant(s) moved into the property

[2] On the   day of   [19][20], I entered into a written tenancy
agreement with the defendant(s). A copy of the first agreement, marked 'A', is exhibited
(attached) to this affidavit. A copy of the current written agreement, marked 'A1', is also
attached.

I confirm that:
• both the tenancy and the agreement were made on or after 15 January 1989.

• I did not let the property mentioned above, or any other property, to the defendant(s)
before 15 January 1989, (and neither did any previous landlord).

• the defendant(s) (is) (are) the original tenant(s) to whom the property was let under the
assured shorthold tenancy agreement. The tenant(s) first occupied the property on

Paragraph 3
Complete this section only if a new tenancy has been agreed **orally** (not in writing)
Delete the words in brackets if the rent and duration of the tenancy are as set out in the written agreement. If either has changed, delete (i) or (ii) as appropriate

[3] The current agreement relates to the same, or substantially the same, property. The
terms are the same as set out in the agreement at paragraph 2
(except for:

    (i) the amount of rent to be paid. The current rent is

        £   per   ;

    (ii) the duration of the tenancy.)

Paragraph 4
Delete paragraphs (a) or (b) as appropriate to show how the latest tenancy agreement came about

[4] The tenancy is an assured tenancy.

(a)   It is subject to the latest written agreement referred to in paragraph 2 above.

(b)   The latest written agreement referred to in paragraph 2 has expired. There is now a
further assured tenancy for an unspecified period. The terms of this tenancy are
the same as in the latest written tenancy except as indicated at paragraph 3. Since the
latest written agreement, there has not been a tenancy which was agreed orally and
which was followed by a statutory periodic tenancy.

Paragraph 5
Delete paragraphs (a)-(e) as appropriate to show the grounds on which you are claiming possession. If paragraph (b) applies, delete the options as applicable to show who bought the property and who intends to live there.

5 The tenancy is an assured tenancy and I am seeking an order for possession on the following grounds:

(a) at some time before the start of the tenancy (I) (a joint landlord) occupied the property as my main home. (The joint landlord's name is   .)

(b) I and/or a joint landlord bought the property before the tenancy started and I and/or my spouse, or a joint landlord and/or the joint landlord's spouse, intend(s) to live in it as the main home. (The joint landlord's name is   .)

(c) The tenancy was for a fixed term of eight months or less and, in the twelve months before the tenancy started, the property was let for a holiday.

(d) The tenancy was for a fixed term of twelve months or less and, in the twelve month period before the tenancy started, the property was let to students by a specified educational establishment.

(e) The property is held for use by a minister of religion as a residence from which to carry out (his) (her) duties and is now needed for this purpose.

Paragraph 6
Give the date on which the notice was served. A copy of the notice must be attached to this affidavit

6 A notice was served on the defendant(s) on the   day of   [19   ][20   ] which said I might ask for possession on the ground(s) claimed in paragraph 5. A copy of this notice, marked 'B', is exhibited (attached) to this affidavit.

Paragraph 7
Give details of how the notice (in paragraph 6) was served eg delivered personally, by post, etc. Attach any proof of service eg recorded delivery slip. Mark it 'B1'.

7

Paragraph 8
Give the date on which the notice was served. A copy of the notice must be attached to this affidavit

8 A further notice, under section 8 of the Housing Act 1988, was served on the defendant(s) on the   day of   [19   ][20   ] which said I intended to make an application for possession of the property on the grounds set out in paragraph 5. A copy of this notice, marked 'C', is exhibited (attached) to this affidavit. The notice of   month(s) has expired.

Paragraph 9
Give details of how the notice (in paragraph 8) was served eg delivered personally, by post, etc. Attach any proof of service eg recorded delivery slip. Mark it 'C1'.

9

Paragraph 10
Give details of further evidence (if any) you wish to use to prove your claim for possession under one or more of the grounds set out in paragraph 5. Attach any written document(s) which support that evidence. Mark them 'D1', 'D2' and so on.

| 10 |

Paragraph 11
Insert address of property and the time within which you want possession. You must not make any claim for rent arrears

| 11 | I ask the court to grant me an order for possession of

within   days and for payment of my costs of making this application

Sworn at

in the

this   day of   [19   ][20   ]

Before me

*Officer of a court appointed
by the Circuit Judge to take affidavits*

CERTIFICATE OF SERVICE

I certify that the summons of which this is a true copy was served by me on

by posting it to the Defendant on

at the address stated on the summons

Officer of the Court

I certify that the summons has not been served for the following reasons:

Officer of the Court

Application for accelerated possession following issue of a notice under section 21 of the Housing Act 1988

Claim No.

In the

County Court

The court office is open from 10am to 4pm Monday to Friday

☎ Telephone

Claimant's full name and address

Name and address for service and payment (if different from above) **Ref/Tel no.**

Defendant's name (including title, eg Mr, Mrs or Miss) **and address**

seal

The claimant (your landlord) is claiming possession of

WHAT THIS MEANS

- The court will be deciding whether or not you have to leave, and if you have to leave, when.

You must act immediately - there will not normally be a court hearing.

- **Read this application,** the information leaflet enclosed and the affidavit

- **Get advice** from an advice agency (a list of agencies is attached) or a solicitor

- **Fill in the form of reply** and return it to the court office

Court fee

Solicitor's costs

Total amount

Application issued on

More information about assured tenancies is available in Housing booklet 'Assured and Assured Shorthold Tenancies: A Guide for Tenants'. The booklet is produced by the Department of the Environment. Your local Citizens Advice Bureau will have a copy.

N5B Application for accelerated possession following issue of a notice under section 21 of the Housing Act 1988 (4.99)   *Printed on behalf of The Court Service*

Affidavit to support my application for accelerated possession following issue of a notice under section 21 of the Housing Act 1988 *(The notes in the margin tell you when you have to delete part of the paragraph)*

Paragraph 1
Insert full name, address and occupation of person making this affidavit. Give the address of the property and delete words in brackets to show whether property is a house or part of one

| 1 | I,

make this affidavit to support my application for an order for possession

of

which is a (dwelling house) (part of a dwelling house).

Paragraph 2
Give the date of the first written tenancy agreement. Attach a copy of the agreement to this affidavit. It must contain all the terms of the agreement. Attach also a copy of the latest written agreement

Delete the words in brackets if there was no previous landlord

Delete as appropriate, to show whether there is one or more defendants. Give date when tenant(s) moved into the property

| 2 | On the   day of   [19   ][20   ], I entered into a written tenancy agreement with the defendant(s). A copy of the first agreement, marked 'A', is exhibited (attached) to this affidavit. A copy of the current written agreement, marked 'A1', is also attached.

I confirm that:
• both the tenancy and the agreement were made on or after 15 January 1989.

• I did not let the property mentioned above, or any other property, to the defendant(s) before 15 January 1989, (and neither did any previous landlord).

• the defendant(s) (is) (are) the original tenant(s) to whom the property was let under the assured shorthold tenancy agreement. The tenant(s) first occupied the property on

---

Paragraph 3
Complete this section only if a new tenancy has been agreed orally (not in writing)
Delete the words in brackets if the rent and duration of the tenancy are as set out in the written agreement. If either has changed, delete (i) or (ii) as appropriate

| 3 | The current agreement relates to the same, or substantially the same, property. The terms are the same as set out in the agreement at paragraph 2 (except for:

(i) the amount of rent to be paid. The current rent is

£   per   ;

(ii) the duration of the tenancy.)

Paragraph 4
Delete paragraphs (a) or (b) as appropriate to show how the latest tenancy agreement came about
If the tenancy is different from either of these two categories, you cannot use the Accelerated Possession Procedure

| 4 | The tenancy is an assured shorthold tenancy.

(a) The latest written agreement referred to in paragraph 2 has expired. There is now a further assured shorthold tenancy for an unspecified period. The terms of this tenancy are the same as in the latest written tenancy except as indicated at paragraph 3. Since the latest written agreement, there has not been a tenancy which was agreed orally and which was followed by a statutory periodic tenancy.

(b) It is subject to the latest written agreement referred to in paragraph 2 above, and it is not for a fixed term.

141

Paragraph 5

[5] The assured shorthold tenancy did not follow an assured non-shorthold tenancy.

Paragraph 6

[6] I did not serve a notice on the defendant(s) before the previous assured shorthold tenancy expired, saying that any new tenancy would not be an assured shorthold tenancy, nor did the tenancy agreement contain a provision saying it was not an assured shorthold tenancy, nor is the tenancy an assured non-shorthold tenancy under any other provision of Schedule 2A to the Housing Act 1988.

Paragraph 7
Delete this paragraph if the tenancy and/or any agreement for it was entered into on or after 28 February 1997

[7] A notice, under section 20 of the Housing Act 1988, was served on the defendant(s) on the day of [19][20] which said that the tenancy was to be an assured shorthold tenancy. A copy of this notice, marked 'B', is exhibited (attached) to this affidavit.

Paragraph 8
Give details of how the notice (in paragraph 7) was served eg delivered personally, by post, etc. Attach any proof of service eg recorded delivery slip. Mark it 'B1'.

[8]

Paragraph 9
Give the date on which the notice was served and the length of notice given. A copy of the notice must be attached to this affidavit

[9] A notice, under section 21 of the Housing Act 1988, was served on the defendant(s) on the day of [19][20] which said possession of the property was required. A copy of that notice, marked 'C', is exhibited (attached) to this affidavit. The notice of month(s) has expired.

Paragraph 10
Give details of how the notice (in paragraph 9) was served eg delivered personally, by post, etc. Attach any proof of service eg recorded delivery slip. Mark it 'C1'.

[10]

142

Paragraph 11
Give details of further evidence (if any) you wish to use to prove your claim for possession. Attach any written document(s) which support that evidence. Mark them 'D1', 'D2' and so on

[11]

Paragraph 12
Insert address of property and the time within which you want possession. You must not make any claim for rent arrears

[12] I ask the court to grant me an order for possession of

within   days and for payment of my costs of making this application   –

Sworn at

in the

this   day of   [19   ][20   ]

Before me

Officer of a court appointed
by the Circuit Judge to take affidavits

CERTIFICATE OF SERVICE

I certify that the summons of which this is a true copy was served by me on

by posting it to the Defendant on

at the address stated on the summons

Officer of the Court

I certify that the summons has not been served for the following reasons:

Officer of the Court

Form for Replying to a Summons (possession of land)

- *Read the notes on the claim form before completing this form. Please use black ink.*
- *Tick the correct boxes and give the other details asked for.*
- *Send or take this completed and signed form immediately to the court office shown on the claim form.*
- *You should keep your copy of the claim form.*
- *For details of where and how to pay see the claim form.*

In the	County Court
Claim Number	
Claimant *(including reference)*	
Defendant	

YOU MUST ANSWER QUESTION 1

1. Do you admit the claimant is entitled to possession of the premises? Yes ☐ ☐ No

Please give below any facts you would like the court to take into consideration when making an order for possession **or** your reasons for disputing the claim.

YOU NEED ONLY ANSWER THE FOLLOWING QUESTIONS IF THERE IS ALSO A MONEY CLAIM AGAINST YOU

2. Do you admit the money claim in full? Yes ☐ No ☐

3. Do you admit only part of the money claim? Yes ☐ No ☐

    Please state the amount admitted £

4. If you dispute all or part of the claimant's money claim please give your reasons for doing so.

continue on a separate sheet if necessary - put the case number in the top right-hand corner

Give an address to which notices about this case should be sent to you	Signed
Post Code	*(To be signed by you or by your solicitor)* Dated

N11 Form of reply - possession summons (4.99)

Printed on behalf of The Court Service

Form of reply to application for accelerated possession following issue

of a notice under section 8 of the Housing Act 1988.

- *Each of the questions in this form relates to a paragraph in the claimant's affidavit. You will find it easier to fill in if you have the affidavit open in front of you*

- *Use **black ink** when you fill in this form*

- *When you have filled it in sign it and send or take it to the court office shown on the application*

In the	
	Court
Claim No.	
Claimant	
Defendant	

1 Are you the tenant named in the tenancy agreement attached to the claimant's affidavit?

☐ Yes ☐ No

2 Does the tenancy agreement referred to at paragraph 2 of the claimant's affidavit:

(a) set out the terms of your tenancy agreement with the claimant?

☐ Yes *If Yes, go to question 4* ☐ No *Give details below*

(b) set out the terms of your tenancy agreement except that the rent you pay, or the duration of the tenancy, have changed (as stated in paragraph 3 of the affidavit)?

☐ Yes *If Yes, go to question 4* ☐ No *Give details below*

3 If you have answered No to either part (a) or (b) of question 2, say which terms of the agreement are different, and how they differ

4 When did you move into the property?

Give date

5 Did you have a tenancy agreement with the claimant (or the previous landlord) for the same, or substantially the same, property, (or another property) before 15 January 1989?

☐ Yes *If Yes, give details below* ☐ No

Say who the landlord was, and give the address of the property (and whether a house or a flat) and details of the previous tenancy (including the dates when you occupied the property). If you have a copy of the agreement, attach a copy to this reply.

6 Do you agree with the claimant's claim to be entitled to have possession of the property?

☐ Yes ☐ No *If No, give details below*

*You must have proper **legal** reasons for not agreeing with the claim for possession. Having nowhere else to live is not a legal reason*

N11A Form of reply to application for accelerated possession following issue of a notice under section 8 of the Housing Act 1988 (Order 49, rule 6) (4.99)
Printed on behalf of The Court Service

7 Did you receive the notice referred to in paragraph 6 of the affidavit which stated that the claimant might ask for possession on the ground(s) given in paragraph 5?

☐ Yes *If Yes, give date below* ☐ No

Give date [ ]

8 Did you receive the notice referred to in paragraph 8 of the affidavit, which stated that the claimant intended to make an application for possession?

☐ Yes *If Yes, give date below* ☐ No

Give date [ ]

9 In the box below, say if you dispute any further evidence the claimant has given in paragraph 10 of the affidavit. If you do, say what you dispute and why.

[ ]

10 If the court decides the claimant should have possession of the property, you will normally be told to leave in 14 days. However, if this would cause you exceptional hardship the court may allow up to 6 weeks (but no longer). If you think you would suffer exceptional hardship, say why in the box below.

[ ]

11 If the court decides you should pay the claimant's costs of making this application would you prefer to pay the costs by instalments?

☐ Yes ☐ No

12 Give an address to which notices about this case should be sent to you

Postcode [ ]

Signed

(To be signed by you or your solicitor)

Dated

Form of reply to application for accelerated possession following issue

of a notice under section 21 of the Housing Act 1988

- *Each of the questions in this form relates to a paragraph in the claimant's affidavit. You will find it easier to fill in if you have the affidavit open in front of you*
- *Use **black ink** when you fill in this form*
- *When you have filled it in sign it and send or take it to the court office shown on the application*

In the	
	Court
Claim No.	
Claimant	
Defendant	

1	Are you the tenant named in the tenancy agreement attached to the claimant's affidavit?	☐ Yes	☐ No

2	Does the tenancy agreement referred to at paragraph 2 of the claimant's affidavit:	☐ Yes *If Yes, go to question 4*	☐ No *Give details below*
	(a) set out the terms of your tenancy agreement with the claimant?		
	(b) set out the terms of your tenancy agreement except that the rent you pay, or the duration of the tenancy, have changed (as stated in paragraph 3 of the affidavit)?	☐ Yes *If Yes, go to question 4*	☐ No *Give details below*

3 If you have answered **No** to either part (a) or (b) of question 2, say which terms of the agreement are different, and how they differ

4 When did you move into the property? *Give date*

5 Did you have a tenancy agreement with the claimant (or the previous landlord) for the same, or substantially the same, property, (or another property) before 15 January 1989?   ☐ Yes *If Yes, give details below*   ☐ No

Say who the landlord was, and give the address of the property (and whether a house or a flat) and details of the previous tenancy (including the dates when you occupied the property). If you have a copy of the agreement, attach a copy to this reply.

6 Do you agree with the claimant's claim to be entitled to have possession of the property?   ☐ Yes   ☐ No *If No, give details below*

*You must have proper **legal** reasons for not agreeing with the claim for possession. Having nowhere else to live is not a legal reason*

N11B Form of reply to application for accelerated possession following issue of a notice under section 21 of the Housing Act 1988 (Order 49, rule 6A) (4.99)
Printed on behalf of The Court Service

You only need to answer question 7 if the claimant says in paragraph 7 of the affidavit that he served a notice.

7   Did you receive the notice referred to in paragraph 7 of the affidavit which stated that the tenancy was to be an assured shorthold? *(This should only apply if your first tenancy, or any agreement for it, was entered into before 28 February 1997)*

☐ Yes   *If Yes, give date below*   ☐ No

Give date [   ]

8   Did you receive the notice referred to in paragraph 9 of the affidavit, which stated that possession was required?

☐ Yes   *If Yes, give date below*   ☐ No

Give date [   ]

9   In the box below, say if you dispute any further evidence the claimant has given in paragraph 11 of the affidavit. If you do, say what you dispute and why.

[   ]

10   If the court decides the claimant should have possession of the property, you will normally be told to leave in 14 days. However, if this would cause you exceptional hardship the court may allow up to 6 weeks (but no longer). If you think you would suffer exceptional hardship, say why in the box below.

[   ]

11   If the court decides you should pay the claimant's costs of making this application would you prefer to pay the costs by instalments.

☐ Yes   ☐ No

12

Give an address to which notices about this case should be sent to you	Signed
	(To be signed by you or your solicitor)
Postcode [ ]	Dated

4. DRAFT PARTICULARS OF CLAIM

Particulars of claim should normally be attached to the claim form, but may be served separately and verified by a statement of truth. The two drafts set out here concern non-shorthold assured tenancies. In Draft 1, the landlord is seeking possession of a dwelling-house where the fixed term tenancy which has been granted has not yet expired. In these circumstances, it is essential to comply with HA 1988, s. 7(6) (see 4.6 above). In Draft 2, possession is sought of a dwelling-house let on periodic tenancy.

IN THE .... COUNTY COURT

Claim No. ....

Between   AA   Claimant

and

BB   Defendant

PARTICULARS OF CLAIM

Draft 1   Fixed-term tenancy which has not yet expired

1. The Claimant is the [freehold] owner and is entitled to possession of residential premises comprising a dwelling-house known as [address].

2. The said premises were let by the Claimant to the Defendant by a lease dated [date] for a term of [two years] from [date] at a rent of [£   ].

3. *Required only if the tenancy was entered into on or after 28 February 1997*
   Prior to the grant of the said lease the Claimant served on the Defendant a notice pursuant to paragraph 1 of Sch. 2A to the Housing Act 1988 stating that the said lease was not to be an assured shorthold tenancy within the meaning of that Act.
   [or] The said lease was an assured shorthold tenancy. After the said lease was entered into the Claimant served on the Defendant a notice pursuant to paragraph 2 of Sch. 2A to the Housing Act 1988 stating that the said lease was no longer an assured shorthold tenancy.
   [or] The said lease contained provision that it was not an assured shorthold tenancy.

149

4. The said lease is an assured tenancy within Part I of the Housing Act 1988.

5. The said lease contained provision whereby the term could be brought to an end in the event of any of Grounds 2, 8, 10 to 15 inclusive or 17 contained in Sch. 2 to the Housing Act 1988 applying or the Defendant being in breach of any covenants contained in the lease.

6. It was a covenant of the said lease that the Defendant would not [specify particular covenant broken].

7. In breach of the said covenant, the Defendant [specify breach].

8. By notice in prescribed form dated [date] the Claimant informed the Defendant that he intended to bring proceedings for possession of the dwelling-house on Ground 12 contained in Sch. 2 to the Housing Act 1988 not earlier than [date] and not later than 12 months from the date of service of the said notice.
[This refers to notice under HA 1988, s. 8, on which see 4.6.1 above.]

9. In the circumstances, the Claimant is entitled to possession of the dwelling-house pursuant to the provisions of Ground 12 of Sch. 2 to the Housing Act 1988.

AND the Claimant claims
    (1)   Possession of the said premises;
    (2)   Rent or mesne profits at the rate of £ ... per month from the date of these proceedings until delivery up of the premises;
    (3)   Interest on the above pursuant to section 69 of the County Courts Act 1984;
    (4)   Costs.
The Claimant believes that the facts stated in these particulars of claim are true.

Draft 2 Periodic tenancy

[In this case there is no need to plead the landlord's right of re-entry (or equivalent). The tenancy may have always been periodic (i.e., in the terminology of this book, a 'contractual periodic tenancy') or the landlord may have granted a fixed term, which has now expired, leaving the tenant holding over as a statutory periodic tenant pursuant to HA 1988, s. 5(2).]

1. The Claimant is the [freehold] owner and is entitled to possession of residential premises comprising a dwelling-house known as [address].

2. The said premises were let by the Claimant to the Defendant on a [weekly/monthly] tenancy dated [date] from [date] at a rent of [£   ].
    [or]
    The said premises were let by the Claimant to the Defendant by a lease dated [date] for a term of [two years] from [date] at a rent of [£   ].
    The said lease came to an end on [state date lease expired by effluxion of time] and thereupon a statutory periodic tenancy arose by virtue of section 5(2) of the Housing Act 1988. The said tenancy is a [weekly/monthly] tenancy and has the same terms as the fixed-term tenancy.

3. *Required only if the tenancy was entered into on or after 28 February 1997*
    Prior to the grant of the said lease the Claimant served on the Defendant a notice pursuant to paragraph 1 of Sch. 2A to the Housing Act 1988 stating that the said lease was not to be an assured shorthold tenancy within the meaning of that Act.
    [or] The said lease was an assured shorthold tenancy. After the said lease was entered into the Claimant served on the Defendant a notice pursuant to paragraph 2 of Sch. 2A to the Housing Act 1988 stating that the said lease was no longer an assured shorthold tenancy.
    [or] The said lease contained provision that it was not an assured shorthold tenancy.

4. The said lease is an assured tenancy within Part I of the Housing Act 1988.

5. The Defendant [or CC, a person residing in or visiting the said premises] has been guilty of conduct causing or likely to cause a nuisance or annoyance to persons residing, visiting or otherwise engaging in a lawful activity in the locality.

PARTICULARS OF NUISANCE

(1) On or about [date] the Defendant [or CC] invited or permitted more than fifty persons into the said premises between the hours of 12 midnight and 5 a.m., and played loud music so as to prevent those nearby from sleeping. The Defendant refused to desist from such behaviour despite being requested to do so on several occasions throughout the night.

151

(2) On or about [date] [give particulars of as many such disturbances as possible].

(3) On or about [date] the Defendant [or CC] threatened to assault DD, who lives in a neighbouring flat, if she complained once more about the Defendant's behaviour.

6. By notice in prescribed form dated [date] the Claimant informed the Defendant that he intended to bring proceedings for possession of the dwelling-house on Ground 14 contained in Sch. 2 to the Housing Act 1988 not earlier than [date] and not later than 12 months from the date of service of the said notice.
[This refers to notice under HA 1988, s. 8, on which see 4.6.1 above.]

7. In the circumstances, the Claimant is entitled to possession of the dwelling-house pursuant to the provisions of Ground 14 of Sch. 2 to the Housing Act 1988.

AND the Claimant claims
[conclude as Draft 1]

Statutes and Statutory Instruments

HOUSING ACT 1988
PART I
RENTED ACCOMMODATION
CHAPTER I
ASSURED TENANCIES

Meaning of assured tenancy etc.

1. Assured tenancies

(1)   A tenancy under which a dwelling-house is let as a separate dwelling is for the purposes of this Act an assured tenancy if and so long as—

(a)   the tenant or, as the case may be, each of the joint tenants is an individual; and

(b)   the tenant or, as the case may be, at least one of the joint tenants occupies the dwelling-house as his only or principal home; and

(c)   the tenancy is not one which, by virtue of subsection (2) or subsection (6) below, cannot be an assured tenancy.

(2)   Subject to subsection (3) below, if and so long as a tenancy falls within any paragraph in Part I of Schedule 1 to this Act, it cannot be an assured tenancy; and in that Schedule—

(a)   'tenancy' means a tenancy under which a dwelling-house is let as a separate dwelling;

(b) Part II has effect for determining the rateable value of a dwelling-house for the purposes of Part I; and

(c) Part III has effect for supplementing paragraph 10 in Part I.

(2A) The Secretary of State may by order replace any amount referred to in paragraphs 2 and 3A of Schedule 1 to this Act by such amount as is specified in the order; and such an order shall be made by statutory instrument which shall be subject to annulment in pursuance of a resolution of either House of Parliament.

(3) Except as provided in Chapter V below, at the commencement of this Act, a tenancy—

(a) under which a dwelling-house was then let as a separate dwelling, and

(b) which immediately before that commencement was an assured tenancy for the purposes of sections 56 to 58 of the Housing Act 1980 (tenancies granted by approved bodies),

shall become an assured tenancy for the purposes of this Act.

(4) In relation to an assured tenancy falling within subsection (3) above—

(a) Part I of Schedule 1 to this Act shall have effect subject to subsection (5) below as if it consisted only of paragraphs 11 and 12; and

(b) sections 56 to 58 of the Housing Act 1980 (and Schedule 5 to that Act) shall not apply after the commencement of this Act.

(5) In any case where—

(a) immediately before the commencement of this Act the landlord under a tenancy is a fully mutual housing association, and

(b) at the commencement of this Act the tenancy becomes an assured tenancy by virtue of subsection (3) above,

then, so long as that association remains the landlord under that tenancy (and under any statutory periodic tenancy which arises on the coming to an end of that tenancy), paragraph 12 of Schedule 1 to this Act shall have effect in relation to that tenancy with the omission of sub-paragraph (1)(h).

2. Letting of a dwelling-house together with other land

(1) If, under a tenancy, a dwelling-house is let together with other land, then, for the purposes of this Part of this Act,—

(a) if and so long as the main purpose of the letting is the provision of a home for the tenant or, where there are joint tenants, at least one of them, the other land shall be treated as part of the dwelling-house; and

(b) if and so long as the main purpose of the letting is not as mentioned in paragraph (a) above, the tenancy shall be treated as not being one under which a dwelling-house is let as a separate dwelling.

(2)   Nothing in subsection (1) above affects any question whether a tenancy is precluded from being an assured tenancy by virtue of any provision of Schedule 1 to this Act.

3.   Tenant sharing accommodation with persons other than landlord

(1)   Where a tenant has the exclusive occupation of any accommodation (in this section referred to as 'the separate accommodation') and—

(a)   the terms as between the tenant and his landlord on which he holds the separate accommodation include the use of other accommodation (in this section referred to as 'the shared accommodation') in common with another person or other persons, not being or including the landlord, and

(b)   by reason only of the circumstances mentioned in paragraph (a) above, the separate accommodation would not, apart from this section, be a dwelling-house let on an assured tenancy,

the separate accommodation shall be deemed to be a dwelling-house let on an assured tenancy and the following provisions of this section shall have effect.

(2)   For the avoidance of doubt it is hereby declared that where, for the purpose of determining the rateable value of the separate accommodation, it is necessary to make an apportionment under Part II of Schedule 1 to this Act, regard is to be had to the circumstances mentioned in subsection (1)(a) above.

(3)   While the tenant is in possession of the separate accommodation, any term of the tenancy terminating or modifying, or providing for the termination or modification of, his right to the use of any of the shared accommodation which is living accommodation shall be of no effect.

(4)   Where the terms of the tenancy are such that, at any time during the tenancy, the persons in common with whom the tenant is entitled to the use of the shared accommodation could be varied or their number could be increased, nothing in subsection (3) above shall prevent those terms from having effect so far as they relate to any such variation or increase.

(5)   In this section 'living accommodation' means accommodation of such a nature that the fact that it constitutes or is included in the shared accommodation is sufficient, apart from this section, to prevent the tenancy from constituting an assured tenancy of a dwelling-house.

4.   Certain sub-lettings not to exclude any part of sub-lessor's premises from assured tenancy

(1)   Where the tenant of a dwelling-house has sub-let a part but not the whole of the dwelling-house, then, as against his landlord or any superior landlord, no part of the dwelling-house shall be treated as excluded from

being a dwelling-house let on an assured tenancy by reason only that the terms on which any person claiming under the tenant holds any part of the dwelling-house include the use of accommodation in common with other persons.

(2) Nothing in this section affects the rights against, and liabilities to, each other of the tenant and any person claiming under him, or of any two such persons.

Security of tenure

5. Security of tenure

(1) An assured tenancy cannot be brought to an end by the landlord except by obtaining an order of the court in accordance with the following provisions of this Chapter or Chapter II below or, in the case of a fixed term tenancy which contains power for the landlord to determine the tenancy in certain circumstances, by the exercise of that power and, accordingly, the service by the landlord of a notice to quit shall be of no effect in relation to a periodic assured tenancy.

(2) If an assured tenancy which is a fixed term tenancy comes to an end otherwise than by virtue of—

(a) an order of the court, or

(b) a surrender or other action on the part of the tenant,

then, subject to section 7 and Chapter II below, the tenant shall be entitled to remain in possession of the dwelling-house let under that tenancy and, subject to subsection (4) below, his right to possession shall depend upon a periodic tenancy arising by virtue of this section.

(3) The periodic tenancy referred to in subsection (2) above is one—

(a) taking effect in possession immediately on the coming to an end of the fixed term tenancy;

(b) deemed to have been granted by the person who was the landlord under the fixed term tenancy immediately before it came to an end to the person who was then the tenant under that tenancy;

(c) under which the premises which are let are the same dwelling-house as was let under the fixed term tenancy;

(d) under which the periods of the tenancy are the same as those for which rent was last payable under the fixed term tenancy; and

(e) under which, subject to the following provisions of this Part of this Act, the other terms are the same as those of the fixed term tenancy immediately before it came to an end, except that any term which makes provision for determination by the landlord or the tenant shall not have effect while the tenancy remains an assured tenancy.

(4) The periodic tenancy referred to in subsection (2) above shall not arise if, on the coming to an end of the fixed term tenancy, the tenant is

entitled, by virtue of the grant of another tenancy, to possession of the same or substantially the same dwelling-house as was let to him under the fixed term tenancy.

(5) If, on or before the date on which a tenancy is entered into or is deemed to have been granted as mentioned in subsection (3)(b) above, the person who is to be the tenant under that tenancy—

(a) enters into an obligation to do any act which (apart from this subsection) will cause the tenancy to come to an end at a time when it is an assured tenancy, or

(b) executes, signs or gives any surrender, notice to quit or other document which (apart from this subsection) has the effect of bringing the tenancy to an end at a time when it is an assured tenancy, the obligation referred to in paragraph (a) above shall not be enforceable or, as the case may be, the surrender, notice to quit or other document referred to in paragraph (b) above shall be of no effect.

(6) If, by virtue of any provision of this Part of this Act, Part I of Schedule 1 to this Act has effect in relation to a fixed term tenancy as if it consisted only of paragraphs 11 and 12, that Part shall have the like effect in relation to any periodic tenancy which arises by virtue of this section on the coming to an end of the fixed term tenancy.

(7) Any reference in this Part of this Act to a statutory periodic tenancy is a reference to a periodic tenancy arising by virtue of this section.

6.   Fixing of terms of statutory periodic tenancy

(1)   In this section, in relation to a statutory periodic tenancy,—

(a) 'the former tenancy' means the fixed term tenancy on the coming to an end of which the statutory periodic tenancy arises; and

(b) 'the implied terms' means the terms of the tenancy which have effect by virtue of section 5(3)(e) above, other than terms as to the amount of the rent; but nothing in the following provisions of this section applies to a statutory periodic tenancy at a time when, by virtue of paragraph 11 or paragraph 12 in Part I of Schedule 1 to this Act, it cannot be an assured tenancy.

(2)   Not later than the first anniversary of the day on which the former tenancy came to an end, the landlord may serve on the tenant, or the tenant may serve on the landlord, a notice in the prescribed form proposing terms of the statutory periodic tenancy different from the implied terms and, if the landlord or the tenant considers it appropriate, proposing an adjustment of the amount of the rent to take account of the proposed terms.

(3)   Where a notice has been served under subsection (2) above,—

(a)   within the period of three months beginning on the date on which the notice was served on him, the landlord or the tenant, as the case may be, may, by an application in the prescribed form, refer the notice to a rent assessment committee under subsection (4) below; and

(b)   if the notice is not so referred, then, with effect from such date, not falling within the period referred to in paragraph (a) above, as may be specified in the notice, the terms proposed in the notice shall become terms of the tenancy in substitution for any of the implied terms dealing with the same subject matter and the amount of the rent shall be varied in accordance with any adjustment so proposed.

(4)   Where a notice under subsection (2) above is referred to a rent assessment committee, the committee shall consider the terms proposed in the notice and shall determine whether those terms, or some other terms (dealing with the same subject matter as the proposed terms), are such as, in the committee's opinion, might reasonably be expected to be found in an assured periodic tenancy of the dwelling-house concerned, being a tenancy—

(a)   which begins on the coming to an end of the former tenancy; and

(b)   which is granted by a willing landlord on terms which, except in so far as they relate to the subject matter of the proposed terms, are those of the statutory periodic tenancy at the time of the committee's consideration.

(5)   Whether or not a notice under subsection (2) above proposes an adjustment of the amount of the rent under the statutory periodic tenancy, where a rent assessment committee determine any terms under subsection (4) above, they shall, if they consider it appropriate, specify such an adjustment to take account of the terms so determined.

(6)   In making a determination under subsection (4) above, or specifying an adjustment of an amount of rent under subsection (5) above, there shall be disregarded any effect on the terms or the amount of the rent attributable to the granting of a tenancy to a sitting tenant.

(7)   Where a notice under subsection (2) above is referred to a rent assessment committee, then, unless the landlord and the tenant otherwise agree, with effect from such date as the committee may direct—

(a)   the terms determined by the committee shall become terms of the statutory periodic tenancy in substitution for any of the implied terms dealing with the same subject matter; and

(b)   the amount of the rent under the statutory periodic tenancy shall be altered to accord with any adjustment specified by the committee;
but for the purposes of paragraph (b) above the committee shall not direct a date earlier than the date specified, in accordance with subsection (3)(b) above, in the notice referred to them.

(8)   Nothing in this section requires a rent assessment committee to continue with a determination under subsection (4) above if the landlord and tenant give notice in writing that they no longer require such a determination or if the tenancy has come to an end.

7.   Orders for possession

(1)   The court shall not make an order for possession of a dwelling-house let on an assured tenancy except on one or more of the grounds set out in Schedule 2 to this Act; but nothing in this Part of this Act relates to proceedings for possession of such a dwelling-house which are brought by a mortgagee, within the meaning of the Law of Property Act 1925, who has lent money on the security of the assured tenancy.

(2)   The following provisions of this section have effect, subject to section 8 below, in relation to proceedings for the recovery of possession of a dwelling-house let on an assured tenancy.

(3)   If the court is satisfied that any of the grounds in Part I of Schedule 2 to this Act is established then, subject to subsections (5A) and (6) below, the court shall make an order for possession.

(4)   If the court is satisfied that any of the grounds in Part II of Schedule 2 to this Act is established, then, subject to subsections (5A) and (6) below, the court may make an order for possession if it considers it reasonable to do so.

(5)   Part III of Schedule 2 to this Act shall have effect for supplementing Ground 9 in that Schedule and Part IV of that Schedule shall have effect in relation to notices given as mentioned in Grounds 1 to 5 of that Schedule.

(5A)   The court shall not make an order for possession of a dwelling-house let on an assured periodic tenancy arising under Schedule 10 to the Local Government and Housing Act 1989 on any of the following grounds, that is to say,—

   (a)   Grounds 1, 2 and 5 in Part I of Schedule 2 to this Act;

   (b)   Ground 16 in Part II of that Schedule; and

   (c)   if the assured periodic tenancy arose on the termination of a former 1954 Act tenancy, within the meaning of the said Schedule 10, Ground 6 in Part I of Schedule 2 to this Act.

(6)   The court shall not make an order for possession of a dwelling-house to take effect at a time when it is let on an assured fixed term tenancy unless—

   (a)   the ground for possession is Ground 2 or Ground 8 in Part I of Schedule 2 to this Act or any of the grounds in Part II of that Schedule, other than Ground 9 or Ground 16; and

   (b)   the terms of the tenancy make provision for it to be brought to an end on the ground in question (whether that provision takes the form of a provision for re-entry, for forfeiture, for determination by notice or otherwise).

(7) Subject to the preceding provisions of this section, the court may make an order for possession of a dwelling-house on grounds relating to a fixed term tenancy which has come to an end; and where an order is made in such circumstances, any statutory periodic tenancy which has arisen on the ending of the fixed term tenancy shall end (without any notice and regardless of the period) on the day on which the order takes effect.

8. Notice of proceedings for possession

(1) The court shall not entertain proceedings for possession of a dwelling-house let on an assured tenancy unless—

(a) the landlord or, in the case of joint landlords, at least one of them has served on the tenant a notice in accordance with this section and the proceedings are begun within the time limits stated in the notice in accordance with subsections (3) to (4B) below; or

(b) the court considers it just and equitable to dispense with the requirement of such a notice.

(2) The court shall not make an order for possession on any of the grounds in Schedule 2 to this Act unless that ground and particulars of it are specified in the notice under this section; but the grounds specified in such a notice may be altered or added to with the leave of the court.

(3) A notice under this section is one in the prescribed form informing the tenant that—

(a) the landlord intends to begin proceedings for possession of the dwelling-house on one or more of the grounds specified in the notice; and

(b) those proceedings will not begin earlier than a date specified in the notice in accordance with subsections (4) to (4B) below; and

(c) those proceedings will not begin later than twelve months from the date of service of the notice.

(4) If a notice under this section specifies in accordance with subsection (3)(a) above Ground 14 in Schedule 2 to this Act (whether with or without other grounds), the date specified in the notice as mentioned in subsection (3)(b) above shall not be earlier than the date of the service of the notice.

(4A) If a notice under this section specifies in accordance with subsection (3)(a) above, any of Grounds 1, 2, 5 to 7, 9 and 16 in Schedule 2 to this Act (whether without other grounds or with any ground other than Ground 14), the date specified in the notice as mentioned in subsection (3)(b) above shall not be earlier than—

(a) two months from the date of service of the notice, and

(b) if the tenancy is a periodic tenancy, the earliest date on which, apart from section 5(1) above, the tenancy could be brought to an end by a notice to quit given by the landlord on the same date as the date of service of the notice under this section.

(4B) In any other case, the date specified in the notice as mentioned in subsection (3)(b) above shall not be earlier than the expiry of the period of two weeks from the date of service of the notice.

(5) The court may not exercise the power conferred by subsection (1)(b) above if the landlord seeks to recover possession on Ground 8 in Schedule 2 to this Act.

(6) Where a notice under this section—

(a) is served at a time when the dwelling-house is let on a fixed term tenancy, or

(b) is served after a fixed term tenancy has come to an end but relates (in whole or in part) to events occurring during that tenancy, the notice shall have effect notwithstanding that the tenant becomes or has become tenant under a statutory periodic tenancy arising on the coming to an end of the fixed term tenancy.

8A. Additional notice requirements: ground of domestic violence

(1) Where the ground specified in a notice under section 8 (whether with or without other grounds) is Ground 14A in Schedule 2 to this Act and the partner who has left the dwelling-house as mentioned in that ground is not a tenant of the dwelling-house, the court shall not entertain proceedings for possession of the dwelling-house unless—

(a) the landlord or, in the case of joint landlords, at least one of them has served on the partner who has left a copy of the notice or has taken all reasonable steps to serve a copy of the notice on that partner, or

(b) the court considers it just and equitable to dispense with such requirements as to service.

(2) Where Ground 14A in Schedule 2 to this Act is added to a notice under section 8 with the leave of the court after proceedings for possession are begun and the partner who has left the dwelling-house as mentioned in that ground is not a party to the proceedings, the court shall not continue to entertain the proceedings unless—

(a) the landlord or, in the case of joint landlords, at least one of them has served a notice under subsection (3) below on the partner who has left or has taken all reasonable steps to serve such a notice on that partner, or

(b) the court considers it just and equitable to dispense with the requirement of such a notice.

(3) A notice under this subsection shall—

(a) state that proceedings for the possession of the dwelling-house have begun,

(b) specify the ground or grounds on which possession is being sought, and

(c) give particulars of the ground or grounds.

9. Extended discretion of court in possession claims

(1) Subject to subsection (6) below, the court may adjourn for such period or periods as it thinks fit proceedings for possession of a dwelling-house let on an assured tenancy.

(2) On the making of an order for possession of a dwelling-house let on an assured tenancy or at any time before the execution of such an order, the court, subject to subsection (6) below, may—

(a) stay or suspend execution of the order, or

(b) postpone the date of possession,

for such period or periods as the court thinks just.

(3) On any such adjournment as is referred to in subsection (1) above or on any such stay, suspension or postponement as is referred to in subsection (2) above, the court, unless it considers that to do so would cause exceptional hardship to the tenant or would otherwise be unreasonable, shall impose conditions with regard to payment by the tenant of arrears of rent (if any) and rent or payments in respect of occupation after the termination of the tenancy (mesne profits) and may impose such other conditions as it thinks fit.

(4) If any such conditions as are referred to in subsection (3) above are complied with, the court may, if it thinks fit, discharge or rescind any such order as is referred to in subsection (2) above.

(5) In any case where—

(a) at a time when proceedings are brought for possession of a dwelling-house let on an assured tenancy, the tenant's spouse or former spouse, having matrimonial home rights under Part IV of the Family Law Act 1996 is in occupation of the dwelling-house, and

(b) the assured tenancy is terminated as a result of those proceedings, the spouse or former spouse, so long as he or she remains in occupation, shall have the same rights in relation to, or in connection with, any such adjournment as is referred to in subsection (1) above or any such stay, suspension or postponement as is referred to in subsection (2) above, as he or she would have if those matrimonial home rights were not affected by the termination of the tenancy.

(5A) In any case where—

(a) at a time when proceedings are brought for possession of a dwelling-house let on an assured tenancy—

(i)   an order is in force under s. 35 of the Family Law Act 1996 conferring rights on a former spouse of the tenant, or

(ii)   an order is in force under s. 36 of that Act conferring rights on a cohabitant or former cohabitant (within the meaning of that Act) of the tenant,

(b)   that cohabitant, former cohabitant or former spouse is then in occupation of the dwelling-house, and

(c)   the assured tenancy is terminated as a result of those proceedings, the cohabitant, former cohabitant or former spouse shall have the same rights in relation to, or in connection with, any such adjournment as is referred to in sub-section (1) above or any such stay, suspension or postponement as is referred to in subsection (2) above as he or she would have if the rights conferred by the order referred to in paragraph (a) above were not affected by the termination of the tenancy.

(6)   This section does not apply if the court is satisfied that the landlord is entitled to possession of the dwelling-house—

(a)   on any of the grounds in Part I of Schedule 2 to this Act; or

(b)   by virtue of subsection (1) or subsection (4) of section 21 below.

10.   Special provisions applicable to shared accommodation

(1)   This section applies in a case falling within subsection (1) of section 3 above and expressions used in this section have the same meaning as in that section.

(2)   Without prejudice to the enforcement of any order made under subsection (3) below, while the tenant is in possession of the separate accommodation, no order shall be made for possession of any of the shared accommodation, whether on the application of the immediate landlord of the tenant or on the application of any person under whom that landlord derives title, unless a like order has been made, or is made at the same time, in respect of the separate accommodation; and the provisions of section 6 above shall have effect accordingly.

(3)   On the application of the landlord, the court may make such order as it thinks just either—

(a)   terminating the right of the tenant to use the whole or any part of the shared accommodation other than living accommodation; or

(b)   modifying his right to use the whole or any part of the shared accommodation, whether by varying the persons or increasing the number of persons entitled to the use of that accommodation or otherwise.

(4)   No order shall be made under subsection (3) above so as to effect any termination or modification of the rights of the tenant which, apart from section 3(3) above, could not be effected by or under the terms of the tenancy.

11. Payment of removal expenses in certain cases

(1)   Where a court makes an order for possession of a dwelling-house let on an assured tenancy on Ground 6 or Ground 9 in Schedule 2 to this Act (but not on any other ground), the landlord shall pay to the tenant a sum equal to the reasonable expenses likely to be incurred by the tenant in removing from the dwelling-house.

(2)   Any question as to the amount of the sum referred in subsection (1) above shall be determined by agreement between the landlord and the tenant or, in default of agreement, by the court.

(3)   Any sum payable to a tenant by virtue of this section shall be recoverable as a civil debt due from the landlord.

12. Compensation for misrepresentation or concealment

Where a landlord obtains an order for possession of a dwelling-house let on an assured tenancy on one or more of the grounds in Schedule 2 to this Act and it is subsequently made to appear to the court that the order was obtained by misrepresentation or concealment of material facts, the court may order the landlord to pay to the former tenant such sum as appears sufficient as compensation for damage or loss sustained by the tenant as a result of the order.

Rent and other terms

13. Increase of rent under assured periodic tenancies

(1)   This section applies to—

(a)   a statutory periodic tenancy other than one which, by virtue of paragraph 11 or paragraph 12 in Part I of Schedule 1 to this Act, cannot for the time being be an assured tenancy; and

(b)   any other periodic tenancy which is an assured tenancy, other than one in relation to which there is a provision, for the time being binding on the tenant, under which the rent for a particular period of the tenancy will or may be greater than the rent for an earlier period.

(2)   For the purpose of securing an increase in the rent under a tenancy to which this section applies, the landlord may serve on the tenant a notice in the prescribed form proposing a new rent to take effect at the beginning of a new period of the tenancy specified in the notice, being a period beginning not earlier than—

(a)   the minimum period after the date of the service of the notice; and

(b)   except in the case of a statutory periodic tenancy, the first anniversary of the date on which the first period of the tenancy began; and

(c)   if the rent under the tenancy has previously been increased by virtue of a notice under this subsection or a determination under section

14 below, the first anniversary of the date on which the increased rent took effect.

(3)   The minimum period referred to in subsection (2) above is—

(a)   in the case of a yearly tenancy, six months;

(b)   in the case of a tenancy where the period is less than a month, one month; and

(c)   in any other case, a period equal to the period of the tenancy.

(4)   Where a notice is served under subsection (2) above, a new rent specified in the notice shall take effect as mentioned in the notice unless, before the beginning of the new period specified in the notice,—

(a)   the tenant by an application in the prescribed form refers the notice to a rent assessment committee; or

(b)   the landlord and the tenant agree on a variation of the rent which is different from that proposed in the notice or agree that the rent should not be varied.

(5)   Nothing in this section (or in section 14 below) affects the right of the landlord and the tenant under an assured tenancy to vary by agreement any term of the tenancy (including a term relating to rent).

14.   Determination of rent by rent assessment committee

(1)   Where, under subsection (4)(a) of section 13 above, a tenant refers to a rent assessment committee a notice under subsection (2) of that section, the committee shall determine the rent at which, subject to subsections (2) and (4) below, the committee consider that the dwelling-house concerned might reasonably be expected to be let in the open market by a willing landlord under an assured tenancy—

(a)   which is a periodic tenancy having the same periods as those of the tenancy to which the notice relates;

(b)   which begins at the beginning of the new period specified in the notice;

(c)   the terms of which (other than relating to the amount of the rent) are the same as those of the tenancy to which the notice relates; and

(d)   in respect of which the same notices, if any, have been given under any of Grounds 1 to 5 of Schedule 2 to this Act, as have been given (or have effect as if given) in relation to the tenancy to which the notice relates.

(2)   In making a determination under this section, there shall be disregarded—

(a)   any effect on the rent attributable to the granting of a tenancy to a sitting tenant;

(b)   any increase in the value of the dwelling-house attributable to a relevant improvement carried out by a person who at the time it was carried out was the tenant, if the improvement—

    (i)   was carried out otherwise than in pursuance of an obligation to his immediate landlord, or

    (ii)   was carried out pursuant to an obligation to his immediate landlord being an obligation which did not relate to the specific improvement concerned but arose by reference to consent given to the carrying out of that improvement; and

    (c)   any reduction in the value of the dwelling-house attributable to a failure by the tenant to comply with any terms of the tenancy.

    (3)   For the purposes of subsection (2)(b) above, in relation to a notice which is referred by a tenant as mentioned in subsection (1) above, an improvement is a relevant improvement if either it was carried out during the tenancy to which the notice relates or the following conditions are satisfied, namely—

    (a)   that it was carried out not more than twenty-one years before the date of service of the notice; and

    (b)   that, at all times during the period beginning when the improvement was carried out and ending on the date of service of the notice, the dwelling-house has been let under an assured tenancy; and

    (c)   that, on the coming to an end of an assured tenancy at any time during that period, the tenant (or, in the case of joint tenants, at least one of them) did not quit.

    (3A)   In making a determination under this section in any case where under Part I of the Local Government Finance Act 1992 the landlord or a superior landlord is liable to pay council tax in respect of a hereditament ('the relevant hereditament') of which the dwelling-house forms part, the rent assessment committee shall have regard to the amount of council tax which, as at the date on which the notice under section 13(2) above was served, was set by the billing authority—

    (a)   for the financial year in which the notice was served, and

    (b)   for the category of dwellings within which the relevant hereditament fell on that date,
but any discount or other reduction affecting the amount of council tax payable shall be disregarded.

    (3B)   In subsection (3A) above—

    (a)   'hereditament' means a dwelling within the meaning of Part I of the Local Government Finance Act 1992.

    (b)   'billing authority' has the same meaning as in that Part of that Act, and

    (c)   'category of dwellings' has the same meaning as in section 30(1) and (2) of that Act.

    (4)   In this section 'rent' does not include any service charge, within the meaning of section 18 of the Landlord and Tenant Act 1985, but, subject to

that, includes any sums payable by the tenant to the landlord on account of the use of furniture, in respect of council tax or for any of the matters referred to in subsection (1)(a) of that section, whether or not those sums are separate from the sums payable for the occupation of the dwelling-house concerned or are payable under separate agreements.

(5) Where any rates in respect of the dwelling-house concerned are borne by the landlord or a superior landlord, the rent assessment committee shall make their determination under this section as if the rates were not so borne.

(6) In any case where—

(a) a rent assessment committee have before them at the same time the reference of a notice under section 6(2) above relating to a tenancy (in this subsection referred to as 'the section 6 reference') and the reference of a notice under section 13(2) above relating to the same tenancy (in this subsection referred to as 'the section 13 reference'), and

(b) the date specified in the notice under section 6(2) above is not later than the first day of the new period specified in the notice under section 13(2) above, and

(c) the committee propose to hear the two references together,
the committee shall make a determination in relation to the section 6 reference before making their determination in relation to the section 13 reference and, accordingly, in such a case the reference in subsection (1)(c) above to the terms of the tenancy to which the notice relates shall be construed as a reference to those terms as varied by virtue of the determination made in relation to the section 6 reference.

(7) Where a notice under section 13(2) above has been referred to a rent assessment committee, then, unless the landlord and the tenant otherwise agree, the rent determined by the committee (subject, in a case where subsection (5) above applies, to the addition of the appropriate amount in respect of rates) shall be the rent under the tenancy with effect from the beginning of the new period specified in the notice or, if it appears to the rent assessment committee that that would cause undue hardship to the tenant, with effect from such later date (not being later than the date the rent is determined) as the committee may direct.

(8) Nothing in this section requires a rent assessment committee to continue with their determination of a rent for a dwelling-house if the landlord and tenant give notice in writing that they no longer require such a determination or if the tenancy has come to an end.

(9) This section shall apply in relation to an assured shorthold tenancy as if in subsection (1) the reference to an assured tenancy were a reference to an assured shorthold tenancy.

14A. Interim increase before 1 April 1994 of rent under assured periodic tenancies in certain cases where landlord liable for council tax

(1) In any case where—

(a) under Part I of the Local Government Finance Act 1992 the landlord of a dwelling-house let under an assured tenancy to which section 13 above applies or a superior landlord is liable to pay council tax in respect of a dwelling (within the meaning of that Part of that Act) which includes that dwelling-house,

(b) under the terms of the tenancy (or an agreement collateral to the tenancy) the tenant is liable to make payments to the landlord in respect of council tax,

(c) the case falls within subsection (2) or subsection (3) below, and

(d) no previous notice under this subsection has been served in relation to the dwelling-house,

the landlord may serve on the tenant a notice in the prescribed form proposing an increased rent to take account of the tenant's liability to make payments to the landlord in respect of council tax, such increased rent to take effect at the beginning of a new period of the tenancy specified in the notice being a period beginning not earlier than one month after the date on which the notice was served.

(2) The case falls within this subsection if—

(a) the rent under the tenancy has previously been increased by virtue of a notice under section 13(2) above or a determination under section 14 above, and

(b) the first anniversary of the date on which the increased rent took effect has not yet occurred.

(3) The case falls within this subsection if a notice has been served under section 13(2) above before 1 April 1993 but no increased rent has taken effect before that date.

(4) No notice may be served under subsection (1) above after 31 March 1994.

(5) · Where a notice is served under subsection (1) above, the new rent specified in the notice shall take effect as mentioned in the notice unless, before the beginning of the new period specified in the notice—

(a) the tenant by an application in the prescribed form refers the notice to a rent assessment committee, or

(b) the landlord and the tenant agree on a variation of the rent which is different from that proposed in the notice or agree that the rent should not be varied.

(6) Nothing in this section (or in section 14B below) affects the right of the landlord and the tenant under an assured tenancy to vary by agreement any term of the tenancy (including a term relating to rent).

14B. Interim determination of rent by rent assessment committee

(1) Where, under subsection (5)(a) of section 14A above, a tenant refers to a rent assessment committee a notice under subsection (1) of that section, the committee shall determine the amount by which, having regard to the provisions of section 14(3A) above, the existing rent might reasonably be increased to take account of the tenant's liability to make payments to the landlord in respect of council tax.

(2) Where a notice under section 14A(1) above has been referred to a rent assessment committee, then, unless the landlord and the tenant otherwise agree, the existing rent shall be increased by the amount determined by the committee with effect from the beginning of the new period specified in the notice or, if it appears to the committee that that would cause undue hardship to the tenant, with effect from such later date (not being later than the date the increase is determined) as the committee may direct.

(3) In any case where—

(a) a rent assessment committee have before them at the same time the reference of a notice under section 13(2) above relating to a tenancy (in this subsection referred to as 'the section 13 reference') and the reference of a notice under section 14A(1) above relating to the same tenancy (in this subsection referred to as 'the section 14A reference'); and

(b) the committee propose to hear the two references together, the committee shall make a determination in relation to the section 13 reference before making their determination in relation to the section 14A reference, and if in such a case the date specified in the notice under section 13(2) above is later than the date specified in the notice under section 14A(1) above, the rent determined under the section 14A reference shall not take effect until the date specified in the notice under section 13(2).

(4) In this section 'rent' has the same meaning as in section 14 above; and section 14(4) above applies to a determination under this section as it applies to a determination under that section.

15. Limited prohibition on assignment etc. without consent

(1) Subject to subsection (3) below, it shall be an implied term of every assured tenancy which is a periodic tenancy that, except with the consent of the landlord, the tenant shall not—

(a) assign the tenancy (in whole or in part); or

(b) sub-let or part with possession of the whole or any part of the dwelling-house let on the tenancy.

(2) Section 19 of the Landlord and Tenant Act 1927 (consents to assign not to be unreasonably withheld etc.) shall not apply to a term which is implied into an assured tenancy by subsection (1) above.

(3)   In the case of a periodic tenancy which is not a statutory periodic tenancy or an assured periodic tenancy arising under Schedule 10 to the Local Government and Housing Act 1989 subsection (1) above does not apply if—

(a)   there is a provision (whether contained in the tenancy or not) under which the tenant is prohibited (whether absolutely or conditionally) from assigning or sub-letting or parting with possession or is permitted (whether absolutely or conditionally) to assign, sub-let or part with possession; or

(b)   a premium is required to be paid on the grant or renewal of the tenancy.

(4)   In subsection (3)(b) above 'premium' includes—

(a)   any fine or other like sum;

(b)   any other pecuniary consideration in addition to rent; and

(c)   any sum paid by way of deposit, other than one which does not exceed one-sixth of the annual rent payable under the tenancy immediately after the grant or renewal in question.

16.   Access for repairs

It shall be an implied term of every assured tenancy that the tenant shall afford to the landlord access to the dwelling-house let on the tenancy and all reasonable facilities for executing therein any repairs which the landlord is entitled to execute.

Miscellaneous

17.   Succession to assured periodic tenancy by spouse

(1)   In any case where—

(a)   the sole tenant under an assured periodic tenancy dies, and

(b)   immediately before the death, the tenant's spouse was occupying the dwelling-house as his or her only or principal home, and

(c)   the tenant was not himself a successor, as defined in subsection (2) or subsection (3) below,

then, on the death, the tenancy vests by virtue of this section in the spouse (and, accordingly, does not devolve under the tenant's will or intestacy).

(2)   For the purposes of this section, a tenant is a successor in relation to a tenancy if—

(a)   the tenancy became vested in him either by virtue of this section or under the will or intestacy of a previous tenant; or

(b)   at some time before the tenant's death the tenancy was a joint tenancy held by himself and one or more other persons and, prior to his death, he became the sole tenant by survivorship; or

(c)   he became entitled to the tenancy as mentioned in section 39(5) below.

(3) For the purposes of this section, a tenant is also a successor in relation to a tenancy (in this subsection referred to as 'the new tenancy') which was granted to him (alone or jointly with others) if—

(a) at some time before the grant of the new tenancy, he was, by virtue of subsection (2) above, a successor in relation to an earlier tenancy of the same or substantially the same dwelling-house as is let under the new tenancy; and

(b) at all times since he became such a successor he has been a tenant (alone or jointly with others) of the dwelling-house which is let under the new tenancy or of a dwelling-house which is substantially the same as that dwelling-house.

(4) For the purposes of this section, a person who was living with the tenant as his or her wife or husband shall be treated as the tenant's spouse.

(5) If, on the death of the tenant, there is, by virtue of subsection (4) above, more than one person who fulfils the condition in subsection (1)(b) above, such one of them as may be decided by agreement or, in default of agreement, by the county court shall be treated as the tenant's spouse for the purposes of this section.

18. Provisions as to reversions on assured tenancies

(1) If at any time—

(a) a dwelling-house is for the time being lawfully let on an assured tenancy, and

(b) the landlord under the assured tenancy is himself a tenant under a superior tenancy; and

(c) the superior tenancy comes to an end,

then, subject to subsection (2) below, the assured tenancy shall continue in existence as a tenancy held of the person whose interest would, apart from the continuance of the assured tenancy, entitle him to actual possession of the dwelling-house at that time.

(2) Subsection (1) above does not apply to an assured tenancy if the interest which, by virtue of that subsection, would become that of the landlord, is such that, by virtue of Schedule 1 to this Act, the tenancy could not be an assured tenancy.

(3) Where, by virtue of any provision of this Part of this Act, an assured tenancy which is a periodic tenancy (including a statutory periodic tenancy) continues beyond the beginning of a reversionary tenancy which was granted (whether before, on or after the commencement of this Act) so as to begin on or after—

(a) the date on which the previous contractual assured tenancy came to an end, or

(b) a date on which, apart from any provision of this Part, the periodic tenancy could have been brought to an end by the landlord by notice to quit,

the reversionary tenancy shall have effect as if it had been granted subject to the periodic tenancy.

(4) The reference in subsection (3) above to the previous contractual assured tenancy applies only where the periodic tenancy referred to in that subsection is a statutory periodic tenancy and is a reference to the fixed-term tenancy which immediately preceded the statutory periodic tenancy.

19. Restriction on levy of distress for rent

(1) Subject to subsection (2) below, no distress for the rent of any dwelling-house let on an assured tenancy shall be levied except with the leave of the county court; and, with respect to any application for such leave, the court shall have the same powers with respect to adjournment, stay, suspension, postponement and otherwise as are conferred by section 9 above in relation to proceedings for possession of such a dwelling-house.

(2) Nothing in subsection (1) above applies to distress levied under section 102 of the County Courts Act 1984.

CHAPTER II

ASSURED SHORTHOLD TENANCIES

19A. Assured shorthold tenancies: post-Housing Act 1996 tenancies

An assured tenancy which—

(a) is entered into on or after the day on which section 96 of the Housing Act 1996 comes into force (otherwise than pursuant to a contract made before that day), or

(b) comes into being by virtue of section 5 above on the coming to an end of an assured tenancy within paragraph (a) above,

is an assured shorthold tenancy unless it falls within any paragraph in Schedule 2A to this Act.

20. Assured shorthold tenancies: pre-Housing Act 1996 tenancies

(1) Subject to subsection (3) below, an assured tenancy which is not one to which section 19A above applies is an assured shorthold tenancy if—

(a) it is a fixed term tenancy granted for a term certain of not less than six months,

(b) there is no power for the landlord to determine the tenancy at any time earlier than six months from the beginning of the tenancy, and

(c)   a notice in respect of it is served as mentioned in subsection (2) below.

(2)   The notice referred to in subsection (1)(c) above is one which—

(a)   is in such form as may be prescribed;

(b)   is served before the assured tenancy is entered into;

(c)   is served by the person who is to be the landlord under the assured tenancy on the person who is to be the tenant under that tenancy; and

(d)   states that the assured tenancy to which it relates is to be a shorthold tenancy.

(3)   Notwithstanding anything in subsection (1) above, where—

(a)   immediately before a tenancy (in this subsection referred to as 'the new tenancy') is granted, the person to whom it is granted or, as the case may be, at least one of the persons to whom it is granted was a tenant under an assured tenancy which was not a shorthold tenancy, and

(b)   the new tenancy is granted by the person who, immediately before the beginning of the tenancy, was the landlord under the assured tenancy referred to in paragraph (a) above,
the new tenancy cannot be an assured shorthold tenancy.

(4)   Subject to subsection (5) below, if, on the coming to an end of an assured shorthold tenancy (including a tenancy which was an assured shorthold but ceased to be assured before it came to an end), a new tenancy of the same or substantially the same premises comes into being under which the landlord and the tenant are the same as at the coming to an end of the earlier tenancy, then, if and so long as the new tenancy is an assured tenancy, it shall be an assured shorthold tenancy, whether or not it fulfils the conditions in paragraphs (a) to (c) of subsection (1) above.

(5)   Subsection (4) above does not apply if, before the new tenancy is entered into (or, in the case of a statutory periodic tenancy, takes effect in possession), the landlord serves notice on the tenant that the new tenancy is not to be a shorthold tenancy.

(5A)   Subsections (3) and (4) above do not apply where the new tenancy is one to which section 19A above applies.

(6)   In the case of joint landlords—

(a)   the reference in subsection (2)(c) above to the person who is to be the landlord is a reference to at least one of the persons who are to be joint landlords; and

(b)   the reference in subsection (5) above to the landlord is a reference to at least one of the joint landlords.

20A. Post-Housing Act 1996 tenancies: duty of landlord to provide statement as to terms of tenancy

(1) Subject to subsection (3) below, a tenant under an assured shorthold tenancy to which section 19A above applies may, by notice in writing, require the landlord under that tenancy to provide him with a written statement of any term of the tenancy which—

(a) falls within subsection (2) below, and

(b) is not evidenced in writing.

(2) The following terms of a tenancy fall within this subsection, namely—

(a) the date on which the tenancy began or, if it is a statutory periodic tenancy or a tenancy to which section 39(7) below applies, the date on which the tenancy came into being,

(b) the rent payable under the tenancy and the dates on which that rent is payable,

(c) any term providing for a review of the rent payable under the tenancy, and

(d) in the case of a fixed term tenancy, the length of the fixed term.

(3) No notice may be given under subsection (1) above in relation to a term of the tenancy if—

(a) the landlord under the tenancy has provided a statement of that term in response to an earlier notice under that subsection given by the tenant under the tenancy, and

(b) the term has not been varied since the provision of the statement referred to in paragraph (a) above.

(4) A landlord who fails, without reasonable excuse, to comply with a notice under subsection (1) above within the period of 28 days beginning with the date on which he received the notice is liable on summary conviction to a fine not exceeding level 4 on the standard scale.

(5) A statement provided for the purposes of subsection (1) above shall not be regarded as conclusive evidence of what was agreed between the parties to the tenancy in question.

(6) Where—

(a) a term of a statutory periodic tenancy is one which has effect by virtue of section 5(3)(e) above, or

(b) a term of a tenancy to which subsection (7) of section 39 below applies is one which has effect by virtue of subsection (6)(e) of that section, subsection (1) above shall have effect in relation to it as if paragraph (b) related to the term of the tenancy from which it derives.

(7) In subsections (1) and (3) above—

(a) references to the tenant under the tenancy shall, in the case of joint tenants, be taken to be references to any of the tenants, and

174

(b)   references to the landlord under the tenancy shall, in the case of joint landlords, be taken to be references to any of the landlords.

21.   Recovery of possession on expiry or termination of assured shorthold tenancy

(1)   Without prejudice to any right of the landlord under an assured shorthold tenancy to recover possession of the dwelling-house let on the tenancy in accordance with Chapter I above, on or after the coming to an end of an assured shorthold tenancy which was a fixed term tenancy, a court shall make an order for possession of the dwelling-house if it is satisfied—

(a)   that the assured shorthold tenancy has come to an end and no further assured tenancy (whether shorthold or not) is for the time being in existence, other than an assured shorthold periodic tenancy (whether statutory or not); and

(b)   the landlord or, in the case of joint landlords, at least one of them has given to the tenant not less than two months' notice in writing stating that he requires possession of the dwelling-house.

(2)   A notice under paragraph (b) of subsection (1) above may be given before or on the day on which the tenancy comes to an end; and that subsection shall have effect notwithstanding that on the coming to an end of the fixed term tenancy a statutory periodic tenancy arises.

(3)   Where a court makes an order for possession of a dwelling-house by virtue of subsection (1) above, any statutory periodic tenancy which has arisen on the coming to an end of the assured shorthold tenancy shall end (without further notice and regardless of the period) on the day on which the order takes effect.

(4)   Without prejudice to any such right as is referred to in subsection (1) above, a court shall make an order for possession of a dwelling-house let on an assured shorthold tenancy which is a periodic tenancy if the court is satisfied–

(a)   that the landlord or, in the case of joint landlords, at least one of them has given to the tenant a notice in writing stating that, after a date specified in the notice, being the last day of a period of the tenancy and not earlier than two months after the date the notice was given, possession of the dwelling-house is required by virtue of this section; and

(b)   that the date specified in the notice under paragraph (a) above is not earlier than the earliest day on which, apart from section 5(1) above, the tenancy could be brought to an end by a notice to quit given by the landlord on the same date as the notice under paragraph (a) above.

(5)   Where an order for possession under subsection (1) or (4) above is made in relation to a dwelling-house let on a tenancy to which

section 19A above applies, the order may not be made so as to take effect earlier than—

(a)   in the case of a tenancy which is not a replacement tenancy, six months after the beginning of the tenancy, and

(b)   in the case of a replacement tenancy, six months after the beginning of the original tenancy.

(6)   In subsection (5)(b) above, the reference to the original tenancy is—

(a)   where the replacement tenancy came into being on the coming to an end of a tenancy which was not a replacement tenancy, to the immediately preceding tenancy, and

(b)   where there have been successive replacement tenancies, to the tenancy immediately preceding the first in the succession of replacement tenancies.

(7)   For the purposes of this section, a replacement tenancy is a tenancy—

(a)   which comes into being on the coming to an end of an assured shorthold tenancy, and

(b)   under which, on its coming into being—

(i)   the landlord and tenant are the same as under the earlier tenancy as at its coming to an end, and

(ii)   the premises let are the same or substantially the same as those let under the earlier tenancy as at that time.

22.   Reference of excessive rents to rent assessment committee

(1)   Subject to section 23 and subsection (2) below, the tenant under an assured shorthold tenancy may make an application in the prescribed form to a rent assessment committee for a determination of the rent which, in the committee's opinion, the landlord might reasonably be expected to obtain under the assured shorthold tenancy.

(2)   No application may be made under this section if—

(a)   the rent payable under the tenancy is a rent previously determined under this section;

(aa)   the tenancy is one to which section 19A above applies and more than six months have elapsed since the beginning of the tenancy or, in the case of a replacement tenancy, since the beginning of the original tenancy; or

(b)   the tenancy is an assured shorthold tenancy falling within subsection (4) of section 20 above (and, accordingly, is one in respect of which notice need not have been served as mentioned in subsection (2) of that section).

(3)   Where an application is made to a rent assessment committee under subsection (1) above with respect to the rent under an assured

shorthold tenancy, the committee shall not make such a determination as is referred to in that subsection unless they consider—

(a) that there is a sufficient number of similar dwelling-houses in the locality let on assured tenancies (whether shorthold or not); and

(b) that the rent payable under the assured shorthold tenancy in question is significantly higher than the rent which the landlord might reasonably be expected to be able to obtain under the tenancy, having regard to the level of rents payable under the tenancies referred to in paragraph (a) above.

(4) Where, on an application under this section, a rent assessment committee make a determination of a rent for an assured shorthold tenancy—

(a) the determination shall have effect from such date as the committee may direct, not being earlier than the date of the application;

(b) if, at any time on or after the determination takes effect, the rent which, apart from this paragraph, would be payable under the tenancy exceeds the rent so determined, the excess shall be irrecoverable from the tenant; and

(c) no notice may be served under section 13(2) above with respect to a tenancy of the dwelling-house in question until after the first anniversary of the date on which the determination takes effect.

(5) Subsections (4), (5) and (8) of section 14 above apply in relation to a determination of rent under this section as they apply in relation to a determination under that section and, accordingly, where subsection (5) of that section applies, any reference in subsection (4)(b) above to rent is a reference to rent exclusive of the amount attributable to rates.

(5A) Where—

(a) an assured tenancy ceases to be an assured shorthold tenancy by virtue of falling within paragraph 2 of Schedule 2A this Act, and

(b) at the time when it so ceases to be an assured shorthold tenancy there is pending before a rent assessment committee an application in relation to it under this section,

the fact that it so ceases to be an assured shorthold tenancy shall, in relation to that application, be disregarded for the purposes of this section.

(6) In subsection (2)(aa) above, the references to the original tenancy and to a replacement tenancy shall be construed in accordance with subsections (6) and (7) respectively of section 21 above.

23. Termination of rent assessment committee's functions

(1) If the Secretary of State by order made by statutory instrument so provides, section 22 above shall not apply in such cases or to tenancies of dwelling-houses in such areas or in such other circumstances as may be specified in the order.

(2)   An order under this section may contain such transitional, incidental and supplementary provisions as appear to the Secretary of State to be desirable.

(3)   No order shall be made under this section unless a draft of the order has been laid before, and approved by a resolution of, each House of Parliament.

CHAPTER III
ASSURED AGRICULTURAL OCCUPANCIES

24.   Assured agricultural occupancies

(1)   A tenancy or licence of a dwelling-house is for the purposes of this Part of this Act an 'assured agricultural occupancy' if—

(a)   it is of a description specified in subsection (2) below; and

(b)   by virtue of any provision of Schedule 3 to this Act the agricultural worker condition is for the time being fulfilled with respect to the dwelling-house subject to the tenancy or licence.

(2)   The following are the tenancies and licences referred to in subsection (1)(a) above—

(a)   an assured tenancy which is not an assured shorthold tenancy;

(b)   a tenancy which does not fall within paragraph (a) above by reason only of paragraph 3, 3A, 3B or paragraph 7 of Schedule 1 to this Act or more than one of those paragraphs and is not an excepted tenancy; and

(c)   a licence under which a person has the exclusive occupation of a dwelling-house as a separate dwelling and which, if it conferred a sufficient interest in land to be a tenancy, would be a tenancy falling within paragraph (a) or paragraph (b) above.

(2A)   For the purposes of subsection (2)(b) above, a tenancy is an excepted tenancy if it is—

(a)   a tenancy of an agricultural holding within the meaning of the Agricultural Holdings Act 1986 in relation to which that Act applies, or

(b)   a farm business tenancy within the meaning of the Agricultural Tenancies Act 1995.

(3)   For the purposes of Chapter I above and the following provisions of this Chapter, every assured agricultural occupancy which is not an assured tenancy shall be treated as if it were such a tenancy and any reference to a tenant, a landlord or any other expression appropriate to a tenancy shall be construed accordingly; but the provisions of Chapter I above shall have effect in relation to every assured agricultural occupancy subject to the provisions of this Chapter.

(4)   Section 14 above shall apply in relation to an assured agricultural occupancy as if in subsection (1) of that section the reference to an assured tenancy were a reference to an assured agricultural occupancy.

25. Security of tenure

(1) If a statutory periodic tenancy arises on the coming to an end of an assured agricultural occupancy—

(a) it shall be an assured agricultural occupancy as long as, by virtue of any provision of Schedule 3 to this Act, the agricultural worker condition is for the time being fulfilled with respect to the dwelling-house in question; and

(b) if no rent was payable under the assured agricultural occupancy which constitutes the fixed term tenancy referred to in subsection (2) of section 5 above, subsection (3)(d) of that section shall apply as if for the words 'the same as those for which rent was last payable under' there were substituted 'monthly beginning on the day following the coming to an end of.'

(2) In its application to an assured agricultural occupancy, Part II of Schedule 2 to this Act shall have effect with the omission of Ground 16.

(3) In its application to an assured agricultural occupancy, Part III of Schedule 2 to this Act shall have effect as if any reference in paragraph 2 to an assured tenancy included a reference to an assured agricultural occupancy.

(4) If the tenant under an assured agricultural occupancy gives notice to terminate his employment then, notwithstanding anything in any agreement or otherwise, that notice shall not constitute a notice to quit as respects the assured agricultural occupancy.

(5) Nothing in subsection (4) above affects the operation of an actual notice to quit given in respect of an assured agricultural occupancy.

CHAPTER IV
PROTECTION FROM EVICTION

27. Damages for unlawful eviction

(1) This section applies if, at any time after 9 June 1988, a landlord (in this section referred to as 'the landlord in default') or any person acting on behalf of the landlord in default unlawfully deprives the residential occupier of any premises of his occupation of the whole or part of the premises.

(2) This section also applies if, at any time after 9 June 1988, a landlord (in this section referred to as 'the landlord in default') or any person acting on behalf of the landlord in default—

(a) attempts unlawfully to deprive the residential occupier of any premises of his occupation of the whole or part of the premises, or

(b) knowing or having reasonable cause to believe that the conduct is likely to cause the residential occupier of any premises—

(i)   to give up his occupation of the premises or any part thereof, or

(ii)   to refrain from exercising any right or pursuing any remedy in respect of the premises or any part thereof,

does acts likely to interfere with the peace or comfort of the residential occupier or members of his household, or persistently withdraws or withholds services reasonably required for the occupation of the premises as a residence,

and, as a result, the residential occupier gives up his occupation of the premises as a residence.

(3)   Subject to the following provisions of this section, where this section applies, the landlord in default shall, by virtue of this section, be liable to pay to the former residential occupier, in respect of his loss of the right to occupy the premises in question as his residence, damages assessed on the basis set out in section 28 below.

(4)   Any liability arising by virtue of subsection (3) above—

(a)   shall be in the nature of a liability in tort; and

(b)   subject to subsection (5) below, shall be in addition to any liability arising apart from this section (whether in tort, contract, or otherwise).

(5)   Nothing in this section affects the right of a residential occupier to enforce any liability which arises apart from this section in respect of his loss of the right to occupy premises as his residence; but damages shall not be awarded both in respect of such a liability and in respect of a liability arising by virtue of this section on account of the same loss.

(6)   No liability shall arise by virtue of subsection (3) above if—

(a)   before the date on which proceedings to enforce the liability are finally disposed of, the former residential occupier is reinstated in the premises in question in such circumstances that he becomes again the residential occupier of them; or

(b)   at the request of the former residential occupier, a court makes an order (whether in the nature of an injunction or otherwise) as a result of which he is reinstated as mentioned in paragraph (a) above;

and, for the purposes of paragraph (a) above, proceedings to enforce a liability are finally disposed of on the earliest date by which the proceedings (including any proceedings on or in consequence of an appeal) have been determined and any time for appealing or further appealing has expired, except that if any appeal is abandoned, the proceedings shall be taken to be disposed of on the date of the abandonment.

(7)   If, in proceedings to enforce a liability arising by virtue of subsection (3) above, it appears to the court—

(a)   that, prior to the event which gave rise to the liability, the conduct of the former residential occupier or any person living with him in the premises concerned was such that it is reasonable to mitigate the damages for which the landlord in default would otherwise be liable, or

(b) that, before the proceedings were begun, the landlord in default offered to reinstate the former residential occupier in the premises in question and either it was unreasonable of the former residential occupier to refuse that offer or, if he had obtained alternative accommodation before the offer was made, it would have been unreasonable of him to refuse that offer if he had not obtained that accommodation,

the court may reduce the amount of damages which would otherwise be payable by such amount as it thinks appropriate.

(8) In proceedings to enforce a liability arising by virtue of subsection (3) above, it shall be a defence for the defendant to prove that he believed, and had reasonable cause to believe—

(a) that the residential occupier had ceased to reside in the premises in question at the time when he was deprived of occupation as mentioned in subsection (1) above or, as the case may be, when the attempt was made or the acts were done as a result of which he gave up his occupation of those premises; or

(b) that, where the liability would otherwise arise by virtue only of the doing of acts or the withdrawal or withholding of services, he had reasonable grounds for doing the acts or withdrawing or withholding the services in question.

(9) In this section—

(a) 'residential occupier', in relation to any premises, has the same meaning as in section 1 of the 1977 Act;

(b) 'the right to occupy', in relation to a residential occupier, includes any restriction on the right of another person to recover possession of the premises in question;

(c) 'landlord', in relation to a residential occupier, means the person who, but for the occupier's right to occupy, would be entitled to occupation of the premises and any superior landlord under whom that person derives title;

(d) 'former residential occupier', in relation to any premises, means the person who was the residential occupier until he was deprived of or gave up his occupation as mentioned in subsection (1) or subsection (2) above (and, in relation to a former residential occupier, 'the right to occupy' and 'landlord' shall be construed accordingly).

28. The measure of damages

(1) The basis for the assessment of damages referred to in section 27(3) above is the difference in value, determined as at the time immediately

before the residential occupier ceased to occupy the premises in question as his residence, between—

(a)   the value of the interest of the landlord in default determined on the assumption that the residential occupier continues to have the same right to occupy the premises as before that time; and

(b)   the value of that interest determined on the assumption that the residential occupier has ceased to have the right.

(2)   In relation to any premises, any reference in this section to the interest of the landlord in default is a reference to his interest in the building in which the premises in question are comprised (whether or not that building contains any other premises) together with its curtilage.

(3)   For the purposes of the valuations referred to in subsection (1) above, it shall be assumed—

(a)   that the landlord in default is selling his interest on the open market to a willing buyer;

(b)   that neither the residential occupier nor any member of his family wishes to buy; and

(c)   that it is unlawful to carry out any substantial development of any of the land in which the landlord's interest subsists or to demolish the whole or part of any building on that land.

(4)   In this section 'the landlord in default' has the same meaning as in section 27 above and subsection (9) of that section applies in relation to this section as it applies in relation to that.

(5)   Section 113 of the Housing Act 1985 (meaning of 'members of a person's family') applies for the purposes of subsection (3)(b) above.

(6)   The reference in subsection (3)(c) above to substantial development of any of the land in which the landlord's interest subsists is a reference to any development other than—

(a)   development for which planning permission is granted by a general development order for the time being in force and which is carried out so as to comply with any condition or limitation subject to which planning permission is so granted; or

(b)   a change of use resulting in the building referred to in subsection (2) above or any part of it being used as, or as part of, one or more dwelling-houses;

and in this subsection 'general development order' has the meaning given in section 56(6) of the Town and Country Planning Act 1990 and other expressions have the same meaning as in that Act.

. . .

33.   Interpretation of Chapter IV and the 1977 Act

(1)   In this Chapter 'the 1977 Act' means the Protection from Eviction Act 1977.

CHAPTER V
PHASING OUT OF RENT ACTS AND OTHER
TRANSITIONAL PROVISIONS

34. New protected tenancies and agricultural occupancies restricted to special cases

(1)   A tenancy which is entered into on or after the commencement of this Act cannot be a protected tenancy, unless—

(a)   it is entered into in pursuance of a contract made before the commencement of this Act; or

(b)   it is granted to a person (alone or jointly with others) who, immediately before the tenancy was granted, was a protected or statutory tenant and is so granted by the person who at that time was the landlord (or one of the joint landlords) under the protected or statutory tenancy; or

(c)   it is granted to a person (alone or jointly with others) in the following circumstances—

(i)   prior to the grant of the tenancy, an order for possession of a dwelling-house was made against him (alone or jointly with others) on the court being satisfied as mentioned in section 98(1)(a) of, or Case 1 in Schedule 16 to, the Rent Act 1977 or Case 1 in Schedule 4 to the Rent (Agriculture) Act 1976 (suitable alternative accommodation available); and

(ii)   the tenancy is of the premises which constitute the suitable alternative accommodation as to which the court was so satisfied; and

(iii)   in the proceedings for possession the court considered that, in the circumstances, the grant of an assured tenancy would not afford the required security and, accordingly, directed that the tenancy would be a protected tenancy; or

(d)   it is a tenancy under which the interest of the landlord was at the time the tenancy was granted held by a new town corporation, within the meaning of section 80 of the Housing Act 1985, and, before the date which has effect by virtue of paragraph (a) or paragraph (b) of subsection (4) of section 38 below, ceased to be so held by virtue of a disposal by the Commission for the New Towns made pursuant to a direction under section 37 of the New Towns Act 1981.

(2)   In subsection (1)(b) above 'protected tenant' and 'statutory tenant' do not include—

(a)   a tenant under a protected shorthold tenancy;

(b)   a protected or statutory tenant of a dwelling-house which was let under a protected shorthold tenancy which has ended before the commencement of this Act and in respect of which at that commencement either there has been no grant of a further tenancy or any grant of a further

tenancy has been to the person who, immediately before the grant, was in possession of the dwelling-house as a protected or statutory tenant;
and in this subsection 'protected shorthold tenancy' includes a tenancy which, in proceedings for possession under Case 19 in Schedule 15 to the Rent Act 1977, is treated as a protected shorthold tenancy.

(3)   In any case where—

(a)   by virtue of subsection (1) and (2) above, a tenancy entered into on or after the commencement of this Act is an assured tenancy, but

(b)   apart from subsection (2) above, the effect of subsection (1)(b) above would be that the tenancy would be a protected tenancy, and

(c)   the landlord and the tenant under the tenancy are the same as at the coming to an end of the protected or statutory tenancy which, apart from subsection (2) above, would fall within subsection (1)(b) above,
the tenancy shall be an assured shorthold tenancy (whether or not, in the case of a tenancy to which the provision applies, it fulfils the conditions in section 20(1) above) unless, before the tenancy is entered into, the landlord serves notice on the tenant that it is not to be a shorthold tenancy.

(4)   A licence or tenancy which is entered into on or after the commencement of this Act cannot be a relevant licence or relevant tenancy for the purposes of the Rent (Agriculture) Act 1976 (in this subsection referred to as 'the 1976 Act') unless—

(a)   it is entered into in pursuance of a contract made before the commencement of this Act; or

(b)   it is granted to a person (alone or jointly with others) who immediately before the licence or tenancy was granted, was a protected occupier or statutory tenant, within the meaning of the 1976 Act, and is so granted by the person who at that time was the landlord or licensor (or one of the joint landlords or licensors) under the protected occupancy or statutory tenancy in question.

(5)   Except as provided in subsection (4) above, expressions used in this section have the same meaning as in the Rent Act 1977.

35.   Removal of special regimes for tenancies of housing associations etc.

(1)   In this section 'housing association tenancy' has the same meaning as in Part VI of the Rent Act 1977.

(2)   A tenancy which is entered into on or after the commencement of this Act cannot be a housing association tenancy unless—

(a)   it is entered into in pursuance of a contract made before the commencement of this Act; or

(b)   it is granted to a person (alone or jointly with others) who, immediately before the tenancy was granted, was a tenant under a housing association tenancy and is so granted by the person who at that time was the landlord under that housing association tenancy; or

(c) it is granted to a person (alone or jointly with others) in the following circumstances—

(i) prior to the grant of the tenancy, an order for possession of a dwelling-house was made against him (alone or jointly with others) on the court being satisfied as mentioned in paragraph (b) or paragraph (c) of subsection (2) of section 84 of the Housing Act 1985; and

(ii) the tenancy is of the premises which constitute the suitable accommodation as to which the court was so satisfied; and

(iii) in the proceedings for possession the court directed that the tenancy would be a housing association tenancy; or

(d) it is a tenancy under which the interest of the landlord was at the time the tenancy was granted held by a new town corporation, within the meaning of section 80 of the Housing Act 1985, and before the date which has effect by virtue of paragraph (a) or paragraph (b) of subsection (4) of section 38 below, ceased to be so held by virtue of a disposal by the Commission for the New Towns made pursuant to a direction under section 37 of the New Towns Act 1981.

(3) Where, on or after the commencement of this Act, a registered social landlord, within the meaning of the Housing Act 1985 (see section 5(4) and (5) of that Act), grants a secure tenancy pursuant to an obligation under section 554(2A) of the Housing Act 1985 (as set out in Schedule 17 to this Act) then, in determining whether that tenancy is a housing association tenancy, it shall be assumed for the purposes only of section 86(2)(b) of the Rent Act 1977 (tenancy would be a protected tenancy but for section 15 or 16 of that Act) that the tenancy was granted before the commencement of this Act.

(4) Subject to section 38(4A) below a tenancy or licence which is entered into on or after the commencement of this Act cannot be a secure tenancy unless—

(a) the interest of the landlord belongs to a local authority, a new town corporation or an urban development corporation, all within the meaning of section 80 of the Housing Act 1985, a housing action trust established under Part III of this Act or the Development Board for Rural Wales; or

(b) the interest of the landlord belongs to a housing co-operative within the meaning of section 27B of the Housing Act 1985 (agreements between local housing authorities and housing co-operatives) and the tenancy or licence is of a dwelling-house comprised in a housing co-operative agreement falling within that section; or

(c) it is entered into in pursuance of a contract made before the commencement of this Act; or

(d) it is granted to a person (alone or jointly with others) who, immediately before it was entered into, was a secure tenant and is so granted by the body which at that time was the landlord or licensor under the secure tenancy; or

(e) it is granted to a person (alone or jointly with others) in the following circumstances—

(i) prior to the grant of the tenancy or licence, an order for possession of a dwelling-house was made against him (alone or jointly with others) on the court being satisfied as mentioned in paragraph (b) or paragraph (c) of subsection (2) of section 84 of the Housing Act 1985; and

(ii) the tenancy or licence is of the premises which constitute the suitable accommodation as to which the court was so satisfied; and

(iii) in the proceedings for possession the court considered that, in the circumstances, the grant of an assured tenancy would not afford the required security and, accordingly, directed that the tenancy or licence would be a secure tenancy; or

(f) it is granted pursuant to an obligation under section 554(2A) of the Housing Act 1985 (as set out in Schedule 17 to this Act).

(5) If, on or after the commencement of this Act, the interest of the landlord under a protected or statutory tenancy becomes held by a housing association, a housing trust, the Housing Corporation or Housing for Wales, nothing in the preceding provisions of this section shall prevent the tenancy from being a housing association tenancy or a secure tenancy and, accordingly, in such a case section 80 of the Housing Act 1985 (and any enactment which refers to that section) shall have effect without regard to the repeal of provisions of that section effected by this Act.

(6) In subsection (5) above 'housing association' and 'housing trust' have the same meaning as in the Housing Act 1985.

36. New restricted contracts limited to transitional cases

(1) A tenancy or other contract entered into after the commencement of this Act cannot be a restricted contract for the purposes of the Rent Act 1977 unless it is entered into in pursuance of a contract made before the commencement of this Act.

(2) If the terms of a restricted contract are varied after this Act comes into force then, subject to subsection (3) below,—

(a) if the variation affects the amount of the rent which, under the contract, is payable for the dwelling in question, the contract shall be treated as a new contract entered into at the time of the variation (and subsection (1) above shall have effect accordingly); and

(b) if the variation does not affect the amount of the rent which, under the contract, is so payable, nothing in this section shall affect the determination of the question whether the variation is such as to give rise to a new contract.

(3)   Any reference in subsection (2) above to a variation affecting the amount of the rent which, under a contract, is payable for a dwelling does not include a reference to—

(a)   a reduction or increase effected under section 78 of the Rent Act 1977 (power of rent tribunal); or

(b)   a variation which is made by the parties and has the effect of making the rent expressed to be payable under the contract the same as the rent for the dwelling which is entered in the register under section 79 of the Rent Act 1977.

(4)   In subsection (1) of section 81A of the Rent Act 1977 (cancellation of registration of rent relating to a restricted contract) paragraph (a) (no cancellation until two years have elapsed since the date of the entry) shall cease to have effect.

(5)   In this section 'rent' has the same meaning as in Part V of the Rent Act 1977.

37.   No further assured tenancies under Housing Act 1980

(1)   A tenancy which is entered into on or after the commencement of this Act cannot be an assured tenancy for the purposes of sections 56 to 58 of the Housing Act 1980 (in this section referred to as a '1980 Act tenancy').

(2)   In any case where—

(a)   before the commencement of this Act, a tenant under a 1980 Act tenancy made an application to the court under section 24 of the Landlord and Tenant Act 1954 (for the grant of a new tenancy), and

(b)   at the commencement of this Act the 1980 Act tenancy is continuing by virtue of that section or of any provision of Part IV of the said Act of 1954,

section 1(3) of this Act shall not apply to the 1980 Act tenancy.

(3)   If, in a case falling within subsection (2) above, the court makes an order for the grant of a new tenancy under section 29 of the Landlord and Tenant Act 1954, that tenancy shall be an assured tenancy for the purposes of this Act.

(4)   In any case where—

(a)   before the commencement of this Act a contract was entered into for the grant of a 1980 Act tenancy, but

(b)   at the commencement of this Act the tenancy had not been granted,

the contract shall have effect as a contract for the grant of an assured tenancy (within the meaning of this Act).

(5)   In relation to an assured tenancy falling within subsection (3) above or granted pursuant to a contract falling within subsection (4)

above, Part I of Schedule 1 to this Act shall have effect as if it consisted only of paragraphs 11 and 12; and, if the landlord granting the tenancy is a fully mutual housing association, then, so long as that association remains the landlord under that tenancy (and under any statutory periodic tenancy which arises on the coming to an end of that tenancy), the said paragraph 12 shall have effect in relation to that tenancy with the omission of subparagraph (1)(h).

(6)   Any reference in this section to a provision of the Landlord and Tenant Act 1954 is a reference only to that provision as applied by section 58 of the Housing Act 1980.

38.   Transfer of existing tenancies from public to private sector

(1)   The provisions of subsection (3) below apply in relation to a tenancy which was entered into before, or pursuant to a contract made before the commencement of this Act if,—

(a)   at that commencement or, if it is later, at the time it is entered into, the interest of the landlord is held by a public body (within the meaning of subsection (5) below); and

(b)   at some time after that commencement, the interest of the landlord ceases to be so held.

(2)   The provisions of subsection (3) below also apply in relation to a tenancy which was entered into before, or pursuant to a contract made before, the commencement of this Act if,—

(a)   at the commencement of this Act or, if it is later, at the time it is entered into, it is a housing association tenancy; and

(b)   at some time after that commencement, it ceases to be such a tenancy.

(3)   Subject to subsections (4) and (4A) below on and after the time referred to in subsection (1)(b) or, as the case may be, subsection (2)(b) above—

(a)   the tenancy shall not be capable of being a protected tenancy, a protected occupancy or a housing association tenancy;

(b)   the tenancy shall not be capable of being a secure tenancy unless (and only at a time when) the interest of the landlord under the tenancy is (or is again) held by a public body; and

(c)   paragraph 1 of Schedule 1 to this Act shall not apply in relation to it, and the question whether at any time thereafter it becomes (or remains) an assured tenancy shall be determined accordingly.

(4)   In relation to a tenancy under which, at the commencement of this Act or, if it is later, at the time the tenancy is entered into, the interest of the landlord is held by a new town corporation, within the meaning of section 80 of the Housing Act 1985 and which subsequently ceases to be so

held by virtue of a disposal by the Commission for the New Towns made pursuant to a direction under section 37 of the New Towns Act 1981, subsections (1) and (3) above shall have effect as if any reference in subsection (1) above to the commencement of this Act were a reference to—

(a) the date on which expires the period of two years beginning on the day this Act is passed; or

(b) if the Secretary of State by order made by statutory instrument within that period so provides, such other date (whether earlier or later) as may be specified by the order for the purposes of this subsection.

(4A) Where, by virtue of a disposal falling within subsection (4) above and made before the date which has effect by virtue of paragraph (a) or paragraph (b) of that subsection, the interest of the landlord under a tenancy passes to a registered social landlord (within the meaning of the Housing Act 1985 (see section 5(4) and (5) of that Act), then, notwithstanding anything in subsection (3) above, so long as the tenancy continues to be held by a body which would have been specified in subsection (1) of section 80 of the Housing Act 1985 if the repeal of provisions of that section effected by this Act had not been made, the tenancy shall continue to be a secure tenancy and to be capable of being a housing association tenancy.

(5) For the purposes of this section, the interest of a landlord under a tenancy is held by a public body at a time when—

(a) it belongs to a local authority, a new town corporation or an urban development corporation, all within the meaning of section 80 of the Housing Act 1985; or

(b) it belongs to a housing action trust established under Part III of this Act; or

(c) it belongs to the Development Board for Rural Wales; or

(d) it belongs to Her Majesty in right of the Crown or to a government department or is held in trust for Her Majesty for the purposes of a government department.

(6) In this section—

(a) 'housing association tenancy' means a tenancy to which Part VI of the Rent Act 1977 applies;

(b) 'protected tenancy' has the same meaning as in that Act; and

(c) 'protected occupancy' has the same meaning as in the Rent (Agriculture) Act 1976.

39. Statutory tenants: succession

(1) ...

(2) Where the person who is the original tenant, within the meaning of Part I of Schedule 1 to the Rent Act 1977, dies after the commencement of

this Act, that Part shall have effect subject to the amendments in Part I of Schedule 4 to this Act.

(3)   Where subsection (2) above does not apply but the person who is the first successor, within the meaning of Part I of Schedule 1 to the Rent Act 1977, dies after the commencement of this Act, that Part shall have effect subject to the amendments in paragraphs 5 to 9 of Part I of Schedule 4 to this Act.

(4)   In any case where the original occupier, within the meaning of section 4 of the Rent (Agriculture) Act 1976 (statutory tenants and tenancies) dies after the commencement of this Act, that section shall have effect subject to the amendments in Part II of Schedule 4 to this Act.

(5)   In any case where, by virtue of any provision of—

(a)   Part I of Schedule 1 to the Rent Act 1977, as amended in accordance with subsection (2) or subsection (3) above, or

(b)   section 4 of the Rent (Agriculture) Act 1976, as amended in accordance with subsection (4) above,

a person (in the following provisions of this section referred to as 'the successor') becomes entitled to an assured tenancy of a dwelling-house by succession, that tenancy shall be a periodic tenancy arising by virtue of this section.

(6)   Where, by virtue of subsection (5) above, the successor becomes entitled to an assured periodic tenancy, that tenancy is one—

(a)   taking effect in possession immediately after the death of the protected or statutory tenant or protected occupier (in the following provisions of this section referred to as 'the predecessor') on whose death the successor became so entitled;

(b)   deemed to have been granted to the successor by the person who, immediately before the death of the predecessor, was the landlord of the predecessor under his tenancy;

(c)   under which the premises which are let are the same dwelling-house as, immediately before his death, the predecessor occupied under his tenancy;

(d)   under which the periods of the tenancy are the same as those for which rent was last payable by the predecessor under his tenancy;

(e)   under which, subject to sections 13 to 15 above, the other terms are the same as those on which, under his tenancy, the predecessor occupied the dwelling-house immediately before his death; and

(f)   which, for the purposes of section 13(2) above, is treated as a statutory periodic tenancy;

and in paragraphs (b) to (e) above 'under his tenancy', in relation to the predecessor, means under his protected tenancy or protected occupancy or in his capacity as a statutory tenant.

(7) If, immediately before the death of the predecessor, the landlord might have recovered possession of the dwelling-house under Case 19 in Schedule 15 to the Rent Act 1977, the assured periodic tenancy to which the successor becomes entitled shall be an assured shorthold tenancy (whether or not, in the case of a tenancy to which the provision applies, it fulfils the conditions in section 20(1) above).

(8) If, immediately before his death, the predecessor was a protected occupier or statutory tenant within the meaning of the Rent (Agriculture) Act 1976, the assured periodic tenancy to which the successor becomes entitled shall be an assured agricultural occupancy (whether or not it fulfils the conditions in section 24(1) above).

(9) Where, immediately before his death, the predecessor was a tenant under a fixed term tenancy, section 6 above shall apply in relation to the assured periodic tenancy to which the successor becomes entitled on the predecessor's death subject to the following modifications—

(a) for any reference to a statutory periodic tenancy there shall be substituted a reference to the assured periodic tenancy to which the successor becomes so entitled;

(b) in subsection (1) of that section, paragraph (a) shall be omitted and the reference in paragraph (b) to section 5(3)(e) above shall be construed as a reference to subsection (6)(e) above; and

(c) for any reference to the coming to an end of the former tenancy there shall be substituted a reference to the date of the predecessor's death.

(10) If and so long as a dwelling-house is subject to an assured tenancy to which the successor has become entitled by succession, section 7 above and Schedule 2 to this Act shall have effect subject to the modifications in Part III of Schedule 4 to this Act; and in that Part 'the predecessor' and 'the successor' have the same meaning as in this section.

CHAPTER VI
GENERAL PROVISIONS

40. Jurisdiction of county courts

(1) A county court shall have jurisdiction to hear and determine any question arising under any provision of—

(a) Chapters I to III and V above, or

(b) sections 27 and 28 above,

other than a question falling within the jurisdiction of a rent assessment committee by virtue of any such provision.

(2) Subsection (1) above has effect notwithstanding that the damages claimed in any proceedings may exceed the amount which, for the time being, is the county court limit for the purposes of the County Courts Act 1984.

(3)   Where any proceedings under any provision mentioned in subsection (1) above are being taken in a county court, the court shall have jurisdiction to hear and determine any other proceedings joined with those proceedings, notwithstanding that, apart from this subsection, those other proceedings would be outside the court's jurisdiction.

41.   Rent assessment committees: procedure and information powers

(1)   ...

(2)   The rent assessment committee to whom a matter is referred under Chapter I or Chapter II above may by notice in the prescribed form served on the landlord or the tenant require him to give to the committee, within such period of not less than fourteen days from the service of the notice as may be specified in the notice, such information as they may reasonably require for the purposes of their functions.

(3)   If any person fails without reasonable excuse to comply with a notice served on him under subsection (2) above, he shall be liable on summary conviction to a fine nor exceeding level 3 on the standard scale.

(4)   Where an offence under subsection (3) above committed by a body corporate is proved to have been committed with the consent or connivance of, or to be attributable to any neglect on the part of, any director, manager or secretary or other similar officer of the body corporate or any person who was purporting to act in any such capacity, he as well as the body corporate shall be guilty of that offence and shall be liable to be proceeded against and punished accordingly.

41A.   Amounts attributable to services

In order to assist authorities to give effect to the housing benefit scheme under Part VII of the Social Security Contributions and Benefits Act 1992, where a rent is determined under section 14 or 22 above, the rent assessment committee shall note in their determination the amount (if any) of the rent which, in the opinion of the committee, is fairly attributable to the provision of services, except where that amount is in their opinion negligible; and the amount so noted may be included in the information specified in an order under section 42 below.

41B.   Provision of information as to exemption from council tax

A billing authority within the meaning of Part I of the Local Government Finance Act 1992 shall, if so requested in writing by a rent officer or rent assessment committee in connection with his or their functions under any enactment, inform the rent officer or rent assessment committee in writing whether or not a particular dwelling (within the meaning of Part I of the Local Government Finance Act 1992) is, or was at any time specified in the request, an exempt dwelling for the purposes of that Part of that Act.

42. Information as to determination of rents

(1) The President of every rent assessment panel shall keep and make publicly available, in such manner as is specified in an order made by the Secretary of State, such information as may be so specified with respect to rents under assured tenancies and assured agricultural occupancies which have been the subject of references or applications to, or determinations by, rent assessment committees.

(2) A copy of any information certified under the hand of an officer duly authorised by the President of the rent assessment panel concerned shall be receivable in evidence in any court and in any proceedings.

(3) An order under subsection (1) above—

(a) may prescribe the fees to be charged for the supply of a copy, including a certified copy, of any of the information kept by virtue of that subsection; and

(b) may make different provision with respect to different cases or descriptions of case, including different provision for different areas.

(4) The power to make an order under subsection (1) above shall be exercisable by statutory instrument which shall be subject to annulment in pursuance of a resolution of either House of Parliament.

...

44. Application to Crown Property

(1) Subject to paragraph 11 of Schedule 1 to this Act and subsection (2) below, Chapters I to IV above apply in relation to premises in which there subsists, or at any material time subsisted, a Crown interest as they apply in relation to premises in relation to which no such interest subsists or ever subsisted.

(2) In Chapter IV above—

(a) sections 27 and 28 do not bind the Crown; and

(b) the reminder binds the Crown to the extent provided for in section 10 of the Protection from Eviction Act 1977.

(3) In this section 'Crown interest' means an interest which belongs to Her Majesty in right of the Crown or of the Duchy of Lancaster or to the Duchy of Cornwall, or to a government department, or which is held in trust for Her Majesty for the purposes of a government department.

(4) Where an interest belongs to Her Majesty in right of the Duchy of Lancaster, then, for the purposes of Chapters I to IV above, the Chancellor of the Duchy of Lancaster shall be deemed to be the owner of the interest.

45. Interpretation of Part I

(1) In this Part of this Act, except where the context otherwise requires,—

'dwelling-house' may be a house or part of a house;

'fixed term tenancy' means any tenancy other than a periodic tenancy;

'fully mutual housing association' has the same meaning as in Part I of the Housing Association Act 1985;

'landlord' includes any person from time to time deriving title under the original landlord and also includes, in relation to a dwelling-house, any person other than a tenant who is, or but for the existence of an assured tenancy would be, entitled to possession of the dwelling-house;

'let' includes 'sub-let';

'prescribed' means prescribed by regulations made by the Secretary of State by statutory instrument;

'rates' includes water rates and charges but does not include an owner's drainage rate, as defined in section 63(2)(a) of the Land Drainage Act 1976;

'secure tenancy' has the meaning assigned by section 79 of the Housing Act 1976;

'statutory periodic tenancy' has the meaning assigned by section 5(7) above;

'tenancy' includes a sub-tenancy and an agreement for a tenancy or sub-tenancy; and

'tenant' includes a sub-tenant and any person deriving title under the original tenant or sub-tenant.

(2)   Subject to paragraph 11 of Schedule 2 to this Act, any reference in this Part of this Act to the beginning of a tenancy is a reference to the day on which the tenancy is entered into or, if it is later, the day on which, under the terms of any lease, agreement or other document, the tenant is entitled to possession under the tenancy.

(3)   Where two or more persons jointly constitute either the landlord or the tenant in relation to a tenancy, then, except where this Part of this Act otherwise provides, any reference to the landlord or to the tenant is a reference to all the persons who jointly constitute the landlord or the tenant, as the case may require.

(4)   For the avoidance of doubt, it is hereby declared that any reference in this Part of this Act (however expressed) to a power for a landlord to determine a tenancy does not include a reference to a power of re-entry or forfeiture for breach of any term or condition of the tenancy.

(5)   Regulations under subsection (1) above may make different provision with respect to different cases or descriptions of case, including different provision for different areas.

. . .

SCHEDULES

Section 1

SCHEDULE 1

TENANCIES WHICH CANNOT BE ASSURED TENANCIES

PART I

THE TENANCIES

Tenancies entered into before commencement

1. A tenancy which is entered into before, or pursuant to a contract made before, the commencement of this Act.

Tenancies of dwelling-houses with high rateable values

2.—(1) A tenancy—

(a) which is entered into on or after 1 April 1990 (otherwise than, where the dwelling-house had a rateable value on 31 March 1990, in pursuance of a contract made before 1 April 1990), and

(b) under which the rent payable for the time being is payable at a rate exceeding £25,000 a year,

(2) In sub-paragraph (1) 'rent' does not include any sum payable by the tenant as is expressed (in whatever terms) to be payable in respect of rates, council tax, services, management, repairs, maintenance or insurance, unless it could not have been regarded by the parties to the tenancy as a sum so payable.

2A. A tenancy—

(a) which was entered into before 1 April 1990, or on or after that date in pursuance of a contract made before that date, and

(b) under which the dwelling-house had a rateable value on 31 March 1990 which, if it is in Greater London, exceeded £1,500 and, if it is elsewhere, exceeded £750.

Tenancies at a low rent

3. A tenancy under which for the time being no rent is payable.

3A. A tenancy—

(a) which is entered into on or after 1 April 1990 (otherwise than, where the dwelling-house had a rateable value on 31 March 1990, in pursuance of a contract made before 1 April 1990, and

(b) under which the rent payable for the time being is payable at a rate of, if the dwelling-house is in Greater London, £1,000 or less a year and, if it is elsewhere, £250 or less a year.

3B. A tenancy—

(a) which was entered into before 1 April 1990 or, where the dwelling-house had a rateable value on 31 March 1990, on or after 1 April 1990 in pursuance of a contract made before that date, and

(b)   under which the rent for the time being payable is less than two-thirds of the rateable value of the dwelling-house on 31 March 1990.

3C.   Paragraph 2(2) above applies for the purposes of paragraphs 3, 3A and 3B as it applies for the purposes of paragraph 2(1).

Business tenancies

4.   A tenancy to which Part II of the Landlord and Tenant Act 1954 applies (business tenancies).

Licensed premises

5.   A tenancy under which the dwelling-house consists of or comprises premises licensed for the sale of intoxicating liquors for consumption on the premises.

Tenancies of agricultural land

6.—(1)   A tenancy under which agricultural land, exceeding two acres, is let together with the dwelling-house.

(2)   In this paragraph 'agricultural land' has the meaning set out in section 26(3)(a) of the General Rate Act 1967 (exclusion of agricultural land and premises from liability for rating).

Tenancies of agricultural holdings [etc.]

7.—(1)   A tenancy under which the dwelling-house—
       (a)   is comprised in an agricultural holding, and
       (b)   is occupied by the person responsible for the control (whether as tenant or as servant or agent of the tenant) of the farming of the holding.
   (2)   A tenancy under which the dwelling-house—
       (a)   is comprised in the holding held under a farm business tenancy, and
       (b)   is occupied by the person responsible for the control (whether as tenant or as servant or agent of the tenant) of the management of the holding.
   (3)   In this paragraph—
       'agricultural holding' means any agricultural holding within the meaning of the Agricultural Holdings Act 1986 held under a tenancy in relation to which that Act applies, and
       'farm business tenancy' and 'holding', in relation to such a tenancy, have the same meaning as in the Agricultural Tenancies Act 1995.

Lettings to students

8.—(1)   A tenancy which is granted to a person who is pursuing, or intends to pursue, a course of study provided by a specified educational institution and is so granted either by that institution or by another specified institution or body of persons.

(2) In sub-paragraph (1) above 'specified' means specified, or of a class specified, for the purposes of this paragraph by regulations made by the Secretary of State by statutory instrument.

(3) A statutory instrument made in the exercise of the power conferred by sub-paragraph (2) above shall be subject to annulment in pursuance of a resolution of either House of Parliament.

Holiday lettings

9.   A tenancy the purpose of which is to confer on the tenant the right to occupy the dwelling-house for a holiday.

Resident landlords

10.—(1)   A tenancy in respect of which the following conditions are fulfilled—

(a)   that the dwelling-house forms part only of a building and, except in a case where the dwelling-house also forms part of a flat, the building is not a purpose-built block of flats; and

(b)   that, subject to Part III of this Schedule, the tenancy was granted by an individual who, at the time when the tenancy was granted, occupied as his only or principal home another dwelling-house which,—

(i)   in the case mentioned in paragraph (a) above, also forms part of the flat; or

(ii)   in any other case, also forms part of the building; and

(c)   that, subject to Part III of this Schedule, at all times since the tenancy was granted the interest of the landlord under the tenancy has belonged to an individual who, at the time he owned that interest, occupied as his only or principal home another dwelling-house which,—

(i)   in the case mentioned in paragraph (a) above, also formed part of the flat; or

(ii)   in any other case, also formed part of the building; and

(d)   that the tenancy is not one which is excluded from this sub-paragraph by sub-paragraph (3) below.

(2) If a tenancy was granted by two or more persons jointly, the reference in sub-paragraph (1)(b) above to an individual is a reference to any one of those persons and if the interest of the landlord is for the time being held by two or more persons jointly, the reference in sub-paragraph (1)(c) above to an individual is a reference to any one of those persons.

(3) A tenancy (in this sub-paragraph referred to as 'the new tenancy') is excluded from sub-paragraph (1) above if—

(a) it is granted to a person (alone, or jointly with others) who, immediately before it was granted, was a tenant under an assured tenancy (in this sub-paragraph referred to as 'the former tenancy') of the same dwelling-house or of another dwelling-house which forms part of the building in question; and

(b) the landlord under the new tenancy and under the former tenancy is the same person or, if either of those tenancies is or was granted by two or more persons jointly, the same person is the landlord or one of the landlords under each tenancy.

Crown tenancies

11.—(1) A tenancy under which the interest of the landlord belongs to Her Majesty in right of the Crown or to a government department or is held in trust for Her Majesty for the purpose of a government department.

(2) The reference in sub-paragraph (1) above to the case where the interest of the landlord belongs to Her Majesty in right of the Crown does not include the case where that interest is under the management of the Crown Estate commissioners.

Local authority tenancies etc.

12.—(1) A tenancy under which the interest of the landlord belongs to—

(a) a local authority, as defined in sub-paragraph (2) below;

(b) the Commission for the New Towns;

(c) the Development Board for Rural Wales;

(d) an urban development corporation established by an order under section 135 of the Local Government, Planning and Land Act 1980;

(e) a development corporation, within the meaning of the New Towns Act 1981;

(f) an authority established under section 10 of the Local Government Act 1985 (waste disposal authorities);

(g) a residuary body, within the meaning of the Local Government Act 1985;

(gg) The Residuary Body for Wales (Corff Gweddilliol Cymru);

(h) a fully mutual housing association; or

(i) a housing action trust established under Part III of this Act.

(2) The following are local authorities for the purposes of sub-paragraph (1)(a) above—

(a) the council of a county, county borough, district or London borough;

(b) the Common Council of the City of London;

(c) the Council of the Isles of Scilly;

(d) the Broads Authority;

(da) a National Park Authority;

(e) the Inner London Education Authority;

(f) a joint authority, within the meaning of the Local Government Act 1985; and

(g) a police authority established under section 3 of the Police Act 1996.

Transitional cases

13.—(1) A protected tenancy, within the meaning of the Rent Act 1977.

(2) A housing association tenancy, within the meaning of Part VI of that Act.

(3) A secure tenancy.

(4) Where a person is a protected occupier of a dwelling-house, within the meaning of the Rent (Agriculture) Act 1976, the relevant tenancy, within the meaning of that Act, by virtue of which he occupies the dwelling-house.

PART II
RATEABLE VALUES

14.—(1) The rateable value of a dwelling-house at any time shall be ascertained for the purposes of Part I of this Schedule as follows—

(a) if the dwelling-house is a hereditament for which a rateable value is then shown in the valuation list, it shall be that rateable value;

(b) if the dwelling-house forms part only of such a hereditament or consists of or forms part of more than one such hereditament, its rateable value shall be taken to be such value as is found by a proper apportionment or aggregation of the rateable value or values so shown.

(2) Any question arising under this Part of this Schedule as to the proper apportionment or aggregation of any value or values shall be determined by the county court and the decision of that court shall be final.

15. Where, after the time at which the rateable value of a dwelling-house is material for the purposes of any provision of Part I of this Schedule, the valuation list is altered so as to vary the rateable value of the hereditament of which the dwelling-house consists (in whole or in part) or forms part and the alteration has effect from that time or from an earlier time, the rateable value of the dwelling-house at the material time shall be ascertained as if the value shown in the valuation list at the material time had been the value shown in the list as altered.

16.   Paragraphs 14 and 15 above apply in relation to any other land which, under section 2 of this Act, is treated as part of a dwelling-house as they apply in relation to the dwelling-house itself.

PART III
PROVISIONS FOR DETERMINING APPLICATION OF PARAGRAPH 10 (RESIDENT LANDLORDS)

17.—(1)   In determining whether the condition in paragraph 10(1)(c) above is at any time fulfilled with respect to a tenancy, there shall be disregarded—

(a)   any period of not more than twenty-eight days, beginning with the date on which the interest of the landlord under the tenancy becomes vested at law and in equity in an individual who, during that period, does not occupy as his only or principal home another dwelling-house which forms part of the building or, as the case may be, flat concerned;

(b)   if, within a period falling within paragraph (a) above, the individual concerned notifies the tenant in writing of his intention to occupy as his only or principal home another dwelling-house in the building or, as the case may be, flat concerned, the period beginning with the date on which the interest of the landlord under the tenancy becomes vested in that individual as mentioned in that paragraph and ending—

(i)   at the expiry of the period of six months beginning on that date, or

(ii)   on the date on which that interest ceases to be so vested, or

(iii)   on the date on which that interest becomes again vested in such an individual as is mentioned in paragraph 10(1)(c) or the condition in that paragraph becomes deemed to be fulfilled by virtue of paragraph 18(1) or paragraph 20 below,
whichever is the earlier; and

(c)   any period of not more than two years beginning with the date on which the interest of the landlord under the tenancy becomes, and during which it remains, vested—

(i)   in trustees as such; or

(ii)   by virtue of section 9 of the Administration of Estates Act 1925, in the Probate Judge or the Public Trustee.

(2)   Where the interest of the landlord under a tenancy becomes vested at law and in equity in two or more persons jointly, of whom at least one was an individual, sub-paragraph (1) above shall have effect subject to the following modifications—

(a)   in paragraph (a) for the words from 'an individual' to 'occupy' there shall be substituted 'the joint landlords if, during that period none of them occupies'; and

(b) in paragraph (b) for the words 'the individual concerned' there shall be substituted 'any of the joint landlords who is an individual' and for the words 'that individual' there shall be substituted 'the joint landlords'.

18.—(1) During any period when—

(a) the interest of the landlord under the tenancy referred to in paragraph 10 above is vested in trustees as such, and

(b) that interest is held on trust for any person who or for two or more persons of whom at least one occupies as his only or principal home a dwelling-house which forms part of the building or, as the case may be, flat referred to in paragraph 10(1)(a),

the condition in paragraph 10(1)(c) shall be deemed to be fulfilled and accordingly, no part of that period shall be disregarded by virtue of paragraph 17 above.

(2) If a period during which the condition in paragraph 10(1)(c) is deemed to be fulfilled by virtue of sub-paragraph (1) above comes to an end on the death of a person who was in occupation of a dwelling-house as mentioned in paragraph (b) of that sub-paragraph, then, in determining whether that condition is at any time thereafter fulfilled, there shall be disregarded any period—

(a) which begins on the date of the death;

(b) during which the interest of the landlord remains vested as mentioned in sub-paragraph (1)(a) above; and

(c) which ends at the expiry of the period of two years beginning on the date of the death or on any earlier date on which the condition in paragraph 10(1)(c) becomes again deemed to be fulfilled by virtue of sub-paragraph (1) above.

19. In any case where—

(a) immediately before a tenancy comes to an end the condition in paragraph 10(1)(c) is deemed to be fulfilled by virtue of paragraph 18(1) above, and

(b) on the coming to an end of that tenancy the trustees in whom the interest of the landlord is vested grant a new tenancy of the same or substantially the same dwelling-house to a person (alone or jointly with others) who was the tenant or one of the tenants under the previous tenancy,

the condition in paragraph 10(1)(b) above shall be deemed to be fulfilled with respect to the new tenancy.

20.—(1) The tenancy referred to in paragraph 10 above falls within this paragraph if the interest of the landlord under the tenancy becomes vested in the personal representatives of a deceased person acting in that capacity.

(2) If the tenancy falls within this paragraph, the condition in paragraph 10(1)(c) shall be deemed to be fulfilled for any period, beginning with the date on which the interest becomes vested in the personal representatives and not exceeding two years, during which the interest of the landlord remains so vested.

21. Throughout any period which, by virtue of paragraph 17 or paragraph 18(2) above, falls to be disregarded for the purpose of determining whether the condition in paragraph 10(1)(c) is fulfilled with respect to a tenancy, no order shall be made for possession of the dwelling-house subject to that tenancy, other than an order which might be made if that tenancy were or, as the case may be, had been an assured tenancy.

22. For the purposes of paragraph 10 above, a building is a purpose-built block of flats if as constructed it contained, and it contains, two or more flats; and for this purpose 'flat' means a dwelling-house which—

(a) forms part only of a building; and

(b) is separated horizontally from another dwelling-house which forms part of the same building.

Section 7   SCHEDULE 2
GROUNDS FOR POSSESSION OF DWELLING-HOUSES LET ON ASSURED TENANCIES

PART I
GROUNDS ON WHICH COURT MUST ORDER POSSESSION

Ground 1

Not later than the beginning of the tenancy the landlord gave notice in writing to the tenant that possession might be recovered on this ground or the court is of the opinion that it is just and equitable to dispense with the requirement of notice and (in either case)—

(a) at some time before the beginning of the tenancy, the landlord who is seeking possession or, in the case of joint landlords seeking possession, at least one of them occupied the dwelling-house as his only or principal home; or

(b) the landlord who is seeking possession or, in the case of joint landlords seeking possession, at least one of them requires the dwelling-house as his or his spouse's only or principal home and neither the landlord (or, in the case of joint landlords, any one of them) nor any other person who, as landlord, derived title under the landlord who gave the notice mentioned above acquired the reversion on the tenancy for money or money's worth.

Ground 2

The dwelling-house is subject to a mortgage granted before the beginning of the tenancy and—

(a)   the mortgagee is entitled to exercise a power of sale conferred on him by the mortgage or by section 101 of the Law of Property Act 1925; and

(b)   the mortgagee requires possession of the dwelling-house for the purpose of disposing of it with vacant possession in exercise of that power; and

(c)   either notice was given as mentioned in Ground 1 above or the court is satisfied that it is just and equitable to dispense with the requirement of notice;

and for the purposes of this ground 'mortgage' includes a charge and 'mortgagee' shall be construed accordingly.

Ground 3

The tenancy is a fixed term tenancy for a term not exceeding eight months and—

(a)   not later than the beginning of the tenancy the landlord gave notice in writing to the tenant that possession might be recovered on this ground; and

(b)   at some time within the period of twelve months ending with the beginning of the tenancy, the dwelling-house was occupied under a right to occupy it for a holiday.

Ground 4

The tenancy is a fixed term tenancy for a term not exceeding twelve months and—

(a)   not later than the beginning of the tenancy the landlord gave notice in writing to the tenant that possession might be recovered on this ground; and

(b)   at some time within the period of twelve months ending with the beginning of the tenancy, the dwelling-house was let on a tenancy falling within paragraph 8 of Schedule 1 to this Act.

Ground 5

The dwelling-house is held for the purpose of being available for occupation by a minister of religion as a residence from which to perform the duties of his office and—

(a)   not later than the beginning of the tenancy the landlord gave notice in writing to the tenant that possession might be recovered on this ground; and

(b) the court is satisfied that the dwelling-house is required for occupation by a minister of religion as such a residence.

Ground 6

The landlord who is seeking possession or, if that landlord is a registered social landlord or charitable housing trust, a superior landlord intends to demolish or reconstruct the whole or a substantial part of the dwelling-house or to carry out substantial works on the dwelling-house or any part thereof or any building of which it forms part and the following conditions are fulfilled—

(a) the intended work cannot reasonably be carried out without the tenant giving up possession of the dwelling-house because—

(i) the tenant is not willing to agree to such a variation of the terms of the tenancy as would give such access and other facilities as would permit the intended work to be carried out, or

(ii) the nature of the intended work is such that no such variation is practicable, or

(iii) the tenant is not willing to accept an assured tenancy of such part only of the dwelling-house (in this sub-paragraph referred to as 'the reduced part') as would leave in the possession of his landlord so much of the dwelling-house as would be reasonable to enable the intended work to be carried out and, where appropriate, as would give such access and other facilities over the reduced part as would permit the intended work to be carried out, or

(iv) the nature of the intended work is such that such a tenancy is not practicable; and

(b) either the landlord seeking possession acquired his interest in the dwelling-house before the grant of the tenancy or that interest was in existence at the time of that grant and neither that landlord (or, in the case of joint landlords, any of them) nor any other person who, alone or jointly with others, has acquired that interest since that time acquired it for money or money's worth; and

(c) the assured tenancy on which the dwelling-house is let did not come into being by virtue of any provision of Schedule 1 to the Rent Act 1977, as amended by Part I of Schedule 4 to this act or, as the case may be, section 4 of the Rent (Agriculture) Act 1976, as amended by Part II of that Schedule.

For the purposes of this ground, if, immediately before the grant of the tenancy, the tenant to whom it was granted or, if it was granted to joint tenants, any of them was the tenant or one of the joint tenants of the dwelling-house concerned under an earlier assured tenancy or, as the case may be, under a tenancy to which Schedule 10 to the Local Government and Housing Act 1989 applied, any reference in paragraph (b) above to the grant of the tenancy is a reference to the grant of the earlier assured tenancy or, as the case may be, to the grant of the tenancy to which the said Schedule 10 applied.

For the purposes of this ground 'registered social landlord' has the same meaning as in the Housing Act 1985 (see section 5(4) and (5) of that Act) and 'charitable housing trust' means a housing trust, within the meaning of the Housing Associations Act 1985 which is a charity, within the meaning of the Charities Act 1993.

Ground 7

The tenancy is a periodic tenancy (including a statutory periodic tenancy) which has devolved under the will or intestacy of the former tenant and the proceedings for the recovery of possession are begun not later than twelve months after the death of the former tenant or, if the court so directs, after the date on which, in the opinion of the court, the landlord or, in the case of joint landlords, any one of them became aware of the former tenant's death.

For the purposes of this ground, the acceptance by the landlord of rent from a new tenant after the death of the former tenant shall not be regarded as creating a new periodic tenancy, unless the landlord agrees in writing to a change (as compared with the tenancy before the death) in the amount of the rent, the period of the tenancy, the premises which are let or any other term of the tenancy.

Ground 8

Both at the date of the service of the notice under section 8 of this Act relating to the proceedings for possession and at the date of the hearing—

(a) if rent is payable weekly or fortnightly, at least eight weeks' rent is unpaid;

(b) if rent is payable monthly, at least two months' rent is unpaid;

(c) if rent is payable quarterly, at least one quarter's rent is more than three months in arrears; and

(d) if rent is payable yearly, at least three months' rent is more than three months in arrears;

and for the purpose of this ground 'rent' means rent lawfully due from the tenant.

PART II
GROUNDS ON WHICH COURT MAY ORDER POSSESSION

Ground 9

Suitable alternative accommodation is available for the tenant or will available for him when the order for possession takes effect.

Ground 10

Some rent lawfully due from the tenant—

(a)   is unpaid on the date on which the proceedings for possession are begun; and

(b)   except where subsection (1)(b) of section 8 of this Act applies, was in arrears at the date of the service of the notice under that section relating to those proceedings.

Ground 11

Whether or not any rent is in arrears on the date on which proceedings for possession are begun, the tenant has persistently delayed paying rent which has become lawfully due.

Ground 12

Any obligation of the tenancy (other than one related to the payment of rent) has been broken or not performed.

Ground 13

The condition of the dwelling-house or any of the common parts has deteriorated owing to acts of waste by, or the neglect or default of, the tenant or any other person residing in the dwelling-house and, in the case of an act of waste by, or the neglect or default of, a person lodging with the tenant or a sub-tenant of his, the tenant has not taken such steps as he ought reasonably to have taken for the removal of the lodger or sub-tenant.

For the purposes of this ground, 'common parts' means any part of a building comprising the dwelling-house and any other premises which the tenant is entitled under the terms of the tenancy to use in common with the occupiers of other dwelling-houses in which the landlord has an estate or interest.

Ground 14

The tenant or a person residing in or visiting the dwelling-house—

(a)   has been guilty of conduct causing or likely to cause a nuisance or annoyance to a person residing, visiting or otherwise engaging in a lawful activity in the locality, or

(b)   has been convicted of—

(i)   using the dwelling-house or allowing it to be used for immoral or illegal purposes, or

(ii)   an arrestable offence committed in, or in the locality of, the dwelling-house.

Ground 14A

The dwelling-house was occupied (whether alone or with others) by a married couple or a couple living together as husband and wife and—

(a)   one or both of the partners is a tenant of the dwelling-house,

(b)   the landlord who is seeking possession is a registered social landlord or a charitable housing trust,

(c)   one partner has left the dwelling-house because of violence or threats of violence by the other towards—

(i)   that partner, or

(ii)   a member of the family of that partner who was residing with that partner immediately before the partner left, and

(d)   the court is satisfied that the partner who has left is unlikely to return.

For the purposes of this ground 'registered social landlord' and 'member of the family' have the same meaning as in Part I of the Housing Act 1996 and 'charitable housing trust' means a housing trust, within the meaning of the Housing Associations Act 1985, which is a charity within the meaning of the Charities Act 1993.

Ground 15

The condition of any furniture provided for use under the tenancy has, in the opinion of the court, deteriorated owing to ill-treatment by the tenant or any other person residing in the dwelling-house and, in the case of ill-treatment by a person lodging with the tenant or by a sub-tenant of his, the tenant has not taken such steps as he ought reasonably to have taken for the removal of the lodger or sub-tenant.

Ground 16

The dwelling-house was let to the tenant in consequence of his employment by the landlord seeking possession or a previous landlord under the tenancy and the tenant has ceased to be in that employment.

For the purposes of this ground, at a time when the landlord is or was the Secretary of State, employment by a health services body, as defined in section 60(7) of the National Health Service and Community Care Act 1990, shall be regarded as employment by the Secretary of State.

Ground 17

The tenant is the person, or one of the persons, to whom the tenancy is granted and the landlord was induced to grant the tenancy by a false statement made knowingly or recklessly by—

(a) the tenant, or

(b) a person acting at the tenant's instigation.

PART III
SUITABLE ALTERNATIVE ACCOMMODATION

1. For the purposes of Ground 9 above, a certificate of the local housing authority for the district in which the dwelling-house in question is situated, certifying that the authority will provide suitable alternative accommodation for the tenant by a date specified in the certificate, shall be conclusive evidence that suitable alternative accommodation will be available for him by that date.

2. Where no such certificate as is mentioned in paragraph 1 above is produced to the court, accommodation shall be deemed to be suitable for the purposes of Ground 9 above if it consists of either—

(a) premises which are to be let as a separate dwelling such that they will then be let on an assured tenancy, other than—

(i) a tenancy in respect of which notice is given not later than the beginning of the tenancy that possession might be recovered on any of Grounds 1 to 5 above, or

(ii) an assured shorthold tenancy, within the meaning of Chapter II of Part I of this Act, or

(b) premises to be let as a separate dwelling on terms which will, in the opinion of the court, afford to the tenant security of tenure reasonably equivalent to the security afforded by Chapter 1 of Part I of this Act in the case of an assured tenancy of a kind mentioned in sub-paragraph (a) above,

and, in the opinion of the court, the accommodation fulfils the relevant conditions as defined in paragraph 3 below.

3.—(1) For the purposes of paragraph 2 above, the relevant conditions are that the accommodation is reasonably suitable to the needs of the tenant and his family as regards proximity to place of work, and either—

(a) similar as regards rental and extent to the accommodation afforded by dwelling-houses provided in the neighbourhood by any local housing authority for persons whose needs as regards extent are, in the opinion of the court, similar to those of the tenant and of his family; or

(b) reasonably suitable to the means of the tenant and to the needs of the tenant and his family as regards extent and character; and

that if any furniture was provided for use under the assured tenancy in question, furniture is provided for use in the accommodation which is either similar to that so provided or is reasonably suitable to the needs of the tenant and his family.

(2)   For the purposes of sub-paragraph (1)(a) above, a certificate of a local housing authority stating—

(a)   the extent of the accommodation afforded by dwelling-houses provided by the authority to meet the needs of tenants with families of such number as may be specified in the certificate, and

(b)   the amount of the rent charged by the authority for dwelling-houses affording accommodation of that extent,

shall be conclusive evidence of the facts so stated.

4.   Accommodation shall not be deemed to be suitable to the needs of the tenant and his family if the result of their occupation of the accommodation would be that it would be an overcrowded dwelling-house for the purposes of Part X of the Housing Act 1985.

5.   Any document purporting to be a certificate of a local housing authority named therein issued for the purposes of this Part of this Schedule and to be signed by the proper officer of that authority shall be received in evidence and, unless the contrary is shown, shall be deemed to be such a certificate without further proof.

6.   In this Part of this Schedule 'local housing authority' and 'district', in relation to such an authority, have the same meaning as in the Housing Act 1985.

PART IV

NOTICES RELATING TO RECOVERY OF POSSESSION

7.   Any reference in Grounds 1 to 5 in Part I of this Schedule or in the following provisions of this Part to the landlord giving a notice in writing to the tenant is, in the case of joint landlords, a reference to at least one of the joint landlords giving such a notice.

8.—(1)   If, not later than the beginning of a tenancy (in this paragraph referred to as 'the earlier tenancy'), the landlord gives such a notice in writing to the tenant as is mentioned in any of Grounds 1 to 5 in Part I of this Schedule, then, for the purposes of the ground in question and any further application of this paragraph, that notice shall also have effect as if it has been given immediately before the beginning of any later tenancy falling within sub-paragraph (2) below.

(2)   Subject to sub-paragraph (3) below, sub-paragraph (1) above applies to a later tenancy—

(a)   which takes effect immediately on the coming to an end of the earlier tenancy; and

(b)   which is granted (or deemed to be granted) to the person who was the tenant under the earlier tenancy immediately before it came to an end; and

(c)   which is of substantially the same dwelling-house as the earlier tenancy.

(3)   Sub-paragraph (1) above does not apply in relation to a later tenancy if, not later than the beginning of the tenancy, the landlord gave notice in writing to the tenant that the tenancy is not one in respect of which possession can be recovered on the ground in question.

9.   Where paragraph 8(1) above has effect in relation to a notice given as mentioned in Ground 1 in Part I of this Schedule, the reference in paragraph (b) of that ground to the reversion on the tenancy is a reference to the reversion on the earlier tenancy and on any later tenancy falling within paragraph 8(2) above.

10.   Where paragraph 8(1) above has effect in relation to a notice given as mentioned in Ground 3 or Ground 4 in Part I of this Schedule, any second or subsequent tenancy in relation to which the notice has effect shall be treated for the purpose of that ground as beginning at the beginning of the tenancy in respect of which the notice was actually given.

11.   Any reference in Grounds 1 to 5 in Part I of this Schedule to a notice being given not later than the beginning of the tenancy is a reference to its being given not later than the day on which the tenancy is entered into and, accordingly, section 45(2) of this Act shall not apply to any such reference.

SCHEDULE 2A
ASSURED TENANCIES: NON-SHORTHOLDS

Tenancies excluded by notice

1.—(1)   An assured tenancy in respect of which a notice is served as mentioned in sub-paragraph (2) below.

(2)   The notice referred to in sub-paragraph (1) above is one which—

(a)   is served before the assured tenancy is entered into,

(b)   is served by the person who is to be the landlord under the assured tenancy on the person who is to be the tenant under that tenancy, and

(c)   states that the assured tenancy to which it relates is not to be an assured shorthold tenancy.

2.—(1)   An assured tenancy in respect of which a notice is served as mentioned in sub-paragraph (2) below.

(2)   The notice referred to in sub-paragraph (1) above is one which—

(a)   is served after the assured tenancy has been entered into,

(b)   is served by the landlord under the assured tenancy on the tenant under that tenancy, and

(c)   states that the assured tenancy to which it relates is no longer an assured shorthold tenancy.

Tenancies containing exclusionary provision

3.   An assured tenancy which contains a provision to the effect that the tenancy is not an assured shorthold tenancy.

Tenancies under section 39

4.   An assured tenancy arising by virtue of section 39 above, other than one to which sub-section (7) of that section applies.

Former secure tenancies

5.   An assured tenancy which became an assured tenancy on ceasing to be a secure tenancy.

Tenancies under Schedule 10 to the Local Government and Housing Act 1989

6.   An assured tenancy arising by virtue of Schedule 10 to the Local Government and Housing Act 1989 (security of tenure on ending of long residential tenancies).

Tenancies replacing non-shortholds

7.—(1)   An assured tenancy which—

(a)   is granted to a person (alone or jointly with others) who, immediately before the tenancy was granted, was the tenant (or, in the case of joint tenants, one of the tenants) under an assured tenancy other than a shorthold tenancy ('the old tenancy'),

(b)   is granted (alone or jointly with others) by a person who was at that time the landlord (or one of the joint landlords) under the old tenancy, and

(c)   is not one in respect of which a notice is served as mentioned in sub-paragraph (2) below.

(2)   The notice referred to in sub-paragraph (1)(c) above is one which—

(a)   is in such form as may be prescribed,

(b)   is served before the assured tenancy is entered into,

(c)   is served by the person who is to be the tenant under the assured tenancy on the person who is to be the landlord under that tenancy (or, in the case of joint landlords, on at least one of the persons who are to be joint landlords), and

(d)   states that the assured tenancy to which it relates is to be a shorthold tenancy.

8.   An assured tenancy which comes into being by virtue of section 5 above on the coming to an end of an assured tenancy which is not a shorthold tenancy.

Assured agricultural occupancies

9.—(1)   An assured tenancy—

(a)   in the case of which the agricultural worker condition is, by virtue of any provision of Schedule 3 to this Act, for the time being fulfilled with respect to the dwelling-house subject to the tenancy, and

(b)   which does not fall within sub-paragraph (2) or (4) below.

(2)   An assured tenancy falls within this sub-paragraph if—

(a)   before it is entered into, a notice—

(i)   in such form as may be prescribed, and

(ii)   stating that the tenancy is to be a shorthold tenancy,

is served by the person who is to be the landlord under the tenancy on the person who is to be the tenant under it, and

(b)   it is not an excepted tenancy.

(3)   For the purposes of sub-paragraph (2)(b) above, an assured tenancy is an excepted tenancy if—

(a)   the person to whom it is granted or, as the case may be, at least one of the persons to whom it is granted was, immediately before it is granted, a tenant or licensee under an assured agricultural occupancy, and

(b)   the person by whom it is granted or, as the case may be, at least one of the persons by whom it is granted was, immediately before it is granted, a landlord or licensor under the assured agricultural occupancy referred to in paragraph (a) above.

(4)   An assured tenancy falls within this sub-paragraph if it comes into being by virtue of section 5 above on the coming to an end of a tenancy falling within sub-paragraph (2) above.

Section 24   SCHEDULE 3
                AGRICULTURAL WORKER CONDITIONS

Interpretation

1.—(1)   In this Schedule—

'the 1976 Act' means the Rent (Agriculture) Act 1976;

'agriculture' has the same meaning as in the 1976 Act; and

'relevant tenancy or licence' means a tenancy or licence of a description specified in section 24(2) of this Act.

(2)   In relation to a relevant tenancy or licence—

(a)   'the occupier' means the tenant or licensee; and

(b)   'the dwelling-house' means the dwelling-house which is let under the tenancy or, as the case may be, is occupied under the licence.

(3)   Schedule 3 to the 1976 Act applies for the purposes of this Schedule as it applies for the purposes of that Act and, accordingly, shall have effect to determine—

(a) whether a person is a qualifying worker;

(b) whether a person is incapable of whole-time work in agriculture, or work in agriculture as a permit worker, in consequence of a qualifying injury or disease; and

(c) whether a dwelling-house is in qualifying ownership.

The conditions

2. The agricultural worker condition is fulfilled with respect to a dwelling-house subject to a relevant tenancy or licence if—

(a) the dwelling-house is or has been in qualifying ownership at any time during the subsistence of the tenancy or licence (whether or not it was at that time a relevant tenancy or licence); and

(b) the occupier or, where there are joint occupiers, at least one of them—

(i) is a qualifying worker or has been a qualifying worker at any time during the subsistence of the tenancy or licence (whether or not it was at that time a relevant tenancy or licence); or

(ii) is incapable of whole-time work in agriculture or work in agriculture as a permit worker in consequence of a qualifying injury or disease.

3.—(1) The agricultural worker condition is also fulfilled with respect to a dwelling-house subject to a relevant tenancy or licence if—

(a) that condition was previously fulfilled with respect to the dwelling-house but the person who was then the occupier or, as the case may be, a person who was one of the joint occupiers (whether or not under the same relevant tenancy or licence) has died; and

(b) that condition ceased to be fulfilled on the death of the occupier referred to in paragraph (a) above (hereinafter referred to as 'the previous qualifying occupier'); and

(c) the occupier is either—

(i) the qualifying widow or widower of the previous qualifying occupier; or

(ii) the qualifying member of the previous qualifying occupier's family.

(2) For the purposes of sub-paragraph (1)(c)(i) above and sub-paragraph (3) below a widow or widower of the previous qualifying occupier of the dwelling-houses is a qualifying widow or widower if she or he was residing in the dwelling-house immediately before the previous qualifying occupier's death.

(3) Subject to sub-paragraph (4) below, for the purposes of sub-paragraph (1)(c)(ii) above, a member of the family of the previous qualifying occupier of the dwelling-house is the qualifying member of the family if—

(a) on the death of the previous qualifying occupier there was no qualifying widow or widower; and

(b) the member of the family was residing in the dwelling-house with the previous qualifying occupier at the time of, and for the period of two years before, his death.

(4) Not more than one member of the previous qualifying occupier's family may be taken into account in determining whether the agricultural worker condition is fulfilled by virtue of this paragraph and, accordingly, if there is more than one member of the family—

(a) who is the occupier in relation to the relevant tenancy or licence, and

(b) who, apart from this sub-paragraph, would be the qualifying member of the family by virtue of sub-paragraph (3) above,

only that one of those members of the family who may be decided by agreement or, in default of agreement by the county court, shall be the qualifying member.

(5) For the purposes of the preceding provisions of this paragraph a person who, immediately before the previous qualifying occupier's death, was living with the previous occupier as his or her wife or husband shall be treated as the widow or widower of the previous occupier.

(6) If, immediately before the death of the previous qualifying occupier, there is, by virtue of sub-paragraph (5) above, more than one person who falls within sub-paragraph (1)(c)(i) above, such one of them as may be decided by agreement or, in default of agreement, by the county court shall be treated as the qualifying widow or widower for the purposes of this paragraph.

4. The agricultural worker condition is also fulfilled with respect to a dwelling-house subject to a relevant tenancy or licence if—

(a) the tenancy or licence was granted to the occupier or, where there are joint occupiers, at least one of them in consideration of his giving up possession of another dwelling-house of which he was then occupier (or one of joint occupiers) under another relevant tenancy or licence; and

(b) immediately before he gave up possession of that dwelling-house, as a result of his occupation the agricultural worker condition was fulfilled with respect to it (whether by virtue of paragraph 2 or paragraph 3 above or this paragraph);

and the reference in paragraph (a) above to a tenancy or licence granted to the occupier or at least one of joint occupiers includes a reference to the case where the grant is to him together with one or more other persons.

5.—(1) This paragraph applies where—

(a) by virtue of any of paragraphs 2 to 4 above, the agricultural worker condition is fulfilled with respect to a dwelling-house subject to a relevant tenancy or licence (in this paragraph referred to as 'the earlier tenancy or licence'); and

(b) another relevant tenancy or licence of the same dwelling-house (in this paragraph referred to as 'the later tenancy or licence') is granted to the person who, immediately before the grant, was the occupier or one of the joint occupiers under the earlier tenancy or licence and as a result of whose occupation the agricultural worker condition was fulfilled as mentioned in paragraph (a) above;

and the reference in paragraph (b) above to the grant of the later tenancy or licence to the person mentioned in that paragraph includes a reference to the case where the grant is to that person together with one or more other persons.

(2) So long as a person as a result of whose occupation of the dwelling-house the agricultural worker condition was fulfilled with respect to the earlier tenancy or licence continues to be the occupier, or one of the joint occupiers, under the later tenancy or licence, the agricultural worker condition shall be fulfilled with respect to the dwelling-house.

(3) For the purposes of paragraphs 3 and 4 above and any further application of this paragraph, where sub-paragraph (2) above has effect, the agricultural worker condition shall be treated as fulfilled so far as concerns the later tenancy or licence by virtue of the same paragraph of this Schedule as was applicable (or, as the case may be, last applicable) in the case of the earlier tenancy or licence.

LOCAL GOVERNMENT AND HOUSING ACT 1989

186. Security of tenure on ending of long residential tenancies

(1) Schedule 10 to this Act shall have effect (in place of Part I of the Landlord and Tenant Act 1954) to confer security of tenure on certain tenants under long tenancies and, in particular, to establish assured periodic tenancies when such long tenancies come to an end.

(2) Schedule 10 to this Act applies, and section 1 of the Landlord and Tenant Act 1954 does not apply, to a tenancy of a dwelling-house—

(a) which is a long tenancy at a low rent, as defined in Schedule 10 to this Act; and

(b) which is entered into on or after the day appointed for the coming into force of this section, otherwise than in pursuance of a contract made before that day.

(3) If a tenancy—

(a) is in existence on 15th January 1999, and

(b) does not fall within subsection (2) above, and

(c)   immediately before that date was, or was deemed to be, a long tenancy at a low rent for the purposes of Part I of the Landlord and Tenant Act 1954,

then, on and after that date (and so far as concerns any notice specifying a date of termination on or after that date and any steps taken in consequence thereof), section 1 of that Act shall cease to apply to it and Schedule 10 to this Act shall apply to it unless, before that date, the landlord has served a notice under section 4 of that Act specifying a date of termination which is earlier than that date.

(4)   The provisions of Schedule 10 to this Act have effect notwithstanding any agreement to the contrary, but nothing in this subsection or that Schedule shall be construed as preventing the surrender of a tenancy.

(5)   Section 18 of the Landlord and Tenant Act 1954 (duty of tenants of residential property to give information to landlords or superior landlords) shall apply in relation to property comprised in a long tenancy at a low rent, within the meaning of Schedule 10 to this Act, as it applies to property comprised in a long tenancy at a low rent within the meaning of Part I of that Act, except that the reference in that section to subsection (1) of section 3 of that Act shall be construed as a reference to sub-paragraph (1) of paragraph 3 of Schedule 10 to this Act.

(6)   Where, by virtue of subsection (3) above, Schedule 10 to this Act applies to a tenancy which is not a long tenancy at a low rent as defined in that Schedule, it shall be deemed to be such a tenancy for the purposes of that Schedule.

Section 186.   SCHEDULE 10

SECURITY OF TENURE ON ENDING OF LONG
RESIDENTIAL TENANCIES

Preliminary

1.—(1)   This Schedule applies to a long tenancy of a dwelling-house at a low rent as respects which for the time being the following condition (in this Schedule referred to as 'the qualifying condition') is fulfilled, that is to say, that the circumstances (as respects the property let under the tenancy, the use of that property and all other relevant matters) are such that, if the tenancy were not at a low rent, it would at that time be an assured tenancy within the meaning of Part I of the Housing Act 1988.

(2)   For the purpose only of determining whether the qualifying condition is fulfilled with respect to a tenancy, Schedule 1 to the Housing Act 1988 (tenancies which cannot be assured tenancies) shall have effect with the omission of paragraph 1 (which excludes tenancies entered into before, or pursuant to contracts made before, the coming into force of Part I of that Act).

(2A)   For the purpose only of determining whether the qualifying condition is fulfilled with respect to a tenancy which is entered into on or after 1st April 1990 (otherwise than, where the dwelling-house has a rateable value on 31st March 1990, in pursuance of a contract made before 1st April 1990), for paragraph 2(1)(b) and (2) of Schedule 1 to the Housing Act 1988 there shall be substituted—

'(b)   where (on the date the contract for the grant of the tenancy was made or, if there was no such contract, on the date the tenancy was entered into) R exceeded £25,000 under the formula—

$$R = \frac{P \times I}{1 - (1 + I)^{-T}}$$

where—
P is the premium payable as a condition of the grant of the tenancy (and includes a payment of money's worth) or, where no premium is so payable, zero,
I is 0.06,
T is the term, expressed in years, granted by the tenancy (disregarding any right to terminate the tenancy before the end of the term or to extend the tenancy).'

(3)   At any time within the period of twelve months ending on the day preceding the term date, application may be made to the court as respects any long tenancy of a dwelling-house at a low rent, not being at the time of the application a tenancy as respects which the qualifying condition is fulfilled, for an order declaring that the tenancy is not to be treated as a tenancy to which this Schedule applies.

(4)   Where an application is made under sub-paragraph (3) above—

(a)   the court, if satisfied that the tenancy is not likely immediately before the term date to be a tenancy to which this Schedule applies but not otherwise, shall make the order; and

(b)   if the court makes the order, then, notwithstanding anything in sub-paragraph (1) above the tenancy shall not thereafter be treated as a tenancy to which this Schedule applies.

(5)   A tenancy to which this Schedule applies is hereinafter referred to as a long residential tenancy.

(6)   Anything authorised or required to be done under the following provisions of this Schedule in relation to a long residential tenancy shall, if done before the term date in relation to a long tenancy of a dwelling-house at a low rent, not be treated as invalid by reason only that at the time at which it was done the qualifying condition was not fulfilled as respects the tenancy.

(7)   In determining for the purposes of any provision of this Schedule whether the property let under a tenancy was let as a separate dwelling,

the nature of the property at the time of the creation of the tenancy shall be deemed to have been the same as its nature at the time in relation to which the question arises, and the purpose for which it was let under the tenancy shall be deemed to have been the same as the purpose for which it is or was used at the last-mentioned time.

(8) The Secretary of State may by order replace the number in the definition of 'I' in sub-paragraph (2A) above and any amount referred to in that sub-paragraph and paragraph 2(4)(b) below by such number or amount as is specified in the order; and such an order shall be made by statutory instrument which shall be subject to annulment in pursuance of a resolution of either House of Parliament.

2.—(1) This paragraph has effect for the interpretation of certain expressions used in this Schedule.

(2) Except where the context otherwise requires, expressions to which a meaning is assigned for the purposes of the 1988 Act or Part I of that Act have the same meaning in this Schedule.

(3) 'Long tenancy' means a tenancy granted for a term of years certain exceeding 21 years, whether or not subsequently extended by act of the parties or by any enactment, but excluding any tenancy which is, or may become, terminable before the end of the term by notice given to the tenant.

(4) A tenancy is 'at a low rent' if under the tenancy—

(a) no rent is payable,

(b) where the tenancy is entered into on or after 1st April 1990 (otherwise than, where the dwelling-house had a rateable value on 31st March 1990, in pursuance of a contract made before 1st April 1990), the maximum rent payable at any time is payable at a rate of—

(i) £1,000 or less a year if the dwelling-house is in Greater London and,

(ii) £250 or less a year if the dwelling-house is elsewhere, or,

(c) where the tenancy was entered into before 1st April 1990 or (where the dwelling-house had a rateable value on 31st March 1990) is entered into on or after 1st April 1990 in pursuance of a contract made before that date, and the maximum rent payable at any time under the tenancy is less than two-thirds of the rateable value of the dwelling-house on 31st March 1990.

(5) Paragraph 2(2) of Schedule 1 to the 1988 Act applies to determine whether the rent under a tenancy falls within sub-paragraph (4) above and Part II of that Schedule applies to determine the rateable value of a dwelling-house for the purposes of that sub-paragraph.

(6) 'Long residential tenancy' and 'qualifying condition' have the meaning assigned by paragraph 1 above and the following expressions shall be construed as follows—

'the 1954 Act' means the Landlord and Tenant Act 1954;

'the 1988 Act' means the Housing Act 1988;

'assured periodic tenancy' shall be construed in accordance with paragraph 9(4) below;

'the date of termination' has the meaning assigned by paragraph 4(4) below;

'disputed terms' shall be construed in accordance with paragraph 11(1)(a) below;

'election by the tenant to retain possession' shall be construed in accordance with paragraph 4(7) below;

'former 1954 Act tenancy' means a tenancy to which, by virtue of section 186(3) of this Act, this Schedule applies on and after 15th January 1999;

'the implied terms' shall be construed in accordance with paragraph 4(5)(a) below;

'landlord' shall be construed in accordance with paragraph 19(1) below;

'landlord's notice' means a notice under sub-paragraph (1) of paragraph 4 below and such a notice is—

(a) a 'landlord's notice proposing an assured tenancy' if it contains such proposals as are mentioned in sub-paragraph (5)(a) of that paragraph; and

(b) a 'landlord's notice to resume possession' if it contains such proposals as are referred to in sub-paragraph (5)(b) of that paragraph;

'specified date of termination', in relation to a tenancy in respect of which a landlord's notice is served, means the date specified in the notice as mentioned in paragraph 4(1)(a) below;

'tenant's notice' shall be construed in accordance with paragraph 10(1)(a) below;

'term date', in relation to a tenancy granted for a term of years certain, means the date of expiry of that term; and

'the terms of the tenancy specified in the landlord's notice' shall be construed in accordance with paragraph 4(6) below; and

'undisputed terms' shall be construed in accordance with paragraph 11(2) below.

Continuation of long residential tenancies

3.—(1) A tenancy which, immediately before the term date, is a long residential tenancy shall not come to an end on that date except by being terminated under the provisions of this Schedule, and, if not then so terminated, shall subject to those provisions continue until so terminated and, while continuing by virtue of this paragraph, shall be deemed to be a long residential tenancy (notwithstanding any change in circumstances).

(2)   Sub-paragraph (1) above does not apply in the case of a former 1954 Act tenancy the term date of which falls before 15th January 1999 but if, in the case of such a tenancy,—

(a)   the tenancy is continuing immediately before that date by virtue of section 3 of the 1954 Act, and

(b)   on that date the qualifying condition (as defined in paragraph 1(1) above) is fulfilled, then, subject to the provisions of this Schedule, the tenancy shall continue until terminated under those provisions and, while continuing by virtue of this paragraph, shall be deemed to be a long residential tenancy (notwithstanding any change in circumstances).

(3)   Where by virtue of this paragraph a tenancy continues after the term date, the tenancy shall continue at the same rent and in other respects on the same terms as before the term date.

Termination of tenancy by the landlord

4.—(1)   Subject to sub-paragraph (2) below and the provisions of this Schedule as to the annulment of notices in certain cases, the landlord may terminate a long residential tenancy by a notice in the prescribed form served on the tenant—

(a)   specifying the date at which the tenancy is to come to an end, being either the term date or a later date; and

(b)   so served not more than twelve nor less than six months before the date so specified.

(2)   In any case where—

(a)   a landlord's notice has been served, and

(b)   an application has been made to the court or a rent assessment committee under the following provisions of this Schedule other than paragraph 6, and

(c)   apart from this paragraph, the effect of the notice would be to terminate the tenancy before the expiry of the period of three months beginning with the date on which the application is finally disposed of, the effect of the notice shall be to terminate the tenancy at the expiry of the said period of three months and not at any other time.

(3)   The reference in sub-paragraph (2)(c) above to the date on which the application is finally disposed of shall be construed as a reference to the earliest date by which the proceedings on the application (including any proceedings on or in consequence of an appeal) have been determined and any time for appealing or further appealing has expired, except that if the application is withdrawn or any appeal is abandoned the reference shall be construed as a reference to the date of withdrawal or abandonment.

(4) In this Schedule 'the date of termination', in relation to a tenancy in respect of which a landlord's notice is served, means,—

(a) where the tenancy is continued as mentioned in sub-paragraph (2) above, the last day of the period of three months referred to in that sub-paragraph; and

(b) in any other case, the specified date of termination.

(5) A landlord's notice shall not have effect unless—

(a) it proposes an assured monthly periodic tenancy of the dwelling-house and a rent for that tenancy (such that it would not be a tenancy at a low rent) and, subject to sub-paragraph (6) below, states that the other terms of the tenancy shall be the same as those of the long residential tenancy immediately before it is terminated (in this Schedule referred to as 'the implied terms'); or

(b) it gives notice that, if the tenant is not willing to give up possession at the date of termination of the property let under the tenancy, the landlord proposes to apply to the court, on one or more of the grounds specified in paragraph 5(1) below, for the possession of the property let under the tenancy and states the ground or grounds on which he proposes to apply.

(6) In the landlord's notice proposing an assured tenancy the landlord may propose terms of the tenancy referred to in sub-paragraph (5)(a) above different from the implied terms; and any reference in the following provisions of this Schedule to the terms of the tenancy specified in the landlord's notice is a reference to the implied terms or, if the implied terms are varied by virtue of this sub-paragraph, to the implied terms as so varied.

(7) A landlord's notice shall invite the tenant, within the period of two months beginning on the date on which the notice was served, to notify the landlord in writing whether,—

(a) in the case of a landlord's notice proposing an assured tenancy, the tenant wishes to remain in possession; and

(b) in the case of a landlord's notice to resume possession, the tenant is willing to give up possession as mentioned in sub-paragraph (5)(b) above;

and references in this Schedule to an election by the tenant to retain possession are references to his notifying the landlord under this sub-paragraph that he wishes to remain in possession or, as the case may be, that he is not willing to give up possession.

5.—(1) Subject to the following provisions of this paragraph, the grounds mentioned in paragraph 4(5)(b) above are—

(a) Ground 6 in, and those in Part II of, Schedule 2 to the 1988 Act, other than Ground 16;

(b) the ground that, for the purposes of redevelopment after the termination of the tenancy, the landlord proposes to demolish or reconstruct the whole or a substantial part of the premises; and

(c) the ground that the premises or part of them are reasonably required by the landlord for occupation as a residence for himself or any son or daughter of his over eighteen years of age or his or his spouse's father or mother and, if the landlord is not the immediate landlord, that he will be at the specified date of termination.

(2) Ground 6 in Schedule 2 to the 1988 Act may not be specified in a landlord's notice to resume possession if the tenancy is a former 1954 Act tenancy; and in the application of that Ground in accordance with sub-paragraph (1) above in any other case, paragraph (c) shall be omitted.

(3) In its application in accordance with sub-paragraph (1) above, Ground 10 in Schedule 2 to the 1988 Act shall have effect as if, in paragraph (b)—

(a) the words 'except where subsection (1)(b) of section 8 of this Act applies' were omitted; and

(b) for the words 'notice under that section relating to those proceedings' there were substituted 'landlord's notice to resume possession (within the meaning of Schedule 10 to the Local Government and Housing Act 1989)'.

(4) The ground mentioned in sub-paragraph (1)(b) above may not be specified in a landlord's notice to resume possession unless the landlord is a body to which section 28 of the Leasehold Reform Act 1967 applies and the premises are required for relevant development within the meaning of that section; and on any application by such a body under paragraph 13 below for possession on that ground, a certificate given by a Minister of the Crown as provided by subsection (1) of that section shall be conclusive evidence that the premises are so required.

(5) The ground mentioned in sub-paragraph (1)(c) above may not be specified in a landlord's notice to resume possession if the interest of the landlord, or an interest which is merged in that interest and but for the merger would be the interest of the landlord, was purchased or created after 18th February 1966.

Interim rent

6.—(1) On the date of service of a landlord's notice proposing an assured tenancy, or at any time between that date and the date of termination, the landlord may serve a notice on the tenant in the prescribed form proposing an interim monthly rent to take effect from a date specified in the notice, being not earlier than the specified date of termination, and to continue while the tenancy is continued by virtue of the preceding provisions of this Schedule.

(2)   Where a notice has been served under sub-paragraph (1) above,—

(a)   within the period of two months beginning on the date of service, the tenant may refer the interim monthly rent proposed in the notice to a rent assessment committee; and

(b)   if the notice is not so referred, then, with effect from the date specified in the notice or, if it is later, the expiry of the period mentioned in paragraph (a) above, the interim monthly rent proposed in the notice shall be the rent under the tenancy.

(3)   Where, under sub-paragraph (2) above, the rent specified in a landlord's notice is referred to a rent assessment committee, the committee shall determine the monthly rent at which, subject to sub-paragraph (4) below, the committee consider that the premises let under the tenancy might reasonably be expected to be let on the open market by a willing landlord under a monthly periodic tenancy—

(a)   which begins on the day following the specified date of termination;

(b)   under which the other terms are the same as those of the existing tenancy at the date on which was given the landlord's notice proposing an assured tenancy; and

(c)   which affords the tenant security of tenure equivalent to that afforded by Chapter I of Part I of the 1988 Act in the case of an assured tenancy (other than an assured shorthold tenancy) in respect of which possession may not be recovered under any of Grounds 1 to 5 in Part I of Schedule 2 to that Act.

(4)   Subsections (2), (3A), (4) and (5) of section 14 of the 1988 Act shall apply in relation to a determination of rent under sub-paragraph (3) above as they apply in relation to a determination under that section subject to the modifications in sub-paragraph (5) below; and in this paragraph 'rent' shall be construed in accordance with subsection (4) of that section.

(5)   The modifications of section 14 of the 1988 Act referred to in sub-paragraph (4) above are that in subsection (2), the reference in paragraph (b) to a relevant improvement being carried out shall be construed as a reference to an improvement being carried out during the long residential tenancy and the reference in paragraph (c) to a failure to comply with any term of the tenancy shall be construed as a reference to a failure to comply with any term of the long residential tenancy.

(6)   Where a reference has been made to a rent assessment committee under sub-paragraph (2) above, then, the rent determined by the committee (subject, in a case where section 14(5) of the 1988 Act applies, to the addition of the appropriate amount in respect of rates) shall be the rent

under the tenancy with effect from the date specified in the notice served under sub-paragraph 910 above or, if it is later, the expiry of the period mentioned in paragraph (1) of sub-paragraph (2) above.

7.—(1) Nothing in paragraph 6 above affects the right of the landlord and the tenant to agree the interim monthly rent which is to have effect while the tenancy is continued by virtue of the preceding provisions of this Schedule and the date from which that rent is to take effect; and, in such a case,—

(a) notwithstanding the provisions of paragraph 6 above, that rent shall be the rent under the tenancy with effect from that date; and

(b) no steps or, as the case may be, no further steps may be taken by the landlord or the tenant under the provisions of that paragraph.

(2) Nothing in paragraph 6 above requires a rent assessment committee to continue with a determination under sub-paragraph (3) of that paragraph—

(a) if the tenant gives notice in writing that he no longer requires such a determination; or

(b) if the long residential tenancy has come to an end on or before the specified date of termination.

(3) Notwithstanding that a tenancy in respect of which an interim monthly rent has effect in accordance with paragraph 6 above or this paragraph is no longer at a low rent, it shall continue to be regarded as a tenancy at a low rent and, accordingly, shall continue to be a long residential tenancy.

Termination of tenancy by the tenant

8.—(1) A long residential tenancy may be brought to an end at the term date by not less than one month's notice in writing given by the tenant to his immediate landlord.

(2) A tenancy which is continuing after the term date by virtue of paragraph 3 above may be brought to an end at any time by not less than one month's notice in writing given by the tenant to his immediate landlord, whether the notice is given before or after the term date of the tenancy.

(3) The fact that the landlord has served a landlord's notice or that there has been an election by the tenant to retain possession shall not prevent the tenant from giving notice under this paragraph terminating the tenancy at a date earlier than the specified date of termination.

The assured periodic tenancy

9.—(1) Where a long residential tenancy (in this paragraph referred to as 'the former tenancy') is terminated by a landlord's notice proposing an assured tenancy, then, subject to sub-paragraph (3) below, the tenant shall be entitled to remain in possession of the dwelling-house and his right to possession shall depend upon an assured periodic tenancy arising by virtue of this paragraph.

(2) The assured periodic tenancy referred to in sub-paragraph (1) above is one—

(a) taking effect in possession on the day following the date of termination;

(b) deemed to have been granted by the person who was the landlord under the former tenancy on the date of termination to the person who was then the tenant under that tenancy;

(c) under which the premises let are the dwelling-house;

(d) under which the periods of the tenancy, and the intervals at which rent is to be paid, are monthly beginning on the day following the date of termination;

(e) under which the rent is determined in accordance with paragraphs 10 to 12 below; and

(f) under which the other terms are determined in accordance with paragraphs 10 to 12 below.

(3) If, at the end of the period of two months beginning on the date of service of the landlord's notice, the qualifying condition was not fulfilled as respects the tenancy, the tenant shall not be entitled to remain in possession as mentioned in sub-paragraph (1) above unless there has been an election by the tenant to retain possession; and if, at the specified date of termination, the qualifying condition is not fulfilled as respects the tenancy, then, notwithstanding that there has been such an election, the tenant shall not be entitled to remain in possession as mentioned in that sub-paragraph.

(4) Any reference in the following provisions of this Schedule to an assured periodic tenancy is a reference to an assured periodic tenancy arising by virtue of this paragraph.

Initial rent under and terms of assured periodic tenancy

10.—(1) Where a landlord's notice proposing an assured tenancy has been served on the tenant,—

(a) within the period of two months beginning on the date of service of the notice, the tenant may serve on the landlord a notice in the prescribed form proposing either or both of the following, that is to say,—

(i) a rent for the assured periodic tenancy different from that proposed in the landlord's notice; and

(ii) terms of the tenancy different from those specified in the landlord's notice, and such a notice is in this Schedule referred to as a 'tenant's notice'; and

(b)   if a tenant's notice is not so served, then, with effect from the date on which the assured periodic tenancy takes effect in possession,—

(i)   the rent proposed in the landlord's notice shall be the rent under the tenancy; and

(ii)   the terms of the tenancy specified in the landlord's notice shall be terms of the tenancy.

(2)   Where a tenant's notice has been served on the landlord under sub-paragraph (1) above—

(a)   within the period of two months beginning on the date of service of the notice, the landlord may by an application in the prescribed form refer the notice to a rent assessment committee; and

(b)   if the notice is not so referred, then, with effect from the date on which the assured periodic tenancy takes effect in possession,—

(i)   the rent (if any) proposed in the tenant's notice, or, if no rent is so proposed, the rent proposed in the landlord's notice, shall be the rent under the tenancy; and

(ii)   the other terms of the tenancy (if any) proposed in the tenant's notice and, in so far as they do not conflict with the terms so proposed, the terms specified in the landlord's notice shall be terms of the tenancy.

11.—(1)   Where, under sub-paragraph (2) of paragraph 10 above, a tenant's notice is referred to a rent assessment committee, the committee, having regard only to the contents of the landlord's notice and the tenant's notice, shall decide—

(a)   whether there is any dispute as to the terms (other than those relating to the amount of the rent) of the assured periodic tenancy (in this Schedule referred to as 'disputed terms') and, if so, what the disputed terms are; and

(b)   whether there is any dispute as to rent under the tenancy;
and where the committee decide that there are disputed terms and that there is a dispute as to the rent under the tenancy, they shall make a determination under sub-paragraph (3) below before they make a determination under sub-paragraph (5) below.

(2)   Where, under paragraph 10(2) above, a tenant's notice is referred to a rent assessment committee, any reference in this Schedule to the undisputed terms is a reference to those terms (if any) which—

(a)   are proposed in the landlord's notice or the tenant's notice; and

(b)   do not relate to the amount of the rent; and

(c)   are not disputed terms.

(3)   If the rent assessment committee decide that there are disputed terms, they shall determine whether the terms in the landlord's notice, the terms in the tenant's notice, or some other terms, dealing with the same subject matter as the disputed terms are such as, in the committee's

opinion, might reasonably be expected to be found in an assured monthly periodic tenancy of the dwelling-house (not being an assured shorthold tenancy)—

(a) which begins on the day following the date of termination;

(b) which is granted by a willing landlord on terms which, except so far as they relate to the subject matter of the disputed terms, are the undisputed terms; and

(c) in respect of which possession may not be recovered under any of Grounds 1 to 5 in Part I of Schedule 2 to the 1988 Act;

and the committee shall, if they consider it appropriate, specify an adjustment of the undisputed terms to take account of the terms so determined and shall, if they consider it appropriate, specify an adjustment of the rent to take account of the terms so determined and, if applicable, so adjusted.

(4) In making a determination under sub-paragraph (3) above, or specifying an adjustment of the rent or undisputed terms under that sub-paragraph, there shall be disregarded any effect on the terms or the amount of rent attributable to the granting of a tenancy to a sitting tenant.

(5) If the rent assessment committee decide that there is a dispute as to the rent under the assured periodic tenancy, the committee shall determine the monthly rent at which, subject to sub-paragraph (6) below, the committee consider that the dwelling-house might reasonably be expected to be let in the open market by a willing landlord under an assured tenancy (not being an assured shorthold tenancy)—

(a) which is a monthly periodic tenancy;

(b) which begins on the day following the date of termination;

(c) in respect of which possession may not be recovered under any of Grounds 1 to 5 in Part I of Schedule 2 to the 1988 Act; and

(d) the terms of which (other than those relating to the amount of the rent) are the same as—

(i) the undisputed terms; or

(ii) if there as been a determination under sub-paragraph (3) above, the terms determined by the committee under that sub-paragraph and the undisputed terms (as adjusted, if at all, under that sub-paragraph).

(6) Subsections (2), (3A), (4) and (5) of section 14 of the 1988 Act shall apply in relation to a determination of rent under sub-paragraph (5) above as they apply in relation to a determination under that section subject to the modifications in sub-paragraph (7) below; and in this paragraph 'rent' shall be construed in accordance with subsection (4) of that section.

(7) The modifications of section 14 of the 1988 Act referred to in sub-paragraph (6) above are that in subsection (2), the reference in

paragraph (b) to a relevant improvement being carried out shall be construed as a reference to an improvement being carried out during the long residential tenancy and the reference in paragraph (c) to a failure to comply with any term of the tenancy shall be construed as a reference to a failure to comply with any term of the long residential tenancy.

(8) Where a reference has been made to a rent assessment committee under sub-paragraph (2) of paragraph 10 above, then,—

(a) if the committee decide that there are no disputed terms and that there is no dispute as to the rent, paragraph 10(2)(b) above shall apply as if the notice had not been so referred,

(b) where paragraph (a) above does not apply then, so far as concerns the amount of the rent under the tenancy, if there is a dispute as to the rent, the rent determined by the committee (subject, in a case where section 14(5) of the 1988 Act applies, to the addition of the appropriate amount in respect of rates) and, if there is no dispute as to the rent, the rent specified in the landlord's notice or, as the case may be, the tenant's notice (subject to any adjustment under sub-paragraph (3) above) shall be the rent under the tenancy, and

(c) where paragraph (a) above does not apply and there are disputed terms, then, so far as concerns the subject matter of those terms, the terms determined by the committee under sub-paragraph (3) above shall be terms of the tenancy and, so far as concerns any undisputed terms, those terms (subject to any adjustment under sub-paragraph (3) above) shall also be terms of the tenancy,

with effect from the date on which the assured periodic tenancy takes effect in possession.

(9) Nothing in this Schedule affects the right of the landlord and the tenant under the assured periodic tenancy to vary by agreement any term of the tenancy (including a term relating to rent).

12.—(1) Subsections (2) to (4) of section 41 of the 1988 Act (rent assessment committees: information powers) shall apply where there is a reference to a rent assessment committee under the preceding provisions of this Schedule as they apply where a matter is referred to such a committee under Chapter I or Chapter II of Part I of the 1988 Act.

(2) Nothing in paragraph 10 or paragraph 11 above affects the right of the landlord and the tenant to agree any terms of the assured periodic tenancy (including a term relating to the rent) before the tenancy takes effect in possession (in this sub-paragraph referred to as 'the expressly agreed terms'); and, in such case,—

(a) the expressly agreed terms shall be terms of the tenancy in substitution for any terms dealing with the same subject matter which would otherwise, by virtue of paragraph 10 or paragraph 11 above, be terms of the tenancy; and

(b) where a reference has already been made to a rent assessment committee under sub-paragraph (2) of paragraph 10 above but there has been no determination by the committee under paragraph 11 above,—

(i) the committee shall have regard to the expressly agreed terms, as notified to them by the landlord and the tenant, in deciding, for the purposes of paragraph 11 above, what the disputed terms are and whether there is any dispute as to the rent; and

(ii) in making any determination under paragraph 11 above the committee shall not make any adjustment of the expressly agreed terms, as so notified.

(3) Nothing in paragraph 11 above requires a rent assessment committee to continue with a determination under that paragraph—

(a) if the long residential tenancy has come to an end; or

(b) if the landlord serves notice in writing on the committee that he no longer requires such a determination;

and, where the landlord serves notice as mentioned in paragraph (b) above, then, for the purposes of sub-paragraph (2) of paragraph 10 above, the landlord shall be treated as not having made a reference under paragraph (a) of that sub-paragraph and, accordingly, paragraph (b) of that sub-paragraph shall, subject to sub-paragraph (2) above, have effect for determining rent and other terms of the assured periodic tenancy.

Landlord's application for possession

13.—(1) Where a landlord's notice to resume possession has been served on the tenant and either—

(a) there is an election by the tenant to retain possession, or

(b) at the end of the period of two months beginning on the date of service of the notice, the qualifying condition is fulfilled as respects the tenancy,

the landlord may apply to the court for an order under this paragraph on such of the grounds mentioned in paragraph 5(1) above as may be specified in the notice.

(2) The court shall not entertain an application under sub-paragraph (1) above unless the application is made—

(a) within the period of two months beginning on the date of the election by the tenant to retain possession; or

(b) if there is no election by the tenant to retain possession, within the period of four months beginning on the date of service of the landlord's notice.

(3) Where the ground or one of the grounds for claiming possession specified in the landlord's notice is Ground 6 in Part I of Schedule 2 to the 1988 Act, then, if on an application made under sub-paragraph (1) above

the court is satisfied that the landlord has established that ground, the court shall order that the tenant shall, on the date of termination, give up possession of the property then let under the tenancy.

(4) Subject to sub-paragraph (6) below, where the ground or one of the grounds for claiming possession specified in the landlord's notice is any of Grounds 9 to 15 in Part II of Schedule 2 to the 1988 Act or the ground mentioned in paragraph 5(1)(c) above, then, if on an application made under sub-paragraph (1) above the court is satisfied that the landlord has established that ground and that it is reasonable that the landlord should be granted possession, the court shall order that the tenant shall, on the date of termination, give up possession of the property then let under the tenancy.

(5) Part III of Schedule 2 to the 1988 Act shall have effect for supplementing Ground 9 in that Schedule (as that ground applies in relation to this Schedule) as it has effect for supplementing that ground for the purposes of that Act, subject to the modification that in paragraph 3(1), in the words following paragraph (b) the reference to the assured tenancy in question shall be construed as a reference to the long residential tenancy in question.

(6) Where the ground or one of the grounds for claiming possession specified in the landlord's notice is that mentioned in paragraph 5(1)(c) above, the court shall not make the order mentioned in sub-paragraph (4) above on that ground if it is satisfied that, having regard to all the circumstances of the case, including the question whether other accommo-dation is available for the landlord or the tenant, greater hardship would be caused by making the order than by refusing to make it.

(7) Where the ground or one of the grounds for claiming possession specified in the landlord's notice is that mentioned in paragraph 5(1)(b) above, then, if on an application made under sub-paragraph (1) above the court is satisfied that the landlord has established that ground and is further satisfied—

(a) that on that ground possession of those premises will be required by the landlord on the date of termination, and

(b) that the landlord has made such preparations (including the obtaining or, if that is not reasonably practicable in the circumstances, preparations relating to the obtaining of any requisite permission or consent, whether from any authority whose permission or consent is required under any enactment or from the owner of any interest in any property) for proceeding with the redevelopment as are reasonable in the circumstances.

the court shall order that the tenant shall, on the date of termination, give up possession of the property then let under the tenancy.

14.—(1)   Where, in a case falling within sub-paragraph (7) of paragraph 13 above, the court is not satisfied as mentioned in that sub-paragraph but would be satisfied if the date of termination of the tenancy had been such date (in this paragraph referred to as 'the postponed date') as the court may determine, being a date later, but not more than one year later, than the specified date of termination, the court shall, if the landlord so requires, make an order as mentioned in sub-paragraph (2) below.

(2)   The order referred to in sub-paragraph (1) above is one by which the court specifies the postponed date and orders—

(a)   that the tenancy shall not come to an end on the date of termination but shall continue thereafter, as respects the whole of the property let under the tenancy, at the same rent and in other respects on the same terms as before that date; and

(b)   that, unless the tenancy comes to an end before the postponed date, the tenant shall on that date give up possession of the property then let under the tenancy.

(3)   Notwithstanding the provisions of paragraph 13 above and the preceding provisions of this paragraph and notwithstanding that there has been an election by the tenant to retain possession, if the court is satisfied, at the date of the hearing, that the qualifying condition is not fulfilled as respects the tenancy, the court shall order that the tenant shall, on the date of termination, give up possession of the property then let under the tenancy.

(4)   Nothing in paragraph 13 above or the preceding provisions of this paragraph shall prejudice any power of the tenant under paragraph 8 above to terminate the tenancy; and sub-paragraph (2) of that paragraph shall apply where the tenancy is continued by an order under sub-paragraph (2) above as it applies where the tenancy is continued by virtue of paragraph 3 above.

Provisions where tenant not ordered to give up possession

15.—(1)   The provisions of this paragraph shall have effect where the landlord is entitled to make an application under sub-paragraph (1) of paragraph 13 above but does not obtain an order under that paragraph or paragraph 14 above.

(2)   If at the expiration of the period within which an application under paragraph 13(1) above may be made the landlord has not made such an application, the landlord's notice to resume possession, and anything done in pursuance thereof, shall cease to have effect.

(3)   If before the expiration of the period mentioned in sub-paragraph (2) above the landlord has made an application under paragraph 13(1) above but the result of the application, at the time when it is finally

disposed of, is that no order is made, the landlord's notice to resume possession shall cease to have effect.

(4) In any case where sub-paragraph (3) above applies, then, if within the period of one month beginning on the date that the application to the court is finally disposed of the landlord serves on the tenant a landlord's notice proposing an assured tenancy, the earliest date which may be specified in the notice as the date of termination shall, notwithstanding any thing in paragraph 4(1)(b) above, be the day following the last day of the period of four months beginning on the date of service of the subsequent notice.

(5) The reference in sub-paragraphs (3) and (4) above to the time at which an application is finally disposed of shall be construed as a reference to the earliest time at which the proceedings on the application (including any proceedings on or in consequence of an appeal) have been determined and any time for appealing or further appealing has expired, except that if the application is withdrawn or any appeal is abandoned the reference shall be construed as a reference to the time of withdrawal or abandonment.

(6) A landlord's notice to resume possession may be withdrawn at any time by notice in writing served on the tenant (without prejudice, however, to the power of the court to make an order as to costs if the notice is withdrawn after the landlord has made an application under paragraph 13(1) above).

(7) In any case where sub-paragraph (6) above applies, then, if within the period of one month beginning on the date of withdrawal of the landlord's notice to resume possession the landlord serves on the tenant a landlord's notice proposing an assured tenancy, the earliest date which may be specified in the notice as the date of termination shall, notwithstanding anything in paragraph 4(1)(b) above, be the day following the last day of the period of four months beginning on the date of service of the subsequent notice or the day following the last day of the period of six months beginning on the date of service of the withdrawn notice, whichever is the later.

Tenancies granted in continuation of long tenancies

16.—(1) Where on the coming to the end of a tenancy at a low rent the person who was the tenant immediately before the coming to an end thereof becomes (whether by grant or by implication of the law) the tenant under another tenancy at a low rent of a dwelling-house which consists of the whole or any part of the property let under the previous tenancy, then, if the previous tenancy was a long tenancy or is deemed by virtue of this paragraph to have been a long tenancy, the new tenancy shall be deemed for the purposes of this Schedule to be a long tenancy, irrespective of its terms.

(2) In relation to a tenancy from year to year or other tenancy not granted for a term of years certain, being a tenancy which by virtue of sub-paragraph (1) above is deemed for the purposes of this Schedule to be a long tenancy, the preceding provisions of this Schedule shall have effect subject to the modifications set out below.

(3) In sub-paragraph (6) of paragraph 2 above for the expression beginning 'term date' there shall be substituted—

'"term date", in relation to any such tenancy as is mentioned in paragraph 16(2) below, means the first date after the coming into force of this Schedule on which, apart from this Schedule, the tenancy could have been brought to an end by notice to quit given by the landlord'.

(4) Notwithstanding anything in sub-paragraph (3) of paragraph 3 above, where by virtue of that paragraph the tenancy is continued after the term date, the provisions of this Schedule as to the termination of a tenancy by notice shall have effect, subject to sub-paragraph (5) below, in substitution for and not in addition to any such provisions included in the terms on which the tenancy had effect before the term date.

(5) The minimum period of notice referred to in paragraph 8(1) above shall be one month or such longer period as the tenant would have been required to give to bring the tenancy to an end at the term date.

6) Where the tenancy is not terminated under paragraph 4 or paragraph 8 above at the term date, then, whether or not it would have continued after that date apart from the provisions of this Schedule, it shall be treated for the purposes of those provisions as being continued by virtue of paragraph 3 above.

Agreements as to the grant of new tenancies

17. In any case where, prior to the date of termination of a long residential tenancy, the landlord and the tenant agree for the grant to the tenant of a future tenancy of the whole or part of the property let under the tenancy at a rent other than a low rent and on terms and from a date specified in the agreement, the tenancy shall continue until that date but no longer; and, in such a case, the provisions of this Schedule shall cease to apply in relation to the tenancy with effect from the date of the agreement.

Assumptions on which to determine future questions

18. Where under this Schedule any question falls to be determined by the court or a rent assessment committee by reference to circumstances at a future date, the court or committee shall have regard to all rights, interests and obligations under or relating to the tenancy as they subsist at the time of the determination and to all relevant circumstances as those

then subsist and shall assume, except in so far as the contrary is shown, that those rights, interests, obligations and circumstances will continue to subsist unchanged until that future date.

Landlords and mortgagees in possession

19.—(1) Section 21 of the 1954 Act (meaning of 'the landlord' and provisions as to mesne landlords) shall apply in relation to this Schedule as it applies in relation to Part I of that Act but subject to the following modifications—

(a) any reference to Part I of that Act shall be construed as a reference to this Schedule; and

(b) subsection (4) (which relates to statutory tenancies arising under that Part) shall be omitted.

(2) Section 67 of the 1954 Act (mortgagees in possession) applies for the purposes of this Schedule except that for the reference to that Act there shall be substituted a reference to this Schedule.

(3) In accordance with sub-paragraph (1) above, Schedule 5 to the 1954 Act shall also apply for the purpose of this Schedule but subject to the following modifications—

(a) any reference to Part I of the 1954 Act shall be construed as a reference to the provisions of this Schedule (other than this sub-paragraph);

(b) any reference to section 21 of the 1954 Act shall be construed as a reference to that section as it applies in relation to this Schedule;

(c) any reference to subsection (1) of section 4 of that Act shall be construed as a reference to sub-paragraph (1) of paragraph 4 above;

(d) any reference to the court includes a reference to a rent assessment committee;

(e) paragraphs 6 to 8 and 11 shall be omitted;

(f) any reference to a particular subsection of section 16 of the 1954 Act shall be construed as a reference to that subsection as it applies in relation to this Schedule;

(g) any reference to a tenancy to which section 1 of the 1954 Act applies shall be construed as a reference to a long residential tenancy; and

(h) expressions to which a meaning is assigned by any provision of this Schedule (other than this sub-paragraph) shall be given that meaning.

Application of other provisions of the 1954 Act

20.—(1) Section 16 of the 1954 Act (relief for tenant where landlord proceeding to enforce covenants) shall apply in relation to this Schedule as it applies in relation to Part I of that Act but subject to the following modifications—

(a) in subsection (1) the reference to a tenancy to which section 1 of the 1954 Act applies shall be construed as a reference to a long residential tenancy;

(b) in subsection (2) the reference to Part I of that Act shall be construed as a reference to this Schedule;

(c) subsection (3) shall have effect as if the words '(without prejudice to section ten of this Act)' were omitted; and

(d) in subsection (7) the reference to subsection (3) of section 2 of the 1954 Act shall be construed as a reference to paragraph 1(6) above.

(2) Section 55 of the 1954 Act (compensation for possession obtained by misrepresentation) shall apply in relation to this Schedule as it applies in relation to Part I of that Act.

(3) Section 63 of the 1954 Act (jurisdiction of court for purposes of Parts I and II of the 1954 Act and of Part I of the Landlord and Tenant Act 1927) shall apply in relation to this Schedule and section 186 of this Act as it applies in relation to Part I of that Act.

(4) Section 65 of the 1954 Act (provisions as to reversions) applies for the purposes of this Schedule except that for any reference to that Act there shall be substituted a reference to this Schedule.

(5) Subsection (4) of section 66 of the 1954 Act (services of notices) shall apply in relation to this Schedule as it applies in relation to that Act.

21.—(1) Where this Schedule has effect in relation to former 1954 Act tenancy the term date of which falls before 15th January 1999, any reference (however expressed) in the preceding provisions of this Schedule to the dwelling-house (or the property) let under the tenancy shall have effect as a reference to the premises qualifying for protection, within the meaning of the 1954 Act.

(2) Notwithstanding that at any time section 1 of the 1954 Act does not, and this Schedule does, apply to a former 1954 Act tenancy, any question of what are the premises qualifying for protection or (in that context) what is the tenancy shall be determined for the purposes of this Schedule in accordance with Part I of that Act.

Crown application

22.—(1) This Schedule shall apply where—

(a) there is an interest belonging to Her Majesty in right of the Crown and that interest is under the management of the Crown Estate Commissioners, or

(b) there is an interest belonging to Her Majesty in right of the Duchy of Lancaster or belonging to the Duchy of Cornwall, as if it were an interest not so belonging.

(2)   Where an interest belongs to Her Majesty in right of the Duchy of Lancaster, then, for the purposes of this Schedule, the Chancellor of the Duchy of Lancaster shall be deemed to be the owner of the interest.

(3)   Where an interest belongs to the Duchy of Cornwall, then, for the purposes of this Schedule, such person as the Duke of Cornwall, or other possessor for the time being of the Duchy of Cornwall, appoints shall be deemed to be the owner of the interest.

THE ASSURED TENANCIES AND AGRICULTURAL OCCUPANCIES (FORMS) REGULATIONS 1997
(SI 1997 No. 194)

1.   Citation and commencement
These Regulations may be cited as the Assured Tenancies and Agricultural Occupancies (Forms) Regulations 1997 and shall come into force on 28 February 1997.

2.   Interpretation
In these Regulations any reference to a section or Schedule is a reference to a section of, or Schedule to, the Housing Act 1988 and any reference to a numbered form is a reference to the form bearing that number in the Schedule to these Regulations, or to a form substantially to the same effect.

3.   Prescribed forms
The forms prescribed for the purposes of Part I (rented accommodation) of the Housing Act 1988 are—

(a)   for a notice under section 6(2) proposing terms of a statutory periodic tenancy different from the implied terms, Form No. 1;

(b)   for an application under section 6(3) referring a notice under section 6(2) to a rent assessment committee, Form No. 2;

(c)   for a notice under section 8 informing a tenant or licensee that the landlord intends to begin proceedings for possession of a dwelling-house let on an assured tenancy or an assured agricultural occupancy, Form No. 3;

(d)   for a notice under section 13(2) proposing a new rent for an assured tenancy or an assured agricultural occupancy, Form No. 4;

(e)   for an application under section 13(4) referring to a rent assessment committee a notice under section 13(2) relating to an assured tenancy or an assured agricultural occupancy, Form No. 5;

(f)   for an application under section 22(1) to a rent assessment committee for a determination of rent under an assured shorthold tenancy, Form No. 6;

(g)   for a notice under section 41(2) requiring a landlord or tenant to give information to a rent assessment committee, Form No. 7;

(h)   for a notice under paragraph 7 of Schedule 2A, by the tenant to the landlord proposing that an assured tenancy be replaced by an assured shorthold tenancy, Form No. 8;

(i)   for a notice under paragraph 9 of Schedule 2A, by the landlord to the prospective tenant, proposing an assured shorthold tenancy where the tenancy meets the conditions for an assured agricultural occupancy, Form No. 9.

4.   Revocations and savings

(1)   The Assured Tenancies and Agricultural Occupancies (Forms) Regulations 1988 ('the 1988 Regulations'), the Assured Tenancies and Agricultural Occupancies (Forms) (Amendment) Regulations 1989, the Assured Tenancies and Agricultural Occupancies (Forms) (Amendment) Regulations 1990 and the Assured Tenancies and Agricultural Occupancies (Forms) (Amendment) Regulations 1993 are hereby revoked.

(2)   Nothing in paragraph (1) affects the validity of a notice served before the coming into force of these Regulations if, at the date of service of the notice, the notice was in the form then prescribed by the 1988 Regulations.

SCHEDULE   Regulation 3

FORMS PRESCRIBED FOR THE PURPOSES OF PART I OF THE
HOUSING ACT 1988

FORM No. 1

Housing Act 1988 section 6(2)

Notice proposing different terms for a Statutory Periodic Tenancy

- Please write clearly in black ink.

- Please tick boxes where appropriate and cross out text marked with an asterisk (*) that does not apply.

- This form can be used by either a landlord or a tenant to propose changes to the terms of a statutory periodic tenancy, which arises when a fixed term of an assured tenancy, an assured shorthold tenancy or an assured agricultural occupancy ends.

- This notice must be served on the landlord or tenant no later than the first anniversary of the day on which the former fixed term tenancy or occupancy ended.

- Do not use this notice if you are a landlord proposing only an increase in rent. Instead, you should use the form headed *Landlord's Notice proposing a new rent under an Assured Periodic Tenancy or Agricultural Occupancy*, which is available from a rent assessment panel or law stationers.

---

1. To: ....

Name(s) of landlord(s)/tenant(s)

Address of premises to which the tenancy relates:

....

....

---

2. This is to give notice that I/we* propose different terms for the statutory periodic tenancy from those of the fixed term assured tenancy which has now ended and that they should take effect from:

....

Insert date which must be at least three months after the date on which this notice is served.

---

3. Changes to the terms

(a) The existing provisions of the tenancy to be changed are:

....

....

Please attach relevant sections of the tenancy agreement if available

(b) The proposed changes are:

....

....

Continue on a separate sheet if necessary

---

4. Changes to the rent (if applicable). Go to section 5 if this does not apply.

- You should not propose a change to the rent on this form unless it is to take account of the proposed new terms at section 3. A change may be made if either the landlord or the tenant considers it appropriate.

(a) The existing rent is   £.......... per ....
                                                (e.g. week, month, year)

(b) Does the rent include council tax?   Yes ☐   No ☐

3

(c) If yes, the amount that is included for council tax is: £.......... per ....
(e.g. week, month, year)

(d) Does the rent include water charges?   Yes ☐   .   No ☐

(e) If yes, the amount that is included for water charges is: £.......... per ....
(e.g. week, month, year)

(f) The new rent which takes into account the proposed
changes in the terms of the tenancy will be: £.......... per ....
(e.g. week, month, year)

(g) Will the new rent include council tax?   Yes ☐   No ☐

(h) If yes, the amount that will be included for council tax is: £.......... per ....
(e.g. week, month, year)

(i) Will the new rent include water charges?   Yes ☐   No ☐

(j) If yes, the amount that will be included for water charges is: £.......... per ....
(e.g. week, month, year)

5. Name and address of landlord or tenant proposing the changes

To be signed and dated by the landlord or his agent (someone acting for him) or the tenant or his agent. If there are joint landlords or joint tenants each landlord/tenant or the agent must sign unless one signs on behalf of the rest with their agreement.

Signed ....   *Date* ....
....
....

Please specify whether: landlord ☐   landlord's agent ☐   tenant ☐   tenant's agent ☐

Name(s) Block Capitals) ....
....
....

Address
....
....
....

Telephone—Daytime ....   Evening ....

What to do if this notice is served on you

- If you agree with the new terms and rent proposed, do nothing. They will become the terms of the tenancy agreement on the date specified in section 2.

- If you don't agree with the proposed terms and any adjustment of the rent (see section 4), and you are unable to reach agreement with your landlord/tenant, or you do not wish to discuss it with him, you may refer the matter directly to your local rent assessment committee, before the date specified in section 2, using the form headed *Application referring a Notice proposing different terms for a Statutory Periodic Tenancy to a Rent Assessment Committee* which you can obtain from a rent assessment panel or a law stationer.

- The rent assessment committee will decide what, if any, changes should be made to the terms of the tenancy and, if applicable, the amount of the new rent.

- If you need help or advice about this notice and what you should do about it, take it immediately to a citizens advice bureau, a housing advice centre, a law centre or a solicitor.

4

FORM No. 2

Housing Act 1988 section 6(3)

Application referring a Notice proposing different terms for a Statutory Periodic Tenancy to a Rent Assessment Committee

- Please write clearly in black ink.

- Please tick boxes where appropriate and cross out text marked with an asterisk (*) that does not apply.

- This form should be used by a landlord or a tenant who has been served with a notice under section 6(2) of the Housing Act 1988, varying the terms of a statutory

periodic tenancy which arises when a fixed term of an assured tenancy, an assured shorthold tenancy or an assured agricultural occupancy ends.

- When you have completed the form, please send it to your local rent assessment panel with a copy of the notice served on you proposing the new terms of the statutory periodic tenancy.

1. Name(s) of tenant(s):
....
....
....

2. Address of premises to which the tenancy relates:
....
....
....

3. Name(s) of landlord(s)/agent*:
....
....
....

Address of landlord(s), agent*:
....
....
....

4. Details of premises.

(a) What type of accommodation is rented?

Room(s) ☐   Flat ☐   Terraced House ☐
Semi-Detached House ☐   Fully Detached House ☐   Other ☐ (*Please specify*)

(b) If it is a flat or room(s) what floor(s) is it on?

Ground ☐   First ☐   Second ☐   Other ☐ (*Please specify*)

(c) Give the number and type of rooms, eg living room, bathroom etc.
....
....

(d) Does the tenancy include any other facilities, eg garden, garage or other separate building or land?

Yes ☐   No ☐

(e) If yes, please give details:
....
....
....

(f) Is any of the accommodation shared with:

(i) the landlord?   Yes ☐   No ☐
(ii) another tenant or tenants?   Yes ☐   No ☐

5

(g) If yes, please give details:

....

....

....

5. When did the statutory periodic tenancy begin?

....

6. Services.

(a) Are any services provided under the tenancy (eg cleaning, lighting, heating, hot water or gardening etc.)?

    Yes ☐   No ☐

(b) If yes, please give details:

....

....

....

(c) Is a separate charge made for services, maintenance, repairs, landlords' costs of management or any other item?

    Yes ☐   No ☐

(d) If yes, what charge is payable?   £..........   per ....

                                                                 (e.g. week, month, year)

(e) Does the charge vary according to the relevant costs?

    Yes ☐   No ☐

(f) If yes, please give details:

....

....

....

7. (a) Is any furniture provided under the tenancy?

    Yes ☐   No ☐

    (b) If yes, please give details. Continue on a separate sheet if necessary or provide a copy of the inventory.

....

....

....

8. What repairs are the responsibility of:

(a) the landlord? Continue on a separate sheet if necessary.

....

....

....

(b) the tenant? Continue on a separate sheet if necessary.

....

....

....

9. Give details (if known) of the other terms of the tenancy, e.g. can you assign the tenancy (pass it on to someone else) and if so is a premium (a payment which is in addition to rent and equivalent to more than two months rent) payable on an assignment? Continue on a separate sheet if necessary.

....

....

....

10. (a) Is there a written tenancy agreement?   Yes ☐   No ☐

    (b) If yes, please attach the tenancy agreement (with a note of any variations). It will be returned to you as soon as possible.

6

11. (a) I/We* attach a copy of the notice proposing changes to the statutory periodic tenancy and, if applicable, an adjustment of the amount of rent and apply for it to be considered by the rent assessment committee.

Signed .... *Date* ....

....

....

To be signed and dated by the landlord or his agent (someone acting for him) or the tenant or his agent. If there are joint landlords or joint tenants each landlord/tenant or the agent must sign unless one signs on behalf of the rest with their agreement.

Please specify whether: landlord ☐   landlord's agent ☐   tenant ☐   tenant's agent ☐

(b) Name and address of landlord or tenant referring to the rent assessment committee.

Name(s) (Block Capitals) ....

....

....

Address

....

....

....

Telephone—Daytime ....

7

FORM No. 3

Housing Act 1988 section 8 as amended by section 151 of the Housing Act 1996

Notice seeking possession of a property let on an Assured Tenancy or an Assured Agricultural Occupancy

- Please write clearly in black ink.
- Please tick boxes where appropriate and cross out text marked with an asterisk (*) that does not apply.
- This form should be used where possession of accommodation let under an assured tenancy, an assured agricultural occupancy or an assured shorthold tenancy is sought on one of the grounds in Schedule 2 to the Housing Act 1988.

- Do not use this form if possession is sought on the "shorthold" ground under section 21 of the Housing Act 1988 from an assured shorthold tenant where the fixed term has come to an end cr. for assured shorthold tenancies with no fixed term which started on or after 28th February 1997, after six months has elapsed. There is no prescribed form for these cases, but you must give notice in writing.

1. To: ....;...

Name(s) of tenant(s)/licensee(s) *

2. Your landlord/licensor* intends to apply to the court for an order requiring you to give up possession of:

....
....
....

Address of premises

3. Your landlord/licensor* intends to seek possession on ground(s) .... in Schedule 2 to the Housing Act 1988. as amended by the Housing Act 1996. which read(s):

....
....
....

Give the full text (as set out in the Housing Act 1988 as amended by the Housing Act 1996) of each ground which is being relied on. Continue on a separate sheet if necessary.

4. Give a full explanation of why each ground is being relied on:

....
....
....

Continue on a separate sheet if necessary.

Notes on the grounds for possession

- If the court is satisfied that any of grounds 1 to 8 is established. it must make an order (but see below in respect of fixed term tenancies).

- Before the court will grant an order on any of grounds 9 to 17, it must be satisfied that it is reasonable to require you to leave. This means that. if one of these grounds is set out in section 3. you will be able to suggest to the court that it is not reasonable that you should have to leave, even if you accept that the ground applies.

- The court will not make an order under grounds 1. 3 to 7. 9 or 16. to take effect during the fixed term of the tenancy (if there is one) and it will only make an order during the fixed term on grounds 2. 8. 10 to 15 or 17 if the terms of the tenancy make provision for it to be brought to an end on any of these grounds.

- Where the court makes an order for possession solely on ground 6 or 9. the landlord must pay your reasonable removal expenses.

8

5. The court proceedings will not begin until after:

....

Give the earliest date on which court proceedings can be brought

- Where the landlord is seeking possession on grounds 1, 2, 5 to 7, 9 or 16, court proceedings cannot begin earlier than 2 months from the date this notice is served on you (even where one of grounds 3, 4, 8, 10 to 13, 14A, 15 or 17 is specified) and not before the date on which the tenancy (had it not been assured) could have been brought to an end by a notice to quit served at the same time as this notice.

- Where the landlord is seeking possession on grounds 3, 4, 8, 10 to 13, 14A, 15 or 17, court proceedings cannot begin earlier than 2 weeks from the date this notice is served (unless one of 1, 2, 5 to 7, 9 or 16 grounds is also specified in which case they cannot begin earlier than two months from the date this notice is served).

- Where the landlord is seeking possession on ground 14 (with or without other grounds), court proceedings cannot begin before the date this notice is served.

- Where the landlord is seeking possession on ground 14A, court proceedings cannot begin unless the landlord has served, or has taken all reasonable steps to serve, a copy of this notice on the partner who has left the property.

- After the date shown in section 5, court proceedings may be begun at once but not later than 12 months from the date on which this notice is served. After this time the notice will lapse and a new notice must be served before possession can be sought.

6. Name and address of landlord/licensor*.

To be signed and dated by the landlord or licensor or his agent (someone acting for him). If there are joint landlords each landlord or the agent must sign unless one signs on behalf of the rest with their agreement.

Signed .... *Date*..

....

Please specify whether: landlord ☐   licensor ☐   joint landlords ☐   landlord's agent ☐

Name(s) (Block Capitals) ....

....

Address

....

....

....

Telephone—Daytime .... Evening ....

What to do if this notice is served on you

- This notice is the first step requiring you to give up possession of your home. You should read it very carefully.

- Your landlord cannot make you leave your home without an order for possession issued by a court. By issuing this notice your landlord is informing you that he intends to seek such an order. If you are willing to give up possession without a court order, you should tell the person who signed this notice as soon as possible and say when you are prepared to leave.

- Whichever grounds are set out in section 3 of this form, the court may allow any of the other grounds to be added at a later date. If this is done, you will be told about it so you can discuss the additional grounds at the court hearing as well as the grounds set out in section 3.

- If you need advice about this notice, and what you should do about it, take it immediately to a citizens' advice bureau, a housing advice centre, a law centre or a solicitor.

9

FORM No. 4

Housing Act 1988 section 13(2)

Landlord's Notice proposing a new rent under an Assured Periodic Tenancy or Agricultural Occupancy

- Please write clearly in black ink.
- Please tick boxes where appropriate.
- This form should be used to propose a new rent under an assured periodic tenancy, including an assured shorthold periodic tenancy.
- This form may also be used to propose a new rent or licence fee for an assured periodic agricultural occupancy. In such cases reference to "landlord"/"tenant" can be read as references to "licensor"/"licensee" etc.

- Do not use this form if there is a current rent fixing mechanism in the tenancy.
- Do not use this form to propose a rent adjustment for a statutory periodic tenancy solely because of a proposed change of terms under section 6(2) of the Housing Act 1988. You should instead use the form headed *Notice proposing different terms for a Statutory Periodic Tenancy* which you can obtain from a rent assessment panel or a law stationer.

1. To: ....

Name(s) of tenant(s)

2. Address of premises to which the tenancy relates:
....
....
....

3. This is to give notice that as from .... your landlord proposes to charge a new rent.

- The new rent must take effect at the beginning of a new period of the tenancy and not earlier than any of the following:

   (a) the minimum period after this notice was served.

      (The minimum period is:

      —in the case of a yearly tenancy, six months;

      —in the case of a tenancy where the period is less than a month, one month;

      —in any other case, a period equal to the period of the tenancy;)

   (b) the first anniversary of the start of the first period of the tenancy except in the case of:

      —a statutory periodic tenancy, which arises when a fixed term assured tenancy ends, or;

      —an assured tenancy which arose on the death of a tenant under a regulated tenancy;

   (c) if the rent under the tenancy has previously been increased by a notice under section 13 or a determination under section 14 of the Housing Act 1988, the first anniversary of the date on which the increased rent took effect.

4. (a) The existing rent is: £.......... per ....
   (e.g. week, month, year)

   (b) Does the rent include council tax? Yes ☐ No ☐

   (c) If yes, the amount that is included for council tax is: £.......... per ....
   (e.g. week, month, year)

   (d) Does the rent include water charges? Yes ☐ No ☐

   (e) If yes, the amount that is included for water charges is: £.......... per ....
   (e.g. week, month, year)

10

245

5. (a) The proposed new rent will be: £.......... per ....
                                                      (e.g. week, month, year)

   (b) Will the new rent include council tax? Yes ☐ . No ☐

   (c) If yes, the amount that will be included for
council tax will be: £.......... per ....
                                                      (e.g. week, month, year)

   (d) Will the new rent include water charges? Yes ☐ No ☐

   (e) If yes, the amount that will be included for
water charges will be: £.......... per ....
                                                      (e.g. week, month, year)

6. Name and address of landlord.

To be signed and dated by the landlord or his agent (someone acting for him). If there are joint landlords each landlord or the agent must sign unless one signs on behalf of the rest with their agreement.

Signed .... *Date* ....

....

Please specify whether: landlord ☐ joint landlords ☐ landlord's agent ☐

Name(s) (Block Capitals) ....

....

Address

....

....

....

Telephone—Daytime .... Evening ....

What to do if this notice is served on you

- You should read this notice carefully. Your landlord is proposing a new rent.

- If you agree with the new rent proposed, do nothing. If you do not agree and you are unable to reach agreement with your landlord or do not want to discuss it directly with him, you may refer this notice to your local rent assessment committee prior to the date specified in section 3, using the form headed *Application referring a Notice proposing a new rent under an Assured Periodic Tenancy or Agricultural Occupancy to a Rent Assessment Committee.* You can obtain this form from a rent assessment panel or a law stationer.

- The rent assessment committee will consider your application and will decide what the rent for the premises will be. The committee may set a rent that is higher, lower or the same as the landlord has proposed in section 5.

- If you are required to include payments for council tax and water charges in your rent, the rent the committee determines will be inclusive of council tax and water charges.

- If you need help or advice please take this notice immediately to a citizens advice bureau, a housing advice centre, a law centre or a solicitor.

11

FORM No. 5

Housing Act 1988 section 13(4)

Application referring a Notice proposing a new rent under an Assured Periodic Tenancy or Agricultural Occupancy to a Rent Assessment Committee

- Please write clearly in black ink.

- Please tick boxes where appropriate and cross out text marked with an asterisk (*) that does not apply.

- This form should be used when your landlord has served notice on you proposing a new rent under an assured periodic tenancy, including an assured shorthold periodic tenancy

- This form may also be used to refer a notice proposing a new rent or licence fee for an assured periodic agricultural occupancy. In such a case references to "landlord"/"tenant" can be read as references to "licensor"/"licensee" etc.

- This form must be completed and sent to your local rent assessment panel—with a copy of the notice served on you proposing the new rent—before the date it is proposed that the new rent will take effect.

1. Address of premises:

....
....
....

2. Name(s) of landlord(s)/agent*:

....
....

Address of landlord(s)/agent*:

....
....
....

3. Details of premises.

(a) What type of accommodation do you rent?

Room(s) □   Flat □   Terraced House □
Semi-Detached House □   Fully Detached House □   Other *(Please specify)* □

(b) If it is a flat or room(s) what floor(s) is it on?

Ground □   First □   Second □   Other □ *(Please specify)*

(c) Give the number and type of rooms, eg living room, bathroom etc.

....
....

(d) Does the tenancy include any other facilities, eg garden, garage or other separate building or land?

Yes □   No □

(e) If yes, please give details:

....
....

(f) Do you share any accommodation with

(i) the landlord?   Yes □   No □

(ii) another tenant or tenants?   Yes □   No □

(g) If yes to either of the above, please give details:

....
....

4. When did the present tenancy begin?

....

12

5. (a) Did you pay a premium?

    Yes ☐   No. ☐

- a premium is a payment which is additional to rent and is equivalent to more than two months rent. It may give you the right to assign the tenancy (pass it on to someone else) unless the tenancy agreement states or implies otherwise.

(b) If yes, please give details:

....
....
....

6. Services

(a) Are any services provided under the tenancy (eg cleaning, lighting, heating, hot water or gardening)?

    Yes ☐   No ☐

(b) If yes, please give details:

....
....
....

(c) If yes, is a separate charge made for services, maintenance, repairs, landlord's costs of management or any other item?

    Yes ☐   No ☐

(d) What charge is payable?   £.......... per ....
                                       (e.g. week, month, year)

(e) Does the charge vary according to the relevant costs?

    Yes ☐   No ☐

(f) If yes, please give details:

....
....
....

7. (a) Is any furniture provided under the tenancy?

    Yes ☐   No ☐

(b) If yes, please give details. Continue on a separate sheet if necessary or attach a copy of the inventory:

....
....
....

8. Improvements

(a) Have you, or any former tenant(s) carried out improvements or replaced fixtures, fittings or furniture for which you or they were not responsible under the terms of the tenancy?

    Yes ☐   No ☐

(b) If yes, please give details. Continue on a separate sheet if necessary:

....
....
....

9. What repairs are the responsibility of:

(a) the landlord?

....
....
....

(b) the tenant?

....
....
....

13

10. (a) Is there a written tenancy agreement?   Yes ☐   No ☐

    (b) If yes, please attach the tenancy agreement (with a note of any variations). It will be returned to you as soon as possible.

11. Do you have an assured agricultural occupancy?

    Yes ☐   No ☐

12. (a) I/we* attach a copy of the notice proposing a new rent under the assured periodic tenancy and I/we* apply for it to be considered by the rent assessment committee.

Signed ....   *Date* ....

                                         ....

                                         ....

To be signed and dated by the tenant or his agent. If there are joint tenants each tenant or the agent must sign unless one signs on behalf of the rest with their agreement.

Please specify whether: tenant ☐   joint tenants ☐   tenant's agent ☐

    (b) Name and address of tenant(s) referring to the rent assessment committee.

Name(s) (Block Capitals) ....

                                      ....

                                      ....

Address

....

....

....

*Telephone—*Daytime ....

14

FORM No. 6

Housing Act 1988 section 22(1) as amended by section 100 of the Housing Act 1996

Application to a Rent Assessment Committee for a determination of a rent under an Assured Shorthold Tenancy

- Please write clearly in black ink.

- Please tick boxes where appropriate and cross out text marked with an asterisk (*) that does not apply.

- This form should be used by a tenant with an assured shorthold tenancy which began (or for which a contract had been made) before 28th February 1997, to apply to the local rent assessment committee, during the fixed term of the original tenancy, to have the rent reduced.

- This form should also be used by a tenant with an assured shorthold tenancy which began on or after 28th February 1997 (unless a contract had been made before that date), to apply to the rent assessment committee within six months of the beginning of the original tenancy, to have the rent reduced.

- This form cannot be used in the cases specified at the end of this form.

- When you have completed the form please send it to your local rent assessment panel.

1. Address of premises:

....

....

....

2. Name(s) of landlord(s)/agent*

....

Address of landlord(s)/agent*

....

....

....

3. Details of premises.

(a) What type of accommodation do you rent?

    Room(s) ☐   Flat ☐   Terraced House ☐
    Semi-Detached House ☐   Fully Detached House ☐   Other ☐ *(Please specify)*

(b) If it is a flat or room(s) what floor(s) is it on?

    Ground ☐   First ☐   Second ☐   Other ☐ *(Please specify)*

(c) Give the number and type of rooms, eg living room, bathroom etc.

....

(d) Does the tenancy include any other facilities, eg garden. garage or other separate building or land?

    Yes ☐   No ☐

(e) If yes. please give details:

....

....

....

(f) Do you share any accommodation with:
    (i) the landlord?   Yes ☐   No ☐

    (ii) another tenant or tenants?   Yes ☐   No ☐

(g) If yes to either of the above, please give details:

....

....

....

4. (a) What is the current rent?   £.......... per ....
        (e.g. week, month, year)

    (b) Does the rent include council tax?   Yes ☐   No ☐

15

(c) If yes, the amount that is included for council tax is: £.......... per ....
(e.g. week, month, year)

(d) Does the rent include water charges? Yes ☐ . No ☐

(e) If yes, the amount that is included for water charges is: £.......... per ....
(e.g. week, month, year)

5. (a) When did the present tenancy begin?
....

(b) When does the present tenancy end?
....

(c) Does the tenancy replace an original tenancy? Yes ☐ No☐

If yes, when did the original tenancy begin ....

6. (a) If the tenancy began before 28th February 1997, please confirm by ticking the box that you received a notice saying that the tenancy was to be an assured shorthold tenancy before the agreement was entered into. ☐

(b) Attach a copy of the notice, if available. It will be returned to you as soon as possible.

7. (a) Did you pay a premium?
Yes ☐ No ☐

● a premium is a payment which is additional to rent and is equivalent to more than two months rent. It may give you the right to assign the tenancy (pass it on to someone else) unless the tenancy agreement states or implies otherwise.

(b) If yes, please give details:
....
....
....

8. Services.

(a) Are any services provided under the tenancy (eg cleaning, lighting, heating, hot water or gardening)?
Yes ☐ No ☐

(b) If yes, please give details:
....
....
....

(c) Is a separate charge made for services, maintenance, repairs, landlord's costs of management or any other item?
Yes ☐ No ☐

(d) If yes, what charge is payable? £.......... per ....
(e.g. week, month, year)

(e) Does the charge vary according to the relevant costs?
Yes ☐ No ☐

(f) If yes, please give details:
....
....
....

9. (a) Is any furniture provided under the tenancy?
Yes ☐ No ☐

(b) If yes, please give details. Continue on a separate sheet if necessary or provide a copy of the inventory.
....
....
....

10. What repairs are the responsibility of:

(a) the landlord. Continue on a separate sheet if necessary:

....
....
....

(b) the tenant. Continue on a separate sheet if necessary:

....
....
....

11. (a) Give details (if known) of the other terms of the tenancy, eg whether the tenancy is assignable and whether a premium may be charged on an assignment. (Continue on a separate sheet if necessary).

....
....
....

(b) Is there a written tenancy agreement?   Yes ☐   No☐

(c) If yes, please attach the tenancy agreement (with a note of any variations). It will be returned to you as soon as possible.

12. (a) I We* apply to the rent assessment committee to determine a rent for the above mentioned premises.

Signed .... *Date* ....

....

To be signed and dated by the tenant or his agent. If there are joint tenants each tenant or the agent must sign unless one signs on behalf of the rest with their agreement.

Please specify whether: tenant ☐   joint tenants ☐   tenant's agent ☐

(b) Name and address of tenant(s) referring to the rent assessment committee.

Name(s) (Block Capitals) ....
....

Address
....
....
....

Telephone—Daytime ....

Cases where this form should not be used

- An application cannot be made if—

  (a) the rent payable under the tenancy is a rent previously determined by a rent assessment committee; or

  (b) the tenancy is a replacement tenancy and more than six months have elapsed since the beginning of the original tenancy. A replacement tenancy is an assured shorthold tenancy that came into being on the ending of a tenancy which had been an assured shorthold of the same, or substantially the same, property and the landlord and tenant under each tenancy were the same at that time.

- The rent assessment committee cannot make a determination unless it considers—

  (a) that there is a sufficient number of similar properties in the locality let on assured tenancies (whether shorthold or not) for comparison; and

  (b) that the rent payable under the shorthold tenancy in question is significantly higher than the rent which the landlord might reasonably be expected to get in comparison with other rents for similar properties let on assured tenancies (whether shorthold or not) in the locality.

17

FORM No.7

Housing Act 1988 section 41(2)

Notice by Rent Assessment Committee requiring further information

1. To:...

☐ landlord(s)　　　☐ tenant(s)
of:

....

....

Address of premises

2. An application has been made to the rent assessment committee for consideration of:

☐ the terms of a statutory periodic assured tenancy

☐ an increase in rent under an assured periodic tenancy

☐ the rent under an assured shorthold tenancy

☐ an increase in rent under an assured agricultural occupancy

of the above property. The committee needs more information from you to consider the application.

3. The information needed is:

....

....

....

....

....

....

4. Please send it to:

....

....

....

no later than ....

5. If you fail to comply with this notice without reasonable cause you will be committing a criminal offence and may be liable to a fine.

6. Signed on behalf of the rent assessment committee.

Signed..　*Date*...

Name (Block Capitals) ....

Address

....

....

Telephone ....

18

253

FORM No. 8

Housing Act 1988 Schedule 2A, paragraph 7(2) as inserted by Schedule 7 to the Housing Act 1996

Tenant's notice proposing that an Assured Tenancy be replaced by an Assured Shorthold Tenancy

- Please write clearly in black ink.

- Please cross out text marked with an asterisk (*) that does not apply.

- This notice should only be used by an assured tenant. You should only use this notice to notify your landlord that you wish your assured tenancy to be replaced by an assured shorthold tenancy.

- This notice must be served by a tenant on a landlord before an assured tenancy can be replaced by an assured shorthold tenancy.

- **You should be aware that by serving this notice, you will be giving up your right to stay in the property after the first six** months of the assured shorthold tenancy or, if you agree a fixed term with your landlord, after the end of the fixed term.

- You do not have to complete this form even if your landlord has asked you to do so. Your existing security of tenure as an assured tenant will be unaffected if you do not complete it.

- If you are in any doubt about whether to complete this form, take it immediately to a citizens' advice bureau, housing advice centre, a law centre or a solicitor.

- Once you are clear that you wish to issue this notice, complete the form and send it to your landlord.

1. To: ....

Name(s) of landlord(s)

2. I/We*, the tenant(s) of:

....

....

....

Address of premises

give notice that I/we* propose that the assured tenancy to which this notice relates should be replaced by a shorthold tenancy.

3. I/We* propose that the new shorthold tenancy should commence on:

......../............/........

day month year

- The new shorthold tenancy cannot commence until after the date this notice is served on the landlord.

4. (a) I/We* understand that under my/our* existing tenancy, I/we* can only be required to give up possession in accordance with the grounds set out in Schedule 2 to the Housing Act 1988, whereas under the new shorthold tenancy, the landlord(s) will be able to recover possession of the premises without being required to prove a ground for possession, after the first six months of the assured shorthold tenancy, or, if there is a fixed term for longer than 6 months, at the end of that fixed term, subject to two months' notice.

Signed .... *Date* ....

....

....

To be signed and dated by the tenant. If there are joint tenants each tenant must sign.

(b) Name and address of tenant.

Name(s) (Block Capitals) ....

....

Address

....

....

Telephone—Daytime .... Evening ....

19

FORM No. 9

Housing Act 1988 Schedule 2A, paragraph 9, as inserted by Schedule 7 to the Housing Act 1996

Landlord's notice proposing an Assured Shorthold Tenancy where the tenancy meets the conditions for an Assured Agricultural Occupancy

- Please write clearly in black ink.

- Please tick boxes where appropriate.

- If the agricultural worker condition in Schedule 3 to the Housing Act 1988 is met with respect to the property to which the proposed assured tenancy relates, and the landlord wishes that tenancy to be an assured shorthold tenancy, he must serve this notice on the tenant before the tenancy is entered into.

- This notice cannot be used where the landlord has already granted to the prospective tenant (or, in the case of joint tenants, to at least one of them) a tenancy or licence under section 24 of the Housing Act 1988 (an assured agricultural occupancy).

- This notice does not commit the tenant to taking the tenancy.

1. To: ....
....
....

Name of the proposed tenant. If a joint tenancy is being offered, enter the names of the joint tenants.

2. You are proposing to take a tenancy at the following address:
....
....
....

commencing on ..../........../..........
          day month year

3. This notice is to tell you that your tenancy is to be an assured shorthold tenancy.

- Provided you keep to the terms of the tenancy, you are entitled to remain in the property for at least six months after the start of the tenancy. Depending on the terms of the tenancy, once the first six months have elapsed, the landlord may have the right to seek possession at any time, subject to two months' notice.

- As an assured shorthold tenant, you have the right to apply to a rent assessment committee for the determination of a reasonable rent for the tenancy. An application to your local rent assessment committee must be made on the form headed *Application to a Rent Assessment Committee for a determination of a rent under an Assured Shorthold Tenancy* within six months of the beginning of the tenancy. You can obtain the form from a rent assessment panel or a law stationer.

- If you need help or advice about this notice, and what you should do about it, take it immediately to a citizens' advice bureau, a housing advice centre, a law centre or a solicitor.

4. Name and address of landlord.

To be signed and dated by the landlord or his agent (someone acting for him). If there are joint landlords each landlord or the agent must sign unless one signs on behalf of the rest with their agreement.

Signed .... *Date* ....
     ....

Please specify whether: landlord ☐   joint landlords ☐   agent ☐

Name(s) (Block Capitals) ....
    ....

Address:
....
....
....

Telephone—Daytime .... Evening ....

20

THE ASSURED AND PROTECTED TENANCIES
(LETTINGS TO STUDENTS)
REGULATIONS 1998
(SI 1998 No. 1967)

1. These Regulations may be cited as the Assured and Protected Tenancies (Lettings to Students) Regulations 1998 and shall come into force on 1 September 1998.

2. In these Regulations—

'assisted' has the same meaning as in section 579(5) and (6) of the Education Act 1996;

'further education' has the meaning assigned to it by section 2(3) and (5) of the Education Act 1996;

'higher education' means education provided by means of a course of any description mentioned in Schedule 6 to the Education Reform Act 1988;

'publicly funded' refers to an institution which is—

(a) provided or assisted by a local education authority;

(b) in receipt of grant under regulations made under section 485 of the Education Act 1996;

(c) within the higher education sector (within the meaning of section 91(5) of the Further and Higher Education Act 1992), other than a university; or

(d) within the further education sector (within the meaning of section 91(3) of the Further and Higher Education Act 1992), and

'the relevant enactments' means section 8 of the Rent Act 1977 and paragraph 8 of Schedule 1 to the Housing Act 1988 (lettings to students).

3. The following institutions are hereby specified as educational institutions for the purposes of the relevant enactments, that is to say—

(a) any university or university college and any constituent college, school or hall or other institution of a university;

(b) any other institution which provides further education or higher education or both and which is publicly funded;

(c) the David Game Tutorial College, London.

4. The following bodies of persons (whether unincorporated or bodies corporate) are hereby specified as bodies for the purposes of the relevant enactments, that is to say—

(a) the governing body of any educational institution specified in regulation 3 above;

(b) the body, other than a local education authority, providing any such educational institution; and

(c) a body listed in Schedule 1 to these Regulations.

5. The following bodies of persons (whether unincorporated or bodies corporate) are hereby specified as bodies for the purposes of paragraph 8 of Schedule 1 to the Housing Act 1988, that is to say—

(a) any housing association (as defined in section 1 of the Housing Associations Act 1985 which is registered by the Housing Corporation or Housing for Wales in accordance with Part I of the Housing Associations Act 1985 and which is not listed in Schedule 1 to these Regulations; and

(b) a body listed in Schedule 2 to these Regulations.

6. The Regulations specified in Schedule 3 to these Regulations are hereby revoked to the extent detailed in that Schedule.

Regulation 4(c)   SCHEDULE 1
SPECIFIED BODIES UNDER REGULATION 4(c)

International Students House
The London Goodenough Trust for Overseas Graduates

Regulation 5(b)   SCHEDULE 2
SPECIFIED BODIES UNDER REGULATION 5(b)

AFSIL Limited
Derbyshire Student Residences Limited
Friendship Housing
Hull Student Welfare Association
International Lutheran Student Centre
International Students Club (Church of England) Limited
International Students' Club (Lee Abbey) Limited
International Students Housing Society
Oxford Brookes Housing Association Limited
Oxford Overseas Student Housing Association Limited
St. Brigid's House Limited
St. Thomas More Housing Society Limited
The House of St. Gregory and St. Macrina Oxford Limited
The London Mission (West London) Circuit Meeting of the Methodist Church
The London School of Economics Housing Association
The Royal London Hospital Special Trustees
The Universities of Brighton and Sussex Catholic Chaplaincy Association
The Victoria League for Commonwealth Friendship
University of Leicester Students' Union
Wandsworth Students Housing Association Limited
York Housing Association Limited

Index